d International

This book examines the international political order in the post-Cold War era, arguing that this order has become progressively more punitive. This is seen as resulting from both a human rights regime that emphasizes legal norms and the aggressive policies of the United States and its allies in the "war on terror."

While punishment can play a key role in creating justice in a political system, serious flaws in the current global order militate against punishment-enforcing global norms. The book argues for the necessary presence of three key concepts – justice, authority and agency – if punishment is to function effectively, and explores three practices in the current international system: intervention, sanctions and counter-terrorism policy. It concludes by suggesting ways to revise the current global political structure in order to enable punitive practices to play a more central role in creating a just world order.

This book will be of much interest to students of International Law, Political Science and International Relations.

Anthony F. Lang, Jr is a Senior Lecturer in the School of International Relations at the University of St Andrews.

Contemporary security studies

Punishment, Justice and International Relations
Ethics and order after the Cold War

Anthony F. Lang, Jr

Routledge
Taylor & Francis Group

LONDON AND NEW YORK

First published 2008
by Routledge
2 Park Square, Milton Park, Abingdon, Oxon OX14 4RN

Simultaneously published in the USA and Canada
by Routledge
270 Madison Ave, New York, NY 10016

Routledge is an imprint of the Taylor & Francis Group, an informa business

Transferred to Digital Printing 2009

© 2008 Anthony F. Lang, Jr

Typeset in Sabon by Wearset Ltd, Boldon, Tyne and Wear

British Library Cataloguing in Publication Data
A catalogue record for this book is available from the British Library

Library of Congress Cataloging in Publication Data
A catalog record for this book has been requested

ISBN10: 0-415-43907-8 (hbk)
ISBN10: 0-415-57031-X (pbk)
ISBN10: 0-203-92714-1 (ebk)

ISBN13: 978-0-415-43907-7 (hbk)
ISBN13: 978-0-415-57031-2 (pbk)
ISBN13: 978-0-203-92714-4 (ebk)

Dedicated to my children,
Theodore, Beatrice and Henry

Contents

Preface and acknowledgements

This book argues that punitive practices take place at the international level but that those practices do not create a just international order. The argument is premised upon the assumption that punishment should create a just society. Because of problems of authority and agency, however, punishment does not function properly at the international level. As a result, attempts to enforce compliance with norms, rules and laws at the international level result in unjust policies and political disorder.

The arguments developed in this book have resulted from the trajectory of my research and thinking about international relations thus far. My first book, *Agency and Ethics*, explored humanitarian intervention by focusing on the question of agency, particularly state agency. I found debates about agency in international relations, inspired by Alexander Wendt's seminal 1987 article on the topic, to be interesting but lacking in their inattention to ethical and political conceptions of agency. That book argued that state agency arises from a process of historical construction. I still agree with some of it, although I now think I was a bit too "statist" in my argument – i.e. that privileging state agency in international affairs reinforces certain conceptual structures that do not support a just world order. Focusing on agency led me to questions of responsibility, questions I have explored through the economic sanctions placed on Iraq and peacekeeping missions undertaken through the United Nations system. Agency and responsibility have led me to questions of punishment.

Another strand of my research and writing has also fed into this book. In my work at the Carnegie Council on Ethics and International Affairs, I engaged in dialogue with a wide range of scholars, activists and policy-makers on the ethics of the use of military force. Some of this work has appeared in print, while some appears for the first time here. I found the just war tradition to be the most interesting and helpful for thinking about the use of military force. In particular, I believe that the question of just authority is the core problem of the tradition, a problem that has been addressed by authors both past and present. Authority, not coincidentally, is also a key issue in punishment, a point I have tried to develop throughout this book.

Yet a third strand of ideas has fed into this research. As a graduate student in political science in the early 1990s, I was fascinated by the methodological debates prompted by post-structuralists and constructivists. This interest can be found in this book in my use of Michel Foucault's work. At the same time, I believe classical realism, particularly the work of Hans Morgenthau, continues to have relevance for international affairs. And, a single course in political theory on the work of Hannah Arendt convinced me that her work has more relevance for the study of global politics than has been commonly appreciated. The influence of these thinkers – admittedly not a normal grouping – will be seen in the chapters of this book.

None of these streams of research and writing arose *de novo* from my own head. A wide range of individuals and institutions have contributed to my thinking on these issues. A few deserve special notice for their insights on this particular book. Nicholas Rengger, my colleague at St Andrews, once described political theory to me as a conversation. His conversations over coffee (which I brew much better than he does) have pointed me in directions I never would have imagined. Chris Brown, who read my first book as a manuscript (and whose advice I largely ignored, much to my later chagrin), has served as a commentator on various papers at conferences that form parts of this book. Chris combines theoretical sophistication with political insight in such a way that every time he has engaged with my work, I always find it much improved. Toni Erskine's work on responsibility and international relations, and her construction of a network of people to pursue that interest, has been profoundly important for the development of my thinking on these themes. Toni's incisive questions on the pursue of punishment have clarified this project. Nicholas Onuf, whose actions as a scholar and teacher have inspired me since I was a graduate student, read substantial portions of this work. Not only has Nick greatly improved what I wanted to say, he has made me realize that I need to say some things I didn't want to, but were necessary for the argument to work. Patrick Hayden, who arrived at St Andrews after I had begun this project, has read through large sections of it and, in so doing, greatly improved its content. Best of all, we have discussed the book not only in my office but on the golf course, which is a much more productive intellectual setting!

A range of other individuals have contributed to this project by commenting on particular chapters: Torsten Michel, Amanda Beattie, Terry Nardin, Patricia Owens, Mark Evans, Gabi Slomp, Harry Gould, Kateri Carmola, Chandra Sriram, Oliver Richmond, Ian Hall, Cian O'Donnell, Sam Harris, Mark Drumbl, Oded Lowenheim, Brent Steele, Sean Molloy, Andrew Neal, Max Taylor, Alex Schmid and Steve Watts. Presentations at ISA meetings, ISA South, University of Glasgow, Cambridge University, University of Edinburgh, London School of Economics and the University of Wales-Swansea added greatly to the ideas developed here. The editorial team at Routledge has been extremely patient and helpful throughout the process. Andrew Humphreys as my editor and his assistant Emily Kindley-sides deserve a great deal of credit for ensuring that this book actually ended up in readers' hands.

My wife, Nicki Wilkins, read some sections and discussed the overall idea with me numerous times. She has challenged me to think about justice and punishment from her perspective as a priest and pastor – a challenge that may not be obvious in every page, but which underlies my attempt to make punishment more just. I am immensely appreciative to her not only for these challenges, but also for making life more bearable while I struggled through the ideas in this book.

This book is dedicated to my children, Theodore, Beatrice and Henry. At various presentations about subjects in this book, I admitted that one of the things that sparked my interest was reading numerous parenting books about how to discipline, punish or impose consequences on children. My wife and I continue to read and think about how to teach our children proper behaviour, knowing that there is not one right answer to how to parent. Through all this, our children continue to respond to our faltering efforts as parents with unconditional love – for which, I am truly thankful.

Introduction

Augusto Pinochet, Slobodan Milosevic and Saddam Hussein. These three leaders have been tried through some combination of international and domestic legal procedures. Only Saddam Hussein was punished in the traditional sense of the word, although both Pinochet and Milosevic suffered by being detained during their trials. All three cases were designed to enforce human rights norms that have emerged at the global level. International lawyers have hailed the fact that they were even brought to trial as evidence of a sea change away from a sovereign system in which leaders are immune from prosecution to a world in which widely accepted norms can be upheld.

Individual leaders are not the only agents that have been punished in the current international system. Iran, Libya, North Korea, Sudan and numerous other countries have been subject to economic sanctions as a result of their failure to comply with UN Security Council Resolutions. Even war has become a form of punishment. The attack on Afghanistan in October 2001 was in part a strategic effort to prevent terrorism in the future, but simultaneously punitive, retribution on both al-Qaeda and the Taliban regime that supported Osama bin Laden and the organization he directs. The network of detention facilities that surround the war on terror that American policymakers refuse to call prisons include both medieval punishments such as torture and more modern ones such as incarceration and surveillance.

War crimes trials, economic sanctions, punitive interventions and counter-terrorism policies – international society has become increasingly punitive in recent years. As these punitive practices increase, however, justice and peace appear no closer. Intended to enforce rules designed to create more justice and peace in the system these punitive practices, in fact, appear to be making the international system more violent and unjust. Especially as these practices are being undertaken by the United States in its strategy of hegemonic leadership, they have increased conflict and unrest throughout the world. The war on Iraq and the trial of Saddam Hussein crystallized these tensions. Very few would deny that Iraq and its ruling regime violated a wide range of global norms concerning weapons of mass destruction, democracy and respect for human rights. But waging war to change the regime and executing the leader have not led to more respect for the rules, but a more fraught international system. What is happening? Can rules not be enforced by punishment at the global level? Or, is there something wrong with the way in which punishment takes place at the international level?

Punishment and international relations

Why do efforts to enforce global norms and rules through punitive practices fail to produce a just world order? To answer this question, a series of subsidiary questions need to be raised: What is a punitive practice at the international level? Are global norms and rules enforced through punitive practices? Can punitive practices be restructured to create a more just world order? These are the questions that this book explores.

War crimes trials, punitive wars and economic sanctions are premised on an assumption that politics requires punishment, an assumption I interrogate in Chapter 1. For political systems to function properly, especially those that are grounded in some form of constitutionalism or law, those who violate the rules of the system must either be punished or be under threat of punishment. Some of the earliest conceptualizations of justice were primarily about punishing those who violate the law.[1] Although today much of the philosophical literature about justice focuses on distributive issues, retributive justice remains an important topic of analysis among philosophers and particularly philosophers of the law. Not only among philosophers is it considered a central issue; nearly everyone in domestic society recognizes the importance of punishment for the functioning of a political order.[2]

While the assumption that punishment is necessary for politics makes sense at the domestic level, it becomes more complicated at the international. Although Martin Wight's admonition that the domestic and international cannot be conflated still has resonance, recent work in international political theory challenges this widely accepted distinction.[3] Yet, even among those challenging the distinction, there remains a lack of attention to the issue of punishment. Perhaps the one place where punishment has been addressed is in the literature on international criminal law.[4] Even here the focus has tended to be on the justifications for creating international courts, universal jurisdiction and the types of rules, norms and laws that should govern international criminal law. There is very little on what constitutes legitimate forms of punishment after individuals have been found guilty of crimes. But while theorists have failed to address this question, international criminal courts and tribunals are finding individuals guilty and sentencing them.

More importantly, as this book demonstrates, individuals are not the only agents in the international system subject to punishment. States are punished through economic sanctions and war. Non-state agents such as terrorist organizations have also been subject to punishments, as have multinational corporations. The problem, then, is that punitive practices continue to take place at the international level. Those practices are justified by reference to an imagined political order that is unreflectively premised upon domestic political order. The differences between the domestic and the international, however, result in practices that are both incoherent and unjust. This book attempts to clarify some of the incoherence and offer some suggestions for how to make the order more just.

In response to these issues, the book has three overarching arguments. First, the current international order relies upon a set of punitive practices. These practices, explored in the chapters to follow, include (but are not limited to) military intervention, economic sanctions, international criminal courts and counter-terrorist policy. These practices play a key role in constituting the legalist, liberal international order embodied in various international institutions and rules. But those who explore the constitution of international order have not explored punishment; instead, those scholars tend to focus on the institutions, rules and norms that are constitutive of the current order.[5] What they fail to explore is how a wide range of practices, punitive practices, give concrete expression to those liberal ideas and institutions. Thus, the first thesis of this book is that to understand the current international order it is essential that a wide range of practices need to be understood as punitive.

Second, while these punitive practices constitute the current international order, they actually hinder the construction of a just and peaceful order. Although these punitive practices often receive their justification through liberal norms – human rights, democracy promotion and non-proliferation of weapons of mass destruction – they do not exist within a just political order. Moreover, they create more conflict than cooperation, thus undermining the potential for peaceful coexistence. This leads to the ironic result that practices designed to promote justice and peace produce unjust and violent outcomes.

Third, in response to the world that these punitive practices are creating, I propose some alternative ways of constructing the world. These range from the theoretical to the concrete. These alternatives are not intended to be specific policy prescriptions to powerful actors, but ways of re-imagining the world in order that rules can be enforced through just forms of punishment.

As will become clear in the following chapters, this book responds to important developments of the last decade of the twentieth century and the first decade of the twenty-first century.[6] The 1990s saw the beginning of a still ongoing conflict between the United States and Iraq, a conflict that has included a range of punitive actions. The decade also saw the explosion of conflict in the Balkans that led to punitive responses by the United States and Europe. It witnessed a series of major terrorist attacks that resulted in a range of punitive counter-terrorism responses. It also saw the reinvigoration of and creation of two international institutions that embody punitive elements: the United Nations Security Council (UNSC), once hampered by the Cold War conflict, but now free to impose both economic and military sanctions on states and the International Criminal Court (ICC), an institution designed to prosecute and punish individuals who violate various international norms. Finally, it has seen debate about the proper sanctions to be imposed on states that pursue weapons of mass destruction in violation of international treaty obligations.

Because of the importance of these developments, many of the cases explored will draw from the last two decades. At the same time, the argument will place these developments in their proper historical context and ensure that parallel past practices will also be explored. The argument will draw upon a wide range of international political theorists in support of its analyses. The next section locates the argument in relation to two ways of understanding the international system.

Punishment, realism and liberalism

The problem to which this book is responding is that the international order includes a wide array of punitive practices, but those engaged in them assume that the practices can accomplish the same ends in the international order as punishment accomplishes in the domestic order. Punishment is not the only concept that has been poorly translated from the domestic to the international. The debate between realists and liberals in the early twentieth century relied upon similar conceptual and normative confusion. Liberals proposed an international political structure in which peace would result from education, cooperation and the operation of a capitalist free market. Realists responded with both analytical and normative critiques of this position.

The debate between these two has dominated twentieth and twenty-first century analyses of international relations. As a result, it is useful to explore how modern inheritors of the realism–liberalism debate conceptualize the problem identified.[7] For scholars of realism, the practices that form the core of this book need not be linked, but exist as strategies employed by powerful actors in pursuit of their interests.[8] For liberal institutionalists, some of these practices – particularly the growth of courts and the use of economic sanctions by the United Nations – evince an attempt by self-interested actors to solve their collective action problems. That is, states still pursue their self-interests, but they do so through institutions they construct.[9] Other liberal theorists might see the growth of the norms underlying these punitive practices as evidence of the power of ideas of human rights and justice.[10] For critical theorists of both realist and liberal stripes, these practices demonstrate the ongoing injustice of the international political system, as powerful actors label some states "rogue" and some individuals "criminal" while they commit the same crimes.[11]

Yet these approaches largely avoid the concept of punishment.[12] They avoid it not in the sense that they avoid describing and explaining things like coercive military strategies, sanctions and war crime tribunals; they avoid it in the sense that they do not describe these policies in punitive terms. Their failure to describe them as such results, I argue here briefly and in the chapters that follow, from certain assumptions about what it means to punish.

Realists, both classical and neorealists, avoid describing the use of force as punitive, for to do so would suggest that there is an authority that can impose sanctions for violations of the law.[13] Such an assumption would violate the primary realist tenet that the international system is anarchic.[14] Even those classical realists who do see the international system as including some normative dimensions, do not describe the use of force in punitive terms. Indeed, some even refuse to see war crimes tribunals as punitive. Hans Morgenthau, a leading realist scholar, argued in response to the Nuremberg Trials that punishment was not an appropriate response to the horrors of the Nazis, claiming that it represented victors' justice rather than a true punitive action.[15] For Morgenthau, this assumption derives in part from his view of ethics as modelled on a divine source.[16] Without that authoritative figure, any use of force, including execution of war criminals, cannot be called punishment, but represents a further instance of the role of power in the international system.

In Chapter 2, I critically assess this assumption concerning authority, examining the function of authority in the practice of punishment. Suffice it to say for now that the assumption that punishment requires a sovereign authority is not a necessary element of a just society. Theorists of international society and natural law – Hedley Bull, Hugo Grotius and John Locke to name a few – see the international system as constituted by state agents who can act to protect what might be called an "international society."

For liberals, both idealists and neoliberals, the lack of attention to theories of punishment is strange. For, if they see institutions as ways to solve collective action problems, little theory is devoted to what happens when an actor chooses to ignore the institution or rules. Rather, the response to those violations is seen as a strategic action – collective security – rather than as a punitive action. The distinction between collective security and punishment may not be clear, for they both involve an infliction of harm on an agent in response to past behaviour. Yet, the rationale underlying collective security is generally not punitive.[17] This seems to be the result of two factors. First, in the idealist strain of liberalism, there is an assumption that human nature is malleable and ultimately cooperative. Rather than needing to punish violators, the proper policy seems to be one of education. In some ways, this idealist assumption has fed into some of the more recent literature on reconciliation in post-conflict societies. It is striking that punishment of wrongdoing rarely appears in the voluminous literature on post-conflict reconciliation except as a shibboleth used to beat back "unjust" responses. The overriding assumption of much of this literature seems to be that punishment equals vengeance, and so does not lead to a just outcome. While this may be true at times, the avoidance of punishment as a possible response to past atrocities is surprising.[18]

A second reason, one explored in greater depth in Chapter 3, concerns agency. The literatures on sanctions and coercive diplomacy, explored in the following chapters, argue that these policies are not punitive, but that they are part of a strategic interaction among agents in an anarchic order. Those who advocated sanctions as an alternative to war with Iraq throughout the 1990s twisted and turned to develop "smart sanctions," i.e. those that did not punish communities but targeted leaders.[19] Smart sanctions certainly did move some of the pain away from the community towards the leaders, but, at the same time, they were still punitive. Strategic interactions put in the service of a normative goal like promoting human rights or ensuring compliance with rules governing weapons of mass destruction – the policies underlying many of the UN sanctions regimes – have clear punitive dimensions. More interestingly, a point explored in Chapter 3, the imposition of sanctions not only punishes agents it creates agents as potentially liable to punishment. That is, agency is not a simple fact at the international level; it is something that is constituted by various policies and outcomes. Imposing sanctions, "smart" or not, creates responsible agents by assuming that this strategy can be used to implement changes in states' policies. Liberals who theorize strategies like economic sanctions and coercive diplomacy fail to appreciate that their policies are not part of a system in which clearly defined agents pursue interests. Rather, those policies constitute responsible agents by engaging in actions that are punitive. Without understanding how punitive strategies constitute agents, we fail to see how the international community functions and might function in a more just way.

Punitive practices

While the first three chapters explore some of the theoretical issues surrounding punishment, the remaining chapters of the book explore the punitive dimensions of various practices in the international system. Chapter 4 begins the study of specific punitive practices that constitute the international order by exploring what I call punitive intervention. Unlike humanitarian intervention, punitive interventions impose harm on a society or use military means to capture individuals in response to violations of human rights. It could thus be considered a subset of humanitarian intervention, in that the harm inflicted is to support a humanitarian purpose. Through the construction of a database of interventions undertaken over the last 60 years, I demonstrate that there has been a rise in this form of military intervention. I suggest that this increase can be partly explained by an increase in American uses of military force, which tend to have a more punitive dimension than others, but also by larger trends in the international system. I also suggest that while these uses of force are undertaken to support liberal goals, they create more conflict because they are not connected to broader institutional structures.

Chapter 5 turns to a non-military practice, but one that is just as punitive as the use of force: economic sanctions. The chapter draws upon a different methodology than the previous one, in that I explore four cases of economic sanctions at four different moments in history: League sanctions on Italy, UN sanctions on Rhodesia, UN sanctions on Iraq and UN targeted sanctions in support of counter-terrorism. I examine these four cases as instances of punitive sanctions. After determining that they are punitive, I point to how they helped construct particular world orders, yet also demonstrate how other elements of those world orders rendered the sanctions regime faulty. I conclude by pointing to how targeted sanctions are a more just form of punishment, but even these fail to integrate norms of criminal justice and due process necessary to protect the rights of those accused of supporting terrorism.

Chapter 6 explores punitive counter-terrorism policy. In this chapter, I focus on US counter-terror practices, examining in more detail three dimensions of that policy: military strikes and war; detention policies; and interrogation and torture. These three practices are identified as punitive, exploring both how the terrorist studies literature and the practices themselves reveal a punitive dimension while simultaneously claiming that they are only designed to protect American citizens. I conclude by arguing that these practices would be more just if they admitted their punitive nature and, more importantly, nested those practices in a judicial order that was more constitutional.

In the final chapter, I begin with a brief review of the arguments made in the three empirical chapters. Having argued that a more judicial and constitutional approach to punishment is necessary, I focus briefly on the international criminal justice regime as an institution that might provide some insights in how to punish more justly. I find some insight here, but also find fault with these institutions as being incapable of responding to the evils that they are designed to punish. Returning to the theoretical arguments made in the first three chapters, I conclude that a rethinking of these courts would provide some alternatives to how evil might be mitigated through more effective judicial and constitutional structures at the global level.

The book combines the empirical with the normative. Throughout these chapters I offer suggestions for how the international system can better respond to conflict and injustice by drawing upon the practice of punishment. Thus, while critiquing the ways in which punishments have been deployed in the current international system, I also argue that they are necessary. This book provides some insights into how new institutions might be designed in order to create a more just and legitimate international order.

1 Punishment, order and justice

What role does punishment play in the constitution of a just international order? This question lies at the heart of this chapter and this book. In brief, my answer is as follows. In the post-Cold War era, punishment takes place at the global level through a series of practices that constitute *an illiberal political order* even though each practice seeks to promote a particular set of liberal norms. A truly liberal order would promote human rights and democracy within the context of a broader rule-governed international system. Instead, the current order promotes human rights in specific contexts and by means of punitive practices but without being nested in a broader rule-governed, or what I call a constitutional, order. In this book, I identify the practices that are creating an illiberal order and propose ways to make that order more constitutional and just.

Punishment is central to the creation of this illiberal order for three reasons. First, punishments at the global level fail to combine retributive and deterrent elements. As this chapter will demonstrate, combining these two functions requires a constitutional structure in which executives, legislatures and judiciaries operate together in the construction of a rule-governed order. The current international system has a proliferation of executives (sovereign states), a broad range of legislatures and legislation, but a dearth of functioning judiciaries. This chapter will demonstrate the importance of the judiciary to the creation of a more just international order, particularly when it comes to punishment.

The second and third ways in which punishment constructs an illiberal global order will be explored in Chapters 2 and 3, but I will briefly mention them here. The second reason is that multiple executive authorities undertake punishment, rendering it closer to vengeance than true punishment. As I demonstrate in the next chapter, however, for punishment to contribute to a truly liberal order, we do not necessarily need a single sovereign authority. Drawing on the theories of natural law theorists such as Hugo Grotius and John Locke, I suggest that punishment can be undertaken by individual executives in the state of nature, but only if there is a strong and effective judicial structure than can adjudicate between competing claimants. Again, I argue we need a more constitutional order for punishment to be an effective part of a liberal international order.

The third reason that punishment fails to contribute to a just liberal order is the failure to identify correctly the proper agents at the international level. This failure results from a conceptual confusion at the global level about agency and responsibility. Punishing individuals through war crimes tribunals, states through sanctions practices, and other groups by means of counter-terrorism activity can all be justified, but the failure to connect these different agents through the role of a single judicial structure makes the various punitive practices appear random and disconnected. This lack of order when determining agency contributes to the construction of an illiberal order.

To understand how punitive practices can be oriented towards the promotion of liberal norms yet contribute to an illiberal international order consider human rights. A human rights regime can be found in the United Nations system, manifested in the UN Charter (1946), Declaration on Human Rights (1948), Covenant on Civil and Political Rights (1966) and Covenant on Social and Economic Rights (1966). These instruments reflect a shared understanding of human rights in the current international system that has become central to the ways in which we understand politics at the global level.[20] They form a foundation for many discursive practices in which liberal states engage to justify their foreign policies. Since the end of the Cold War, the international community has invoked human rights as so important that military force can be employed to defend them in situations where they are being violated. This argument has formed the core of many justifications for humanitarian intervention.[21]

The four practices explored in more detail in the chapters to follow have all been deployed in the post-Cold War era to promote human rights. Humanitarian interventions, economic sanctions, counter-terrorism policies and war crimes tribunals have all been invoked as ways to protect the human rights of individuals in situations of conflict or post-conflict. They form the core of an aggressive liberal attempt to create a more just international order. The problem, however, is that they operate outside of a constitutional structure in which judgements are made about wrongs and criminal culpability. Certainly, there exist judicial structures – the International Criminal Court and the International Court of Justice are the two most important. Yet, these two institutions operate in different spheres and sometimes at cross-purposes with each other. Moreover, various human rights structures in regional and even national contexts tend to undermine any kind of single judicial order.

This book focuses on this broader need for a more just constitutional order within which punishment can be justified. The next section provides some clarity about the concept of punishment, focusing in particular on its deterrent and retributive dimensions. The section also clarifies how punishment can be understood as a practice as opposed to an official policy of an authoritative sovereign, a description that comes closer to how punishment functions at the international level. The following section examines the concept of order, particularly as it has been understood at the international level and the role that punishment plays in constituting that order. The final section examines the concept of justice, explaining what it would mean for punishment to contribute to a just political order, and proposing the idea of a global constitutional political order. The conclusion points to the conceptual problems of authority and agency that will be addressed in Chapters 2 and 3.

Punishment

A punishment is the infliction of harm in response to a violation of a norm or rule. Punishment differs from vengeance because it is a response to a general rule and not a single act of harm. This distinction is important to emphasize, for many assume that vengeance differs from punishment because a non-sovereign undertakes the former while a sovereign undertakes the latter. For an infliction of harm to count as punishment it must be intended to support, in some way, a general rule of behaviour for a society. This is why criminal trials differ from civil trails in Anglo-American law; in a criminal trial, the prosecution is the state, which, although an individual has been harmed by the crime, sees it as a violation of its norms and rules and so deems punishment should be necessary to uphold those rules and norms.

Some definitions of punishment assume that it must be undertaken by an "authority" which results from the desire to avoid the abuse of force by powerful individuals in a state of nature. This concern is a valid one, but ensuring that there exists a single sovereign authority will not necessarily prevent this problem – indeed, sovereign authority figures can abuse the practice of punishment as much as powerful individuals. Instead, what is required is an institutional structure that is legitimate, grounded in a clearly defined set of rules that fairly adjudicates about which agents can be punished. Especially in a political system that is formally anarchic (as the current international system is), punishment can take place as long as it is arises from an institutional framework. This point is expanded upon in Chapter 2, where I draw upon a diverse range of theorists to explore how institutions at the global level can be seen as legitimate agents of punishment.

The overriding purpose of punishment is twofold: return the community to the balance that existed prior to the violation of the norm, and prevent such violations in the future. But the decision to inflict harm in order to halt that violation is a contestable practice, since the infliction of harm is "something we regard as morally prohibited under normal circumstances."[22] Much of the philosophical literature, then, has been devoted to justifying this practice with deterrence and retribution having been offered as the primary justifications.[23]

Deterrence is the idea that by punishing agents who violate norms future violations will be prevented. Deterrence can be either specific or general. If it is specific, it is an attempt to deter a particular agent from violating the same norm again. If it is general, it is an attempt to deter others from violating the law by using the individual case as an example. Punishment premised on deterrence is largely unconcerned with the welfare or character of the agent being harmed. Instead, the practice aims to alter the agent's behaviour and to demonstrate a larger point to the community. Deterrence can be evaluated in terms of whether or not the same crimes continue to occur. If they do, the deterrence approach may not be working; if they do not, one would have a reason, though not a conclusive one, for thinking that deterrence does work. The general deterrent justification arises from a utilitarian philosophy, in that it seeks to justify punishment on the basis of contributing to a greater good for the entire society.

Retribution as the justification for punishment is more difficult to capture. It is, perhaps, the most common-sense notion of punishment. As one author suggests, it is the "idea that wrongdoers should be 'paid back' for their wicked deeds."[24] This idea considers both the community and the criminal. It seeks to restore a sense of balance to a community by punishing wrongdoers. It differs from deterrence in not seeking to use the agent to teach a larger lesson. Retributive punishment respects the moral autonomy of the agent more than does punishment aimed at deterrence. Retribution assumes that the agent is not a tool to be used to convince a community of a lesson; instead, an agent is presumed to be morally autonomous and therefore responsible for his or her actions.

The philosophical literature on punishment has sought to develop these justifications, especially in combination with each other. Critics of the general deterrent or utilitarian justification have argued that, according to this justification, there is no need actually to punish the agent who committed the crime. Instead, a utilitarian justification could lead to the punishment of random individuals whenever a norm is violated.[25] A related problem is that a utilitarian or deterrent punishment, while actually focusing on the individual agent who committed the violation, might engage in excessive forms of violence to make the point. For example, one might execute individuals for jaywalking according to an extreme form of utilitarianism or deterrence.[26] Others have levelled important criticisms at the retributive model. While retribution might address the problems raised by the utilitarian model – that is, it can better connect the agent to the violation – critics have suggested that it "confuses the irrational thirst for vengeance with a rational ground for punishment."[27]

These debates continue among both theorists and policymakers. In the United Kingdom, for instance, justifications for domestic punishment have oscillated among a variety of justifications. After the popularity of rehabilitation as the central principle of punishment in the 1960s, the perceived rise in crime during the 1970s and 1980s led to a renewed interest in retributive justifications. The Criminal Justice Act of 1991 made the "retributivist principle of just deserts as the primary principle of sentencing, where by the focus is on proportionate punishment rather than treatment or deterrence *per se*."[28] The 2002 White Paper, Justice for All and the 2003 Criminal Justice Act continued this emphasis on retribution, although seeking to locate punishment within a wider social context in which the rights of victims, criminals and society were balanced.[29]

While public discourse oscillates among these different justifications in different domestic political contexts, rarely are these concepts addressed at the international level. Certainly, the idea of deterrence is commonplace among theorists of international relations. At the same time, its invocation in strategic debates rarely conceptualizes it as a form of punishment. Retribution is perhaps the most commonly invoked justification for punishing at the international level, usually in uses of force. Retributive justifications, usually verging on the vengeful, have been an important part of the discourse surrounding war. One study of public opinion attitudes in the United States links support for the death penalty with support for retributive uses of military force.[30]

The lack of direct reference to these justifications for punishment at the global level does not mean they are not operative in different contexts. In other words, what makes certain actions punitive or not is precisely the discourse of justification that seeks to link them to prevention of harm for the community as a whole. So, when activists invoke "ending impunity" by bringing Sudanese militia members before the ICC, they are drawing upon deterrent and retributive logics. When American soldiers carry with them flags from New York City in the prosecution of the war on terror in Afghanistan, they are engaging in retributive actions. When economic sanctions were imposed on Iraq during the 1990s, especially when they were targeted at leaderships rather than whole communities, a deterrent and perhaps even a rehabilitative logic were at work.

Simply suggesting how these diverse actions might be understood as punitive requires more clarification. The next section locates punishment more centrally in international affairs through the idea of punitive practices, or the wide ranging set of actions that reinforce global rules and enforce a hierarchy of states.

Punitive practices

The political practices that are the subject of this book – intervention, economic sanctions and counter-terrorism policy – are not often described as punitive. If they are, especially in the post-conflict justice literature, the term punitive is not used in a descriptive sense but in an evaluative, usually negative, sense.[31] One reason that punitive is not used to describe these actions is that those who undertake them rarely describe them as such.

Political leaders who undertake military interventions do not describe their efforts as a means to "punish" those who violate international norms. Even when economic sanctions are employed (a term that is conceptually linked to punishment), policymakers do not emphasize the punitive nature of their policy and seek instead to frame it in terms of coercing the leaders of the opposing state.[32]

A central argument of this book is that such practices should be described as punitive. While this case will be made in each chapter in which a specific practice is explored, I want to introduce briefly the overall method I employ in making these claims. To describe these policies as punitive relies on the concept of a practice. Practices as I use the term in this book are the intentions, justifications, events and outcomes that delimit a certain area of reality at the global level. Such practices get labelled through a discourse that constitutes them, a discourse in which scholars, policymakers and commentators all play a part. A practice cannot be reduced to a single dimension or a single scholarly account of that reality – instead, a conglomeration of different agents play a role in creating it as a reality.

This conception of a practice draws partly from the work of Michel Foucault. For Foucault, "discursive practices are characterized by the delimitation of a field of objects, the definition of a legitimate perspective for the agent of knowledge, and the fixing of norms for the elaboration of concepts and theories."[33] Foucault explored a range of such practices, including punishment, madness and sexuality. His work revealed that these terms are not simple descriptions of a reality, but categories that result from various social and economic structures, political projects and scholarly discourses. For Foucault, connecting these specific practices to wide realms of social reality meant locating them in the larger social and political systems that constitute daily life. Practices result in part from the nexus of power and knowledge.

Since he explored punishment as one such practice, briefly describing Foucault's views here will help clarify the idea of a practice as I will use it. At one level, in *Discipline and Punish*, Foucault provided a history of punishment in France from the seventeenth to the twentieth centuries.[34] He begins by describing how punishment was the infliction of pain on the body in a public spectacle in order to demonstrate the power of the sovereign. As a result of Enlightenment reformers like Cesare Beccaria, attempts to teach the criminal the error of his ways by reformation became the focus.[35] Further reforms, particularly the ideas of Jeremy Bentham, shifted the focus to observing and classifying the prisoner, thus not only reforming him but also analysing and studying him. Bentham's ideas linked the power of the prison to emerging forms of knowledge, thus reinforcing the power/knowledge link that animated much of Foucault's work. The architectural design of Bentham's model prison, the panopticon, in which the prisoners were separated from each other but could be constantly observed, captures these ideas.

But, at another level, Foucault is not just interested in the penal reforms that spread throughout Europe. Instead, he uses these penal reforms as a means to analyse other changes in society. For instance, the shift from the infliction of pain on the body to a focus on the inner character of the prisoner reflected the growth of capitalist modes of production and the associated need for an organized and regimented workforce. Yet even this was not the end point for Foucault's exploration of punishment (indeed, others had made this point prior to his work);[36] rather, Foucault linked punitive techniques to the ways in which society disciplined itself, with examples drawn from education, the military and, especially, psychiatry. He demonstrates that the panopticon was not simply an architectural model for the prison, but a model for how society could be governed and constituted through the constant observation, administration and disciplining of its members. Through this tool, the "inmates [or members of society] should be caught up in a power situation of which they themselves are the bearers."[37] He expands this analysis by exploring how the prison created the category of a "delinquent," an idea that reinforces what is normal in society and thus allows it to function. In other words, punishment is not simply about preventing crime and creating security in a society; it is also about the construction of society and its members.

Foucault's work demonstrates how to conceptualize punishment as a practice that reveals wider social and political dynamics, but that does not rely on a purely legalistic or ethical framework. But, I differ in important ways from Foucault. First, my ambition in this book is both less and more than Foucault's. It is less in that I do not explore a power/knowledge nexus for punishment at the global level. Instead, I want to locate punitive practices in relation to various developments in international relations that have coalesced in the post-Cold War era, particularly those that point to the construction of a liberal world order. So, the next section will explore briefly the debates about order and international affairs, locating punitive practices therein. Because this study is about global and international punitive practices, it extends beyond Foucault's focus primarily on European and North American social structures.

Second, and perhaps more importantly, I differ from Foucault in my belief that punishment is not simply about the circulation of power in society. Rather, I argue that punishment is necessary for a just political order, and social and political institutions can be proposed and constructed to sustain such political orders. From his political activism on behalf of prisoners, it is clear that Foucault was not the amoral individual that some of his critics paint him as. But his description of the prison as "the only place where power is manifested in its naked state, in its most excessive form, and where it is justified as moral force"[38] suggests that he did not see attempts to evaluate punishment morally as anything other than another discourse that should be subject to intense scrutiny and exposed for the power relations that it reveals.[39]

As the third section of this chapter on justice and punishment indicates, I cannot follow Foucault here. I believe that it is possible to propose alternatives to the current political practices operative at the international level. This means critically assessing them and revealing how their failures create unjust political structures and outcomes. So, while Foucault helps to orient this book towards some of its (re)descriptions of certain practices as punitive, I argue that some of those practices can be redesigned to further certain just political ends. I realize that in using Foucault in this way, I will satisfy neither those who see in his work the bane of social science and philosophy, nor those who find in him liberation from constraints imposed by those same disciplines. My only reply to those concerns is to note that Foucault is not the primary theoretical inspiration for this study, but that without his work I would not have been able to see these practices as punitive.

Punishment and order

Practices construct order in a political system. The chapters in this book explore punitive practices in the military and economic realms. But what I describe as punitive is rarely called this in the practice and study of international affairs; rather, we have intervention, economic sanctions, counter-terrorism policy and war crimes tribunals being undertaken to provide security, enforce human rights and bring about peace. Ultimately, however, these goals – security, protection of rights and peace – underlie the practice of punishment in a domestic political system. While the Foucauldian approach I have described above demonstrates how these practices can be understood as punitive, connecting them to particular conceptions of political order requires some clarification of what order means and the particular order (or orders) operative in the current international context.

What is political order? Political order can be understood in one of two ways, what Andrew Hurrell calls order as fact and order as value. First, it is simply a pattern of regular and predictable behaviour, one that provides a level of certainty that allows individuals to conduct their affairs. Second, order is a normative goal that individuals within a polity seek to achieve by designing their institutions to constitute a particular set of ends.[40] These two conceptions of order often appear together and end up being conflated by those who deploy them, but they assume different things about politics. The first meaning of order assumes that politics is an ongoing practice that does not have a particular end point, while the second assumes politics is a goal-oriented project that will achieve some final end point, even if only in a utopian formula.[41]

For some, political order stands in contrast to justice, as famously stated by Hedley Bull in his Hagey Lectures.[42] The argument here is that the pursuit of regularized interactions among individuals requires that some of those individuals will not have their rights respected. The need to obtain peaceful interactions among agents cannot constantly succumb to the demands of those who feel disenfranchised by the existing relations. In order to establish order, according to this view, powerful agents must set the parameters of what can and cannot be done in the political sphere and must continuously manage it to prevent radical change. Even if the political sphere solidifies in certain ways around the interests of the powerful, order requires that those whose interests are not being respected do not demand radical change.

To create order, compliance with rules is necessary.[43] Because agents do not always comply of their own free will, authorities exist to ensure such compliance. The means by which authorities ensure compliance can be through reward or sanction. While rewards are theoretically possible as a means to ensure order, the more common means are punitive. This may be because the "reward" to be gained by compliance is the simple existence of an ordered system in which agents can pursue their own individual wants and plans. Whatever the case, it would appear that in most political systems, the primary means of enforcing compliance with a particular order is through punitive measures.

Punishment to create order can be of two types. First, the common-sense understanding of legal punishment, which is that agents know the rules and when they violate them are subject to a criminal justice procedure that, if they are found guilty, leads to them being punished in some way. The alternative is the Foucauldian notion of constituting order suggested in the previous section. Here, order results not from the conscious decisions of institutional actors, but from a wide range of political and social practices that internalize the rules in agents. This internalization process is not one that they would even recognize, but comes about through various evolutions in the daily practice of politics.

This book demonstrates that both sorts of punishment – formal, legal punishment and punitive practices – support the current international order. Institutions exist that impose order through the imposition of punishment. These institutions are both formal – the International Criminal Court (ICC) is the most prominent example – and informal – the role of great powers in enforcing the rules of the system.[44] The chapters that follow explore some of these institutions and their role in various political regimes. The following section suggests how such institutions should be understood in order that they embody justice. Punitive practices not necessarily linked to any specific institutional structure also play a role in creating the global political order. As Chapter 4 demonstrates, punitive intervention, while sometimes authorized by institutions such as the United Nations Security Council, also results from shared assumptions about which agents are legitimate. In the early 1990s intervention in Somalia, the assumption on the part of the UN, US and various human rights groups that certain warlords did not count as legitimate agents and could thus be subject to punishment and exclusion from the political realm led, in part, to the collapse of the intervention after the attacks on American soldiers in October 1993. Again, while decisions were made in this intervention in official institutions, they also resulted from political practices that construct the state as the only legitimate institution, thus preventing certain actors from playing any part in the political process.

Finally, what characterizes the current international order that is sustained by these political practices? To find a single "order" in the current international system is not really possible. Indeed, competing visions of order often motivate ideological conflict among various actors in the system. At the same time, the existence of an order that is both a pattern and a normative goal can be roughly outlined. It is perhaps best described as a liberal order, one based on two premises: that individuals have basic rights and that those rights can be best supported through the creation of sovereign states. Corollary to these assumptions are a range of others: peace between states is necessary and can only come about through the abandonment of aggressive war; economic development should take place at the national level and it is necessary for states to protect the rights of individuals; and communities should be able to create their own states, but only if they respect the needs of minority populations within those states.

A number of theorists have explored this liberal world order. Standard bearers of this model of world order include Stanley Hoffmann[45] and G. John Ikenberry.[46] Surprisingly, some realist authors assume that this liberal world order is the best model, even though they see it arising from a balance of power rather than from the creation of institutional structures.[47] Critical theorists have pointed to the tensions in this model or world order, yet, in so doing, they seek to construct an order that is similar in many respects.[48]

One of the leading theorists of international liberalism is Robert Keohane, whose recent work suggests a parallel to some of the issues described in this book. While sometimes characterized as a neoliberal, Keohane's recent work promotes what he calls "sophisticated liberalism" which combines the economic focus of commercial liberalism with the regulatory approach of more legal liberal ideas.[49] Keohane presents a powerful argument that a liberal world order has come into existence as states pursue their interests yet recognize the necessity of working together through institutions. In the late 1990s, Keohane turned more directly to international law as a source for understanding state interactions, helping to popularize the idea of "legalization" as a description of how various international institutions are becoming more legalistic in their operations.[50] Not only has his work become more focused on law in recent years, it has also turned towards the importance of ensuring compliance with international legal norms and rules rather than simply assuming that states will comply with those norms out of their own self-interest. In a series of recent articles, Keohane has described and promoted various mechanisms in international institutions for ensuring greater compliance with norms and holding agents accountable when they violate those norms.[51]

While his previous work examined how and why states follow various norms because it is in their self-interest to do so,[52] these recent articles demonstrate an understanding that agents do not comply with norms unless they are forced to do so. Perhaps because his concerns in the past have been with refuting the realist claim that rules and norms play no role in international affairs, this more recent work stands in contrast to his previous analyses. The shift from examining why states might comply with liberal norms because it benefits them to a focus on how institutions might be better designed to compel compliance is an important, albeit subtle, shift. While not exploring punishment directly, Keohane's work has begun to explore some of the themes being developed in this book – that is, how compliance with international norms and rules does not arise simply from the self-interest of agents (which it certainly does sometimes), but also comes about through more coercive or punitive practices.

Keohane and others, however, have not directly addressed punishment, the oldest means of ensuring compliance with rules and norms. This results in large part from the fact that the international system remains formally anarchic, thus occluding punitive practices that play a key role in sustaining that order. Without a sovereign authority issuing punishments on those who violate the rules, it would appear that the liberal order springs from the good will of member states and individual agents who work hard to create it. But, although such good will undoubtedly exists and individuals play a key role in creating and promoting that order, it also relies on the punishment of those who violate it. Highlighting how institutions and practices create order through punishment is one of the central aims of this book.

The order that is being created, however, is not the liberal one advocated by Keohane and others. Rather, it is what I would call an illiberal order, one that reinforces various liberal norms and rules in specific contexts, but does not connect those instances within a larger framework. This is not the same as claiming that the order is a realist one, for I do not believe that states simply pursue their self-interests with no concern for the role of rules and norms. Rather, I would argue that it is the pursuit of enforcement both selectively and violently that contributes to the illiberal international system. The 1999 coercive diplomacy used against Yugoslavia to protect the human rights of Albanian Kosovars[53] and the 2003 war against Iraq to enforce compliance with UN Security Council Resolutions concerning disarmament demonstrate how the aggressive pursuit of rules through enforcement mechanisms can lead to further violence and injustice.[54] Punishment, in other words, has enforced certain norms and rules in particular places, but it has not created a just international order.

Punishment, justice and constitutionalism

Punitive practices are currently constructing an illiberal political order. In order for them to contribute to a more just liberal order, they need to be nested in a larger, coherent framework. In this book I do not completely describe such an order, but I do want to demonstrate how the problem of punishment in the global order can be ameliorated by attending to a different political structure than the liberal ideas examined above; what I call a constitutional order. Before turning to how such an order might operate, let me detour into a brief discussion of the relationship between punishment and justice.

Justice is the cardinal political virtue. At its core, justice is the fair distribution of goods across a community. That distribution must be in accordance with some standard or metric that can be morally justified. It should reflect a balance, an equalling of status among agents in a community, although it does not necessarily mean that all agents should be equal in every sense. In terms of punishment, justice demands that the agent who has been harmed, along with the entire community of agents, must be taken into account when punishing the violator. It must also include attention to the rights of the criminal,[55] although those rights are diminished by the fact of having harmed others.

Because politics is an ongoing process, not one that has a single end point, most theorists of justice focus on the process more than the final outcome in determining that fair distribution. John Rawls' theory of justice focuses on the process by which goods are distributed, but uses a set of ideals to provide a critique of outcomes.[56] Others focus much more directly on the process, with libertarian arguments being almost solely devoted to justifying political practices on the basis of historical accounts.[57] Some equate justice with adherence to human rights standards, or the construction of a world in which human rights are protected.[58]

How does punishment relate to these standards of justice? The "good" punishment seeks to distribute is not wealth, even though in some cases punishments take wealth from one and give it to the state. Rather, the good that punishment seeks to promote is protection from harm or security.[59] Harm can be defined in terms of human rights, i.e. harm is inflicted when one's human rights are violated, but it need not be defined in such a way. By ensuring that individuals obey the rules and laws of a system, punishment ensures that those rules and laws continue to provide the good of protection. One could take this point even further and argue that the infliction of harm that punishment entails cannot conceptually be called punishment unless it is intended to protect others. That is, inflicting harm is simply violence unless it is connected to ensuring justice, i.e. protecting persons from harm.

This description of just punishment, however, focuses on how specific acts can be considered just. What of the justice of an entire punitive system, or what might be called criminal justice more broadly defined? For a political order to be just, it must protect the society or group as a whole from harm, not just individuals in specific cases. This would mean the inclusion of those who are potential criminals; i.e. the system should be designed not simply to inflict harm after a violation has occurred, but to construct a system in which individuals will not be put into a position to violate the rules in the first place. Furthermore, it is important to consider how a just system will not only ensure that agents are not in a position to violate certain norms, they must also be protected from being construed as criminals or outlaws by those with more power. A just political system, in other words, not only punishes those who violate norms, but also seeks to ensure that attributions of responsibility result from a fair political process.

The international system does not currently conform to such a definition of justice, especially when it comes to the ways in which states are constructed as responsible agents. This is not a new phenomenon, as Gerry Simpson has recently argued.[60] Simpson traces the ways in which great powers and, crucially, international lawyers have compromised their rhetoric about sovereign equality in the international legal order with a category of outlaw, pariah or rogue states. This has resulted in what Simpson calls a legalized hierarchy of states. Current American foreign policy only provides the most recent evidence for this trend, with the doctrine of "rogue states" and an "axis of evil" as guiding principles for its post-Cold War foreign policy.[61] This is not to say that states that are labelled as rogue or pariah have not violated certain norms, and that they might well deserve punishment. Rather, the process by which their responsibility is established fails to account for either their lack of agency[62] or their decisions being the result of acting within a structure dominated by legal and moral regimes from which they are systematically excluded.

Does this mean we are left without any just punishment? I would argue that it is possible to retain a conception of justice that is sensitive to these political dimensions. John Rawls, in a paper originally delivered in 1954, proposes a novel way to understand punishment, one that suggests a way to construct a political system that both recognizes the political dimensions of power yet also ensures that those who violate the rules can be punished. Rawls begins his essay by noting that there exist two types of rules: those that justify a practice as a whole and those that justify a particular application of that practice. He uses this distinction to make the case that punishment can be justified in both utilitarian and retributive ways. The practice of punishment as a means of enforcing justice in a society – that is, as an institution – is utilitarian. But the particular application of punishment in specific cases – the action of punishment – is best understood as retributive. One way to see this distinction is through the different roles played by a legislator and a judge:

One can say, then, that the judge and the legislator stand in different positions and look in different directions: one to the past, the other to the future. The justification of what the judge does, qua judge, sounds like the retributive view; the justification of what the (ideal) legislator does, qua legislator, sounds like the utilitarian view.[63]

Rawls' concern in writing this essay was to intervene in the philosophical debates I identified earlier in the chapter. My purpose in invoking him here is slightly different, although it overlaps. I interpret Rawls' conception of the legislator as the international community's role in constituting itself through legal and political practices, while the particular decisions made about guilt and innocence as part of a judicial process punish those who can fairly be considered as responsible agents. The current international system has been seeking to develop a judicial system in its creation of international criminal tribunals and the ICC. This remains an important part of constructing a just political system. At the same time, the international community needs to reconsider the legislative function that Rawls identifies. Resolutions passed by the Security Council and judgements made by the International Court of Justice provide two sources of law-making in the current order. As I have argued elsewhere, the former institution tends to constitute the powers of some over others, while the latter has not been effectively utilized, especially in possibly punishing states that violate international norms.[64]

Rawls' essay does not answer the question of how to construct a just punitive system, especially one that will be sensitive to the unequal distribution of power at the international level. What it does do, however, is demonstrate that if judicial institutions arise from a political system in which there is not sufficient attention being paid to the constitution of agents as responsible through discourses of power, such judicial institutions (like the ICC) may assuage our desire to inflict vengeance, but may not be just.

One way to make Rawls' ideas about punishment and justice relevant at the global level is to locate punishment in a constitutional order. Constitutionalism is a wide-ranging term that has been applied across different political contexts.[65] At its core, constitutionalism revolves around two central ideas: rule of law and a balance of power. In terms of the first, political decisions should be made in reference to a body of law that has been established within a political community, as opposed to making decisions on the basis of individual whim or personal interest. In terms of the second, a constitutional order needs to provide a balance of power among decision-makers within a particular political community, the classic being a balance between legislature, executive and judiciary. Constitutionalism, in other words, seeks to balance the need for adherence to rules with recognition that individuals within a political system will pursue their own interests in opposition to those rules, so that structural constraints need to be built into the system along with the rules. Constitutionalism does not necessarily require a "constitution" as a single text, with the United Kingdom demonstrating how a political system can function without such a text.

Constitutionalism has begun to appear more often amongst those exploring international affairs. International lawyers have only started exploring constitutionalism, often through an engagement with issues arising from the relations of international institutions with their constituent members.[66] Among those exploring questions of international relations more broadly, some of these themes have appeared in an emerging literature on republicanism.[67] This emerging literature, and the broader topic of constitutionalism, provides one way to think about Rawls' need for a political order in which the judiciary and legislature act together. A constitutional order provides legitimacy by ensuring that the law rules, rather than the whims of individuals, and that the most powerful can be constrained by both the rules and structures of the system. Enforcement is not automatic in a constitutional order but arises from the interactions between the different branches of government. And constitutions are defined by their adaptability, with the capacity of democratic process creating and recreating new constitutions through an amendment or complete rewriting of the constitution.

Creating constitutions is no easy matter, and governing according to a constitution will not solve all the problems that I have identified in terms of punishment.[68] The international system is also not on the verge of suddenly becoming a constitutional system. Perhaps what is needed, as a first step, is the inculcation of a spirit of constitutionalism rather than a full-fledged constitutional order. This would mean encouraging international agents to think critically about how they engage in punitive practices and how those practices might connect to each other rather than remain detached.

Two issues that are explored in the following two chapters – authority and agency – might be places to start in terms of creating a more constitutional spirit at the global level. First, judicial institutions need to be capable of trying both individual persons and corporate entities. A more robust ICJ, one that could actually try and punish states, could complement the ICC. The passage of the Articles on State Responsibility by the International Law Commission suggests that states can be considered responsible agents, although their refusal to include punitive sanctions as part of those articles vitiates their impact.[69] A more invigorated and conceptually coherent judicial structure would most certainly contribute towards the construction of a constitutional order.

Second, while empowering the ICJ to undertake such punishments would move determinations of responsibility and punishment away from institutions where power differentials determine outcomes, such as the Security Council, more judicial institutions will not solve all the problems of punishment. This requires greater political participation by the international community in the construction of the rules and norms that determine blame and responsibility. This is not a suggestion that Burma should serve on the Human Rights Council in the United Nations; rather, it is that institutions such as the United Nations need to be made more effective and participatory for various members of international society in the formulation of international norms. Powerful agents will always play a strong role in rule making, but incorporating more and diverse structures and institutions in which states and non-state actors can play a role in determining political norms is a first step.

Third, we need to think more critically about agency and responsibility. Only when we understand that the structures within which we are enmeshed, whether those are domestic or international, constitute us as responsible agents will we be less willing to engage in unthinking punitive actions.

This book does not provide the only answer to what a just punitive system might look like. Rather, it suggests some considerations that are necessary in constructing such a system. The chapters that follow provide some suggestions for new institutional arrangements that are not too idealistic to be achieved, but that do pay more attention to the differences among agents and the importance of justice. In describing the various ways in which punishment operates in the international system, this book will seek to reveal how far from or close to these ideals of a just punitive system the current international order actually is. Understanding both the importance and dangers of punishment for a just international order can result from being aware of the nuances involved in authority and agency, nuances explored in the chapters to follow.

2 Authority

The "war on terror" of recent years has seen the invocation of punishment as a justification for the use of force.[70] For many, however, this renewed interest in punishment appears as a retrograde development, something to be avoided rather than embraced. In particular, at the international level punishment is seen as highly problematic because there is no sovereign authority that can undertake just punishments. According to this line of argument, rather than a disinterested party that will punish and support the order of the community, states that engage in punitive wars are exacerbating tensions in an already anarchic system. Revenge leads to increased hostilities, a tit-for-tat mentality that results in unrestrained uses of military force by state and non-state actors alike. The one thing that separates punishment from revenge – an impartial authority – is the one thing that is missing at the international level.

Yet, as argued in the previous chapter, an increase in punishment at the global level might not be a bad thing. Punishment plays a central role in politics by enforcing compliance with the rules. Without punishment, rules can progressively lose their meaning and force. Especially when it is properly administered and part of a just political system, punishment can play an important role in reinforcing and stabilizing that system. If punishment is an important part of a just political order, but the international order lacks a sovereign authority, can we have justice? Without a sovereign, will attempts to "right wrongs" be nothing more then revenge?

This chapter addresses this problem by exploring the relationship between punishment and authority. Those concerned with the increase of punitive uses of force at the international level assume a particular type of authority, an executive sovereign whose primary goal is the creation of peace and security – a Hobbesian sovereign. Such a sovereign uses punishment to deter any future violations, ruling through fear. Punishment on this account would most certainly create security of a sort, but it might not contribute to a just order.

Such a sovereign authority does not exist at the international level, nor is there any prospect of one appearing any time soon. Instead, the international order does have other institutional arrangements that provide some glimpses as to what punishment might look like in a just constitutional system. If we relax our assumptions about the type of authority necessary for impartial punishment, alternative conceptions of political order become apparent.

The remainder of the book suggests ways in which current institutional arrangements, and the global public policies that those institutions promote, can be revised to incorporate a more just form of punishment. But before making those arguments (found in Chapters 4, 5 and 6), it is necessary to demonstrate that the authority necessary can be something different than a Hobbesian all-powerful sovereign. This chapter provides some of the theoretical foundation for those institutional modifications by reviewing three political theorists – Thomas Hobbes, John Locke and Hugo Grotius. I find Hobbes' arguments about punishment and authority problematic with their emphasis on deterrence, while I find in Locke and Grotius suggestions for how individual agents might punish each other. While Grotius proposes a system in which the decision to punish arises solely from a shared understanding of natural law, Locke proposes that the central institution of a just political order should be the judiciary. Such a constitutional order, while precarious because of the ever-present danger of revenge, does provide a means by which a political system without an executive authority might be able to engage in punitive actions that can promote justice. The chapter concludes by turning to the legal theory of Hans Kelsen. Kelsen's emphasis on the judicial element of international law, and suggestions for how such a judiciary might function at the global level, provide a means by which the ideas of Locke and Grotius could be turned into viable institutional arrangements.

Punishment, revenge and authority

Before turning to Hobbes, Locke and Grotius, a brief example of the danger of punishment turning into revenge without a sovereign authority is helpful. As noted above, the current US-led war on terror demonstrates what happens when a state takes on the role of punishing those who have violated its rights. In the case of the United States, however, its use of force against Afghanistan and then Iraq has been portrayed not just as an attempt to defend itself, but also in the context of its self-assumed role as the guarantor of the international order. As various American administration spokespersons have argued, the American fight against al-Qaeda is good not just for Americans but also for the entire international order.

One perceptive critic of this emerging punitive discourse is the philosopher Paul Gilbert. Gilbert argues that the US war on terror is part of an increasingly punitive international order, an order that is fostering not only "new wars" but new forms of terror.[71] He argues that while international law has made punitive war unjustifiable, the rise of terrorism and "new wars" has made punitive war more acceptable again – a development he finds highly problematic.[72] Gilbert's critique of punitive uses of force relies, in part, upon his assumption that an authority's primary role is to provide security rather than justice:

> Here it is important to distinguish the way that authority to fight operates in modern defensive just war theory from its place in older doctrines. In its Christian origins, the authority to fight was given to princes because they were supposed to derive their authority to administer justice from God, and war itself represented a means of delivering justice by punishing wrongdoers. In the defensive theory [what Gilbert sees in modern international law], by contrast, authority to fight derives from being placed in a position to defend a territory and its people, for which a resort to war may be necessary.

Gilbert's assumption is that a sovereign that is authorized to use force must only use it for self-defence purposes, for to do otherwise would be to impose justice, something he believes cannot be achieved through force of arms at the global level.[73]

Gilbert argues that attempts to punish arise from identity politics, particularly religiously derived identity politics, a path that can eventually lead to terrorism and the kind of counter-terrorism policies that have been in effect since the attacks of 11 September 2001. He sees these policies as retributive, although in fact much closer to revenge than the idea of retribution I introduced in the previous chapter. For Gilbert, retribution does not make sense in the international order, primarily because there can be no neutral arbiter between competing conceptions of what is right and just. Relying on international law and its ability to codify norms for which punishment can be justified, Gilbert finds very few legal norms that would justify punitive military actions.

Gilbert's critique is important and powerful. But for all its relevance, it is intimately tied to his conception of authority, a conception that deserves greater scrutiny. For Gilbert, and for many others, both supporters and critics of the war on terror, punitive military actions in the war on terror should not be considered punishment but revenge. Because the United States is one state among many, with no more sovereign rights than any other, its attacks on Afghanistan and Iraq can only be justified through a self-defence argument. In both cases, much more so in Iraq,[74] such arguments fail miserably, leaving the war on terror without any normative justifications.

Chapter 6 addresses in more detail the punitive nature of counter-terrorism policies. This chapter merely uses this example as a starting point from which to explore the relationship between punishment and authority. I next turn to three political theorists of the seventeenth century, who wrote from similar starting points, but came to very different conclusions about the relationship between authority and punishment.

Authority in Hobbes and Locke

Justifying authority is a central concern of political philosophy.[75] As a result, any theorist could be chosen to explore the question of authority since almost all, in one way or another, deal with the topic. In order to capture some of the most important philosophical elements of this debate, however, I will turn to two particular theorists of authority whose writings have, in many ways, framed modern debates about political authority and punishment: Thomas Hobbes and John Locke.[76]

Writing in the midst of the English civil wars, Thomas Hobbes (1588–1679) confronted a world in which the old markers of certainty – church and monarch in particular – were being challenged. His life was shaped in many ways by those wars – as a supporter of monarchy, he served as a tutor to Charles II and was forced to live in exile in Paris for some time. Yet, political authority was not the only standard being challenged in Hobbes' time; the sources of knowledge were also under attack, especially the authority of tradition. In his writing, Hobbes excoriates "the schoolmen" for their reliance on the authority of Aristotle and church fathers in their philosophy. He concluded that only direct experience and science could lead to truth and he saw geometry as a master science, leading to an approach that focused on defining concepts in order to achieve certainty.

While he wrote widely on politics in both Latin and English, I concentrate here on his most well known work, *Leviathan*, published in 1651. He sought to develop an argument that would explain why individuals should abdicate their rights to a powerful sovereign, or Leviathan as Hobbes called it. Hobbes argued that without the Leviathan, society could not function. Not only would social and political norms be overridden, normal social intercourse and even language would not be possible – leading to the famous description of human existence as solitary, poor, nasty, brutish and short.

While he emphasized the sovereign's absolute power and authority, it is important to remember that Hobbes' ideas of governance and authority are grounded in a liberal conception of the human person, that is, one that relies upon the rights of individual persons.[77] The nature of the human person, however, produces the need for a sovereign to whom those rights will be abdicated. Those individuals pursue power in order to protect themselves since they have an equal ability to kill each other.[78] This description of the human person leads Hobbes to propose a series of natural laws, the first two of which are the most important. First, every man seeks peace. Second, every man will defend himself.[79] The result of these natural laws is that man must submit to a sovereign authority that will ensure the protection of all.

That sovereign has authority over all members of the society, the result of a contract of sorts between the individual and the authority.[80] That authority manifests itself in the ability of the sovereign to issue commands. Commands are orders to obey rules based purely on the will of the authority, which Hobbes differentiates from counsels, which are orders to obey based on reasons for what would be good for the individual.[81] This distinction is central to Hobbes' conception of obligation. I am obliged to follow the dictates of the sovereign not because he gives me reasons to do so, but simply because he has ordered me to do so. If the sovereign is forced to justify his orders and debate with individuals, then his authority is weakened. This obligation to obey the sovereign is, ultimately, grounded in Hobbes' natural law arguments – obedience is necessary to protect us from each other, a point that arises from Hobbes' natural laws, particularly the first two.[82] But, once we have entered into the contract with the sovereign, we no longer need to have our obedience justified by reference to those reasons but simply because the sovereign wishes it to be that way.

One of the central ways in which the sovereign ensures the protection of all is through the use of punishment; indeed, in his introduction, Hobbes highlights the centrality of punishment, "by which fastened to the seat of Soveraignty, every joynt and member is moved to peforme his duty."[83] Hobbes does not define punishment until much later into the text, after he has established his theories of man and the commonwealth:

> A Punishment is an Evill inflicted by publique Authority, on him that hath done, or omitted that which is Judged by the same Authority to be of a Transgression of the Law; to the end that the will of men may thereby the better be disposed to obedience.[84]

The sovereign authority is central to Hobbes' conception of punishment. As he goes on to argue, those "evils" inflicted by private authorities cannot be called punishment but should rather be called "hostilities." He argues as well that punishment must only be deterrent and not retributive; in his words, the point of punishment is "terror not revenge," which means its purpose is to frighten men into acting in accordance with the law and not to satisfy the desire for revenge. His seventh law of nature states this most clearly:

> That in revenges (this retribution of evil for Evil), Men not look at the greatnesse of the evill past, but the greatnesse of the good to follow. Whereby we are forbidden to inflict punishment with any other designe, than for the correction of the offender, or direction of others.[85]

For one commentator, this focus on deterrence and the future places Hobbes closer to modern theories of punishment such as those of Beccaria and Bentham.[86]

Hobbes also argues that "evils" inflicted on those who are not in the political community should not be considered punishment. Because Hobbes is a theorist of the social contract, only those in that contract can be subject to the demands of the sovereign, i.e. foreigners cannot be subject to punishment.[87] This does not mean he is against war, for he believes that wars are necessary to protect the community from harm. Rather, any use of force outside the boundaries of the commonwealth is war and not punishment, for the latter is only to be inflicted by the sovereign. He defines infliction of harm by a sovereign on those outside the community as a hostility that can only be issued upon an "enemy."[88]

From this brief overview, a few points are worth reiterating. First, the foundation of Hobbes' account is the need for peace rather than justice.[89] Punishment is designed not to create a just political order – one in which various goods are fairly distributed – but one in which individuals do not harm each other. This leads him to emphasize the deterrent function of punishment much more highly than the retributive one. This emphasis on deterrence supports his view that punishment cannot be committed by anyone other than the sovereign. When individuals enact "evil" on each other they are engaged in revenge. As a corollary to this, the sovereign cannot punish anyone outside the borders of the community, for to do so would mean inflicting harm on an agent who is not part of the community and thus not part of the social contract.

Hobbes' account of punishment stands in tension with some of the arguments I am making in this book. As the previous chapter suggested and as later chapters will demonstrate, the infliction of harms on various agents in the international system by non-sovereign agents can be considered punitive. My dispute with Hobbes is not, however, in his argument that the human person pursues power. Nor do I dispute the importance of sovereign power in preventing individuals from harming each other in that relentless pursuit of power. Finally, as I have argued in the previous chapter, the role of an authority is central to ensuring that deterrence functions.

My difference with Hobbes is on two interrelated points. First, Hobbes' emphasis on peace over justice leads to a deterrent conception of punishment. Punishment, as an infliction of harm, does not always contribute to peace. What it does, however, is ensure justice. Hobbes' resistance to retribution reveals how the emphasis on peace over justice manifests itself in his conception of punishment. If peace is the primary goal of governance, then punitive actions designed to create a more just society will be less important. In my account, punishment must be both deterrent and retributive. As a result, punishment might be meted out by non-sovereign authorities or legitimate institutions, a point I explore further below.

Second, Hobbes' view that the infliction of harm on those outside the community can never be considered punishment results from his social contract framework and, importantly, from his emphasis on the sovereign as the sole legitimate agent of punishment. Sovereigns only exist, according to Hobbes, because they are in a particular relationship with the commonwealth. Without that relationship, there can be no punishment. But, while the relationship between authority and community is important, more important is the fact of a violation of the law. That is, rather than define punishment in terms of the relationship among the various agents, it is more important to focus on the nature of the violation that is to be punished.

One theorist who shares Hobbes' social contract ideas yet differs on the matter of punishment, in part because he differs in his conception of authority that arises from that contract, is John Locke (1632–1704).[90] As with Hobbes, Locke wrote in the context of the English civil wars, albeit somewhat later. His concerns were also with the collapse of political authority, although he did not see monarchy as the answer to those concerns as Hobbes did. Indeed, Locke also spent time in exile against the monarch; he was involved with those who objected to Charles II's attempts to place his brother James, a Roman Catholic, on the throne. He returned to England in 1689 as a supporter of the Whig Revolution that put William on the throne in place of James II. In the same year he published his most important works, *An Essay on Human Understanding* and *Two Treatises on Government*. While he was more known for the first during his lifetime, the second, particularly the *Second Treatise*, solidified his fame as a political theorist who gave support to those advocating for their rights against unjust rule.[91]

Locke began at a similar point as Hobbes; individuals have certain natural rights, particularly the right to defend themselves and exist in a state of equality. Unlike Hobbes' assumption that individuals pursue power, Locke argues that individuals in the state of nature pursue their own happiness. Locke believes that in that state of nature, individuals can coexist peacefully. They do not need the Leviathan of Hobbes' account, one that is overpowering and not subject to question. In fact, Locke warns against absolute power granted to the Leviathan, a warning not found in Hobbes:

> [S]o that such a man, however intitled, Czar, or Grand Seignior, or how you please, is as much in the state of nature, with all under his dominion, as he is with the rest of mankind: for where-ever any two men are, who have not standing rule, and common judge to appeal to on earth, for the determination of controversies of right between them there they are still in the state of nature, and under all the inconveniences of it, with only this woeful difference to the subject, or rather slave of an absolute prince: that whereas in the ordinary state of nature, he has a liberty to judge of his right, and according to the best of his power, to maintain it; now, whenever his property is invaded by the will and order of his monarch, he has not only no appeal, as those in society ought to have, but as if he were degraded from the common

state of rational creatures, is denied a liberty to judge of or to defend his right; and so is exposed to all the misery and inconveniences, that a man can fear from one, who being the unrestrained state of nature, is yet corrupted with flattery, and armed with power.[92]

This warning results in Locke proposing a more constitutional structure than Hobbes, one that includes separate legislative, executive and judicial powers. Hobbes also distinguished these powers, but in *Leviathan*, at least, they seem a more functional distinction than a necessary theoretical one. While a full-fledged balance of power within a governing structure would have to wait for Montesquieu, Locke's constitutional framework provides more protection against the abuse of authority by the single sovereign than is found in Hobbes.

Locke also adds an important natural right that is largely lacking from Hobbes: the right to property.[93] Locke devotes all of Book V in the *Second Treatise* to a defence of property as a right that must be protected by civil society and the authority that is eventually established. His focus on private property while not unique in the context of his day, does stand out from other theorists.

As with Hobbes, punishment plays a central role in Locke's overall argument. Book I of the Second Treatise defines political power as

A right of making laws with penalties of death, and consequently all less penalties, for the regulating and preserving of property, and of employing the force of the community, in the execution of such laws, and in the defence of the commonwealth from foreign injury, and all this only for the common good.[94]

Locke argues that this political power is inherent in all individuals in the state of nature, meaning they all have the right to punish. This "natural right to punish" fundamentally distinguishes Locke from Hobbes; A. John Simmons claims it is at the "heart of Locke's political philosophy."[95] As Locke states in Book II:

all men may be restrained from invading others rights, and from doing hurt to one another, and the law of nature be observed, which willeth the peace and preservation of all mankind, the execution of the law of nature is in that state, put into every mans hands, whereby every one has a right to punish the transgressors of that Law to such a degree as may hinder its violation: for the law of nature would, as all other laws that concern men in this world, be in vain, if there were no body that in the state of nature had a power to execute that law, and thereby preserve the innocent and restrain offenders.[96]

Simmons reiterates this point:

Imagine that, for whatever reason, your society "dissolved" into disorder and chaos. Once again in your natural state, unprotected by the rule of law, you witness a man brutally robbing and murdering a defenseless victim. If it were within your power to do so, would you not feel justified in seeing to it that the murderer suffered for his crime? Would there be anything morally objectionable in your inflicting on him some harm, either to save others from his atrocities or (supposing you somehow know that he will commit no more) simply as a response to what he did? Would not anyone in that state of nature have a right to punish him for his crime?[97]

It is important to note that Locke is not arguing for retaliation but for punishment. If individuals have rights in a state of nature, and if no sovereign exists to ensure the protection of those rights, individuals can undertake punishment to ensure their rights remain protected. Locke goes on to say that only a sovereign should punish, but does note that individuals retain their natural rights to resist the government, and, at some level, retain the right to punish.

Locke's ideas about punishment, then, suggest that it may be undertaken by individuals in a state of nature. But this situation cannot endure, and civil societies are formed which provide an authority who can enact punishments. Importantly, however, Locke's authority is not simply an executive, but a judicial authority, one that can make judgements between those whose rights have been violated and those who have done the violating. Locke's concern with the power of the sovereign, in other words leads him to emphasize the judicial function of the authority.[98] Locke also makes an intriguing comment, one that has relevance for the thesis of this book. When describing the creation of the commonwealth, he states:

And thus the commonwealth comes by a power to set down what punishment shall belong to the several transgressions which they think worthy of it, committed amongst the members of that society, (which is the power making laws) as well as it has the power to punish any injury done unto any of its members, by anyone not of it (which is the power of war and peace); and all this for the preservation of the property of all the members of that society, as far as is possible.[99]

Locke, in other words, sees war as a form of punishment. He also hints that foreigners can be punished by a political community, a point rejected by Hobbes.[100] All this results from the fact that, unlike Hobbes, Locke finds the meaning for punishment in the violation and not in the sovereign.

Most important, however, is the link between Locke's emphasis on property and his ideas of punishment. As noted above, the preservation of property is central to Locke's theory of governance and to his justification for punishment. Along with the need to stop the individual who violated the law, those who punish have a right to seek reparation for the property that they lost in the crime. This second element of punishment is so important that it cannot be abrogated by the sovereign:

> From these two distinct rights, the one of punishing the crime for restraint and preventing the like offence, which right of punishing is in everybody; the other of taking reparation, which belongs only to the injured party, comes it to pass that the magistrate, who by being magistrate hath the common right of punishing put into his hands, can often, where the public good demands not the execution of the law, remit the punishment of the criminal offences by his own authority, but yet cannot remit the satisfaction due to any private man for the damage he has received.[101]

The next section makes a case for a retributive form of punishment, noting that "each transgression may be punished to that degree, and with so much severity, as will suffice it to make an ill bargain to the offender."[102]

For Locke, punishment not only deters, it also returns the world to what it was like before the violation. An important part of that return is the return of property that has been taken. Property, for Locke, is actual property, goods and money that might have been lost through a crime. The idea of retribution, however, is also a form of returning things to the way they were. Retribution and reparations are both ways of achieving justice. While Hobbes' emphasis on deterrence as the primary justification for punishment arose from his emphasis on peace, Locke's emphasis on reparation and retribution arises from his emphasis on property and, as a result, justice.

In the end, Locke provides some important alternatives to Hobbes on the relationship between punishment and authority. First, because his emphasis is on the violation of natural law rather than on the need for peace, Locke believes punishment can be undertaken by any agent in a state of nature, which he admits is a "strange doctrine."[103] While the creation of civil society and the commonwealth move that right from individuals to the commonwealth, that move is premised upon the importance of a judicial authority that can make judgements between individuals rather than an all-powerful executive. Second, punishments can be exacted upon those not within the political community, either foreigners living among them or even those outside of the boundaries of the commonwealth in war. Third, just as important as deterrence, retribution or ensuring that the right proportionate punishment is inflicted on the right agent ensures that justice prevails even when laws have been violated. This concern with justice and retribution arises, in part, from Locke's emphasis on the restoration of property that has been lost when natural laws are violated.

To simplify their arguments radically, Hobbes' account of punishment emphasizes deterrence and Locke's emphasizes justice. Their disagreement comes from their account of authority, for they share a similar social contract basis as their starting point. In the case of Hobbes, authority is to create peace and security, while for Locke authority is to create justice, primarily through the protection of property. Because of these different overriding tasks, Hobbes' authority combines all the powers into one sovereign, while Locke sees the importance of separating the judicial and executive authority, and places an important burden on the judicial authority in matters of punishment.

Writing in the context of a civil war, both authors focus more on domestic social arrangements than on international ones. Yet, they both incorporate international themes into their accounts; Hobbes claims that authority is limited outside the sphere of the commonwealth, and so punishment cannot take place outside one's borders, while Locke, with his emphasis on natural law as the determinant of what is a violation, suggests that those who use force outside their borders can justify it on punitive grounds.

Grotius on authority and punishment

An author who starts from similar themes yet whose focus is much more clearly on the international is Hugo Grotius. Grotius demonstrates how conceptualizing political relations at the global level leads to yet a different conception of the relationship between authority and punishment. More specifically, while he shares with Locke the view that agents in a state of nature who understand natural law may punish, because he was writing as lawyer in the context of relations between communities, Grotius takes the Lockean emphasis on justice and punishment to develop an account of how states can punish each other through war.

Hugo Grotius (1583–1645) was a Dutch lawyer whose work spanned theology, politics and statecraft. He published widely in these fields, but two publications are most relevant for international affairs: *De Jure Praedae* (1605) and *De Jure Belli ac Pacis* (1625). The former was not published in its entirety during Grotius' lifetime, although a chapter was published in 1609 as *Mare Liberum*. *De Jure Praedae* was written while he was a lawyer for the Dutch East Indies Company, which had requested a report on the law of prize when the company captured a Portuguese ship in the Indian Ocean. Grotius argued in that book, which became widely known through the publication of *Mare Liberum*, that the Portuguese had no exclusive rights to trade in the Indies, neither based on first trading there or on the basis of authorization from the Pope. In making this argument, Grotius drew on a wide range of classical sources, but less on Biblical sources, thus grounding his arguments in secular natural law rather than divine law. Moreover, in response to a critique by the Scottish scholar

William Welwod, Grotius explored the natural law basis of property, largely to argue that the sea could not be property of anyone. His natural law arguments, in other words, while finding a basis in property, did not place it in the same central position as Locke did.[104]

Grotius is most well known for his *De Jure Belli ac Pacis* which he wrote while a prisoner, the result of his political activities in The Netherlands. Grotius had aligned himself with Jan van Oldenbarnevelt, a leading politician in The Netherlands, who was seeking to counter the extreme Calvinism of the political authorities of the day. Grotius and his ally lost in that battle, resulting in the beheading of Oldenbarnevelt and the imprisonment of Grotius in 1618, from which he escaped in 1621. Like Hobbes and Locke, then, Grotius wrote his most important works in the midst of civil and religious conflict.

De Jure Belli ac Pacis is divided into three books. The preface provides the basis for the text as a whole, building upon the natural law arguments of *Mare Liberum*. Book I defines war, justice and right, drawing upon a wide range of Christian and classical authors. Book II begins by extending the just causes of war introduced in Book I, but then explores the foundations of right, property and punishment. These foundations result from the fact that Grotius, like the just war tradition within which he was writing, assumed that there were three just causes for war: self-defence, retaking of property unlawfully taken and punishment of wrongdoing.[105] Book III then examines what may be justly undertaken in war, or what is today called *jus in bello*.

While Grotius has much to offer in understanding war, peace and international law, I will be focusing on his arguments concerning war as a form of punishment. Grotius was not the first to make an argument that force could be used for punitive purposes. Both Augustine and Aquinas argue for punishment as legitimate reasons for using force. Pope Innocent IV also argued, in the context of the Crusades, that adherence to natural law demanded that punishments be undertaken by monarchs against those who violated the moral law. For Innocent, using force for purposes of punishment should come from an authority, in this case the papacy; indeed, it is perhaps because he feared the ways in which this obligation would be twisted by sovereigns for their own purposes that he emphasized the importance of papal authority.[106] The rise of Protestantism, along with the humanist tradition of intellectual thought, undercut the importance of papal authorization for the use of force.[107] Moreover, not only Protestants, but Catholic writers as well raised questions about papal claims to authority when it came to matters of war and peace.[108] At the same time, however, using force to uphold the moral law did not disappear. Instead, the growth of natural law theory moved towards formulations in which individuals in a state of nature, rather than a defined properly constitute society, could be authorized to punish.

Grotius does not simply list punishment as a potential cause for war.

Rather, he develops a much larger and extensive analysis of the philosophical purpose behind punishment. It is in Book II, Chapters 20 and 21, "On Punishment" and "On the Sharing of Punishments" that Grotius extends the argument that war can be waged for purposes of punishment. He begins his discussion of punishment by linking it to justice, in which he seeks to determine what kind of justice is being pursued through punishment. In Book I Grotius introduces the distinction that the justice relevant to punishment is called "expletive justice," a concept he draws from Aristotle:

> Tis expletive Justice, Justice properly and strictly taken, which respects the Faculty, or perfect Right and is called by Aristotle sunalktika, Justice of Contracts, but this does not give us an adequate Idea of that Sort of Justice. For, if I have a Right to Demand Restitution of my Goods, which are in the Possession of another, it is not by vertue of any Contract, and yet it is the Justice in question that gives such a Right.[109]

Whether or not Grotius accurately captures Aristotle's idea of justice here is not my concern; rather, Grotius' own understanding of this idea is important because it informs his idea of punishment.[110] Expletive or restorative justice is close to, but not the exact same as a civil law approach to contract violations. That is, expletive justice seeks to restore a balance between two parties that has been disrupted, but that balance should not be understood purely in terms of business dealings. This distinction, while subtle, is important for understanding Grotius' view on what punishment seeks to do. He points out that punishment "comes near to the Nature of Contracts" but avoids making punishment an attempt to simply enforce a contract.[111]

This fine line between enforcing a contract and restoring a balance informs Grotius' next important point about punishment. Unlike Hobbes, and like Locke, Grotius does not assume the necessity of a single community headed by a sovereign who has the responsibility to punish. Rather than argue that the right to punish derives from the inherent dignity or authority of the sovereign, he posits that punishment derives from the character of the violation:

> But the Subject of this Right, that is, the Person to whom the Right of Punishing belongs, is not determined by the Law of Nature. For natural reason informs us, that a Malefactor may be punished, but not who ought to punish him. It suggests indeed so much, that it is the fittest to be done by a Superior, but yet does not shew that to be absolutely necessary, unless by Superior we mean him who is innocent and detrude the Guilty below the Rank of Men, which is the Doctrine of some Divines.[112]

Rather than punishment being defined by the existence of a sovereign, it is instead defined by the objective fact of a criminal violation.

Here we see similarities between Locke and Grotius. Like Locke, Grotius sees punishment as somehow a restoration of what has been lost, retribution of a sort. Also, like Locke, the right to punish does not derive solely from authority or its need to deter others in the future (although this might also take place). Rather, punishment derives from the wrong that has been committed.

In Section 37 of Chapter 20 Grotius turns to the question of war being waged to inflict punishment. He notes "the Desire for inflicting Punishment is often the Occasion of War."[113] He then turns to the question of whether a king whose subjects have not been harmed may launch a war to punish one who has harmed another community. He argues that yes, those who commit crimes "against nature" may be punished by any sovereign state through war. This claim, which he admits is not allowed by some of his predecessors such as Vitoria, leads him to an examination of the law of nature and what justifies such actions.[114] This expands the justification for war as punishment away from vengeance, i.e. punishing one who has wronged you, and more towards the types of punitive actions that can be seen as supporting the norms of an international community of sorts. Here Grotius goes beyond Locke, for he now moves away from the state of nature conception that informs Locke's justification for punishment, to something closer to Christian charity as a justification for using force.

Grotius is careful to specify that not every agent can punish. Writing as he was in the midst of the Thirty Years War, he undoubtedly understood the dangers of so many different agents using force to defend themselves and to seek justice. In a chapter entitled, "War as Publick and Private" Grotius argues that a "solemn" or justified war can only be undertaken by "the Authority of those who have Sovereign power in the State."[115] For Grotius, this means that states are justified in using force to defend and punish, with other uses of force being private war. Authority is not disconnected from punishment, then. At the same time, in the anarchic system of international affairs, Grotius clearly sees a justification for the use of force by sovereign states in their relations with each other, provided it fulfils the criteria of just war.

Grotius, then, parallels Locke in that both see individual agents as justified in using force to punish. But Grotius extends Locke's arguments in two ways. First, his focus on war as punishment in the context of an international order moves Locke's largely domestic arguments to a different level. Second, and more important, Grotius makes a stronger case for punishment as an action that can contribute to a just order by claiming that force can be used to punish those who violate the rights of their own citizens. In a sense, Grotius provides us with the first[116] justification for a punitive intervention to support human rights (of course, he would not use those same terms).

Grotius does warn against the dangers of hypocrisy in justifying force as a punitive measure.[117] His reliance on Christian charity as a way to keep the line firm between vengeance and punishment is problematic, however. Rather than rely on Grotius' hope for Christian charity here, however, let me turn to one final author who both updates some of these arguments and provides more concrete specifications for how punishment can be undertaken without an authoritative figure.

Adjudicating punishments

So far in this chapter, I have argued that punishment does not require the type of sovereign authority imagined by Thomas Hobbes. Rather, drawing on the arguments of John Locke and Hugo Grotius, I have suggested that agents in a state of nature can undertake punishment. Grotius locates this argument in the context of war between states, arguing that a war for punitive reasons can be a just war. He also adds the important element that punishments can be undertaken by just agents in situations where their own interests are not involved, i.e. to punish those who violate the rights of their own people.

Grotius, however, does not provide any means for limiting the punitive impulse that can easily slip into vengeance. Locke, on the other hand, suggests a way that such impulses can be contained with the introduction of the judicial power. Rather than the executive authority to punish, Locke places greater emphasis on the impartial judge who can prevent individuals from making judgements in which they might be involved and can control the impulses of vengeance.

Neither Grotius nor Locke, however, gives a concrete expression to how such a judicial system might work at the international level. This is especially surprising in the case of Grotius, whose work addresses relations between states. In the remainder of this chapter, I suggest a form for that judicial structure at the global level. One of the central tenets I draw from Locke and Grotius is the fact that authority is not the justification for punishment, but something about the character of the society and the violation. This point is central to the legal theory of positivism. One theorist who developed this idea at some length was Hans Kelsen.

Kelsen (1881–1973) is considered one of the central figures of twentieth-century positivist law. He was rare among legal theorists for placing international law at the centre of his theory. For Kelsen, "law is a coercive order."[118] Unlike Austin and other positivists, however, Kelsen argues that the coercive force of law does not derive from the existence of a sovereign authority. Employing what he called a "scientific" analysis of law, Kelsen argued that the very nature of legal norms and the rules they create include sanctions; that is, a law is not a law unless it leads to a sanction. As a result, it is not the existence of a sovereign that creates punishments; it is the very nature of law itself that leads to punishment for violations.

This approach to law led Kelsen to posit that punishment, or what he called sanction, can take place in international law as well as in domestic law. Because sanction arises from the very nature of legal norms and rules and not from sovereign authorities, the use of military force in response to a violation of the existing law (what Kelsen calls a delict) is punishment. For Kelsen, sanctions in international law are either war or reprisals:

> The sanctions of international law, especially war, it is true, are usually not interpreted as punishments; but they have nevertheless, in principle, the same character as the sanctions of criminal law – forcible deprivation of life and freedom of individuals.[119]

One might conclude from this that Kelsen's world would be one in which states are constantly at war with each other, deciding on their own when a violation has occurred. Indeed, a similar critique could be made of Grotius; who is to decide when a violation occurs? David Rodin has recently criticized the possibility of punitive war on precisely these grounds. Rodin points out that if individuals who are not sovereign punish, they need to be seen as impartial by those who are being punished if punishment is considered a just practice. As he notes, "The requirement that administrators of justice be impartial seems to stem directly from the nature of justice itself. Indeed, justice is only defined in opposition to the partisan and the partial."[120]

Kelsen's solution to this problem is to construct an institutional order in which judicial bodies have a more important place. During the Second World War, Kelsen gave concrete specificity to such an institution in a short monograph.[121] He argued that rather than an executive or even legislative institution, the international community needed a judicial institution that could adjudicate among competing claims, and, more importantly, make judgements as to when a delict has occurred. Once such decisions were made, this court would authorize the punishment of the violating state through military means if necessary. He critiques the League of Nations for placing the legislative function before the judicial one, leading it to issue normative statements rather than make judgements grounded in existing international law. In describing that institution, Kelsen constructs a court that is representative of different legal traditions and includes the best legal minds.[122] Of course, no judge can be truly impartial, at least according to the criteria set out by Rodin. Nevertheless, by creating a court and ensuring that its justices come from different legal traditions and represent different nationalities, a closer semblance of impartiality can be found than exists today.

Kelsen is not denying the need for laws. Rather, his argument is that there exists a body of international law already, laws that have arisen from various sources in the international system. The concern of Kelsen is that creating a new legislative institution whose legitimacy will be questioned would undermine the laws it might produce. Instead, Kelsen believes that a legal structure needs a judiciary at the global level to ensure that punishments are imposed.

For Kelsen, then, international law does allow for, and even requires, punishment. Like Grotius, Kelsen sees the need for military punishment if states violate the legal norms of the international system. Crucially, again like Grotius, punishment does not arise from the authority of a sovereign, but from the character of the legal order and from the fact of a violation of the law. Without punishment, the legal order would no longer be legal, but something altogether different. To avoid the abuse of punishment as a justification for self-interested war, Kelsen adds to his theoretical idea the centrality of a judicial institution that can adjudicate among claimants.

Constitutionalism, authority and punishment

Kelsen's emphasis on the judiciary parallels some recent works in international political theory. As noted in the previous chapter, Robert Keohane, for instance, has proposed a series of institutional designs for collective adjudication of threats to international security. These have included suggestions for ways to judge whether preemptive action is necessary and structures to control the use of force by non-state actors. Keohane has progressively moved towards a greater interest in international law and what he calls "legalization" or the process by which law becomes central to the international order.[123] This move towards a greater attention to questions of law and institutional design by a leading figure in international relations theory suggests that alternative ways of imagining the international order, ones more closely connected to some of the themes being addressed in this volume, are becoming more central to the study of international affairs.

These suggestions are not necessarily new. They are close to the ideas of collective security that were built into both the League of Nations and the United Nations structure. What was missing from these designs, however, and to some extent from these recent writings, is a place for a judicial structure to make decisions about when a violation of norms has taken place. The emphasis in both structures and in the recent proposals from Keohane and others is on the executive means to undertake collective security actions. Kelsen's arguments remind us that what is more important is the need for judicial authorities to consider evidence and make judgements according to existing international law.

Another dimension of Keohane's arguments about law and legalization that differs from mine is his concern in finding out how states will come to accept law because it is in their interest to do so. My concern in this volume is precisely those cases where agents in the international system do not accept norms and need to be coerced into following the rules. This means proposals for alternatives must confront the fact that powerful agents must both see the benefits but also be put in situations where they may be forced to follow the rules. The neoliberal tradition from which Keohane is writing, in which self-interested behaviour is the overriding presumption, often ends up addressing the concerns of those agents which are the most powerful, i.e. the United States. To convince powerful agents to accept a new institutional design in which they may be punished will be difficult, but it should not mean tailoring proposals to the sole concerns of the most powerful agent.

The difficulty, in other words, is constructing a political order in which powerful agents will agree to be constrained and sometimes punished, but in which the rule of law is ultimately the final determinant of behaviour. Combining the balance of power with the rule of law is not a problem unique to the international level, but one that has long been central to creating just and peaceful political orders. One alternative way to conceptualize the global political order that places a strong emphasis on both power and law is constitutionalism, an idea introduced in Chapter 1. Constitutionalism developed as a means to limit the power of arbitrary government, the dangers of the sovereign whom Hobbes believes is essential to the governance of a community. Locke is often considered a central figure in the development of constitutional government. The emphasis that Locke placed on the judiciary in the *Second Treatise* is testament to the fact that he saw constitutional government as the foundation of the protection of liberty.

The international level does not have a dangerous sovereign authority that needs to be constrained by constitutional rules, but it most certainly has powerful individual agents who take on the mantle of authority and, in so doing, make decisions that lack legitimacy. The United States, certainly since the end of the Cold War, has become the embodiment of that agent that sees itself as having the means and the will to govern and save others from themselves, but in the process overrides international law and rules.[124] As a result of American foreign policy, many have turned to international law and international rules more broadly defined as a means to limit the sovereign. But international law does not always clearly define what should be done, and debates over how to interpret those laws have left many with the feeling that there does not exist a clear international legal structure to restrain the powerful.[125]

One immediate assumption is that the UN Charter and various law-making functions of the United Nations are the source of a constitution in the international order.[126] While the United Nations does provide a structure of sorts, constitutionalism can be found in a wider range of institutions and processes at the international level. Philip Allot has argued that there exists a constitutional order in various international institutions.[127] Jose Alveraz has demonstrated how judicial interpretation, to return to Kelsen's emphasis on the role of the judiciary, has played an important role in the construction of international legal order.[128] Jan Klabbers has also described the potential for international organizations to play a greater role in an international constitutional order, but has also cautioned against an excessive enthusiasm about their potential.[129]

Constitutionalism does not provide clear answers on what types of punishment are justified. Rather, constitutionalism privileges the role of the judge in making decisions about the rules and how they should be enforced. There is much to be said about constitutionalism and punishment, which this chapter has only briefly explored. The point of this section has been to suggest that rather than a Hobbesian authority, the international society might be better served by a constitutional order that places an important emphasis on the role of international jurists who can make judgements about when rules have been violated or not. Enforcing those judgements raises other questions, ones that I will explore in the chapters to follow. Following the examples of Locke and Grotius, I would argue that in the state of nature, it is more important to ensure that rules are enforced by the community after a judgement has been made that such rules have indeed been violated.

Conclusion

This chapter has argued that there does not need to be a sovereign authority for punishment to be just. As long as punitive actions are lodged within a just constitutional structure, one that includes a judicial body that can make clear judgements about what norms have been violated and what consequences should exist for such violations, punishments might well be undertaken at the global level. By comparing the political philosophies of Hobbes, Locke and Grotius, I have demonstrated that the current assumption in the international system that punishment cannot take place without a sovereign authority rests on the assumption, found most clearly articulated in Hobbes, that punishment should primarily be about deterrence. Locke's work demonstrates that punishment is about both deterrence and retribution, and the retributive element connects punishment to justice. Grotius parallels Locke here, but demonstrates how individuals can punish not only in response to violations of their own rights, but the rights of others, again without a sovereign impartial authority undertaking that punishment. This results from the fact that the right to punish for both Locke and Grotius arises from the character of the violation and not from the sovereign authority.

The chapter concludes with a brief reference to Hans Kelsen, whose ideas about law and the importance of the judiciary place these arguments in the context of positive international law. Connecting Kelsen to recent works on constitutionalism at the global level, I highlighted some ways in which the international system might already contain the potential for punishing without a sovereign authority.

Some of these institutional designs will appear in Chapters 4, 5 and 6.

Before turning to how punishment operates and how it might be under-taken more justly, there is one further conceptual issue that needs develop-ment. This chapter has explored which agents ought to decide and punish when a violation takes place, but I have not explored who ought to be punished. The question of agency, particularly in the international system in which agents include states, people, NGOs, corporations and inter-national organizations, raises important questions of responsibility and punishment. To these questions I now turn.

3   Agency[130]

The last chapter explored the problem of authority as it relates to punishing in the international sphere. I argued that punishment can take place without a Hobbesian authority figure by turning to Locke, Grotius and Kelsen, and proposed the idea of constitutionalism as a way to organize the international order. In the chapters to follow, I will explore various punitive practices to see whether or not they assume a Hobbesian sovereign, which would render them unjust, or whether they assume a more Lockean constitutional order which might bring them closer to a just political practice.

Authority, however, is not the only conceptual confusion surrounding punishment at the global level. In domestic legal systems, determining who gets punished depends on two broad assumptions about ethics and politics. First, that individuals are moral agents who intend certain actions and can be held responsible for those actions. Second, that individuals have a particular status in the community that assumes they know their responsibilities before the law and are, to some extent, participants in the political community that holds them responsible. Underlying both of these assumptions are ideas about moral and political agency, i.e. the capacity of particular sorts of persons being considered capable of action in a morally and legally significant way.

Punishment at the global level, however, raises important challenges to these assumptions. The first problem is the wide range of agents that exist, not all of whom can be held responsible in the same way. In domestic political systems, such as the United States, there exist different types of agents that can be held responsible for crimes; for instance, corporations became legitimate agents before the law in the late nineteenth century, allowing individuals to avoid criminal responsibility for certain types of financial and commercial crime. But at the global level, the expansive range of agents – individual persons, nation-states, non-governmental organizations, multinational corporations and international organizations – create even more problems in terms of agency and responsibility. These different agents can be held responsible for different kinds of actions, some of which might deserve punishment. The variety of punishments available further complicates the international political system, with military attack, economic sanctions, coercive diplomacy, service of time in jail and diplomatic isolation as possible punishments depending on the type of agent.

These confusions sometimes result in parallel punitive processes taking place without a clear sense of how such practices ought to fit together. Consider briefly the case of Darfur, Sudan. With the adoption of Security Council Resolution 1593 on 31 March 2005, the Security Council referred the situation in Sudan to the Prosecutor of the International Criminal Court (ICC). As a result of the resolution, the Prosecutor determined on 14 December 2006 that there was sufficient evidence to undertake a criminal trial of individuals responsible for the violations of human rights, arguing that there are "reasonable grounds to believe that the individuals identified have committed crimes against humanity and war crimes, including the crimes of persecution, torture, murder and rape." In that same report, however, the Prosecutor also points out that:

> The restoration of security in Darfur is the responsibility of the Government of the Sudan and the Security Council, working with the African Union and other relevant organisations. Justice for past and present crimes will contribute to enhancing security and send an important warning to those individuals who might otherwise continue to resort to violence and criminality as a means of achieving their aims.[131]

The report adds a further complication to the determination of responsibility by pointing out that the individuals it will put on trail are not necessarily the same individuals who have been subject to travel restrictions and economic sanctions that were imposed by the Security Council as a result of its passage of Resolution 1591 on 29 March 2005 (although they might be, depending on the outcome of his investigation and the decisions of the sanctions committee created by UNSCR 1591).[132]

Thus, two sorts of agents have been identified as holding some level of responsibility for the situation in Sudan, the Government of Sudan and individuals in both the government of Sudan and some of the rebel groups. Moreover, two types of punishment have been proposed for the individuals, sanctions through the passage of Resolution 1591 and whatever punishment is determined by the judgement of the ICC. The need to ensure that justice will be served, as the Prosecutor stated, perhaps demands that these different types of agents and punishments be undertaken simultaneously. Nevertheless, the parallel processes suggest confusion in the international system about agency, responsibility and punishment, a confusion that this chapter uses as a starting point.

In this chapter, I introduce what I call political agency as a concept that allows us to account for the various types of agents and forms of responsibility that operate at the global level. This concept of agency begins with some standard assumptions about agency and responsibility: an agent is an individual who intentionally acts to change the world around her. Also, a moral agent is one who understands that she exists in different types of social spheres that have correspondingly different assumptions about proper behaviour. The capacity to understand in which sphere one is operating is an important requirement of standard moral agency. After developing these assumptions about agency through an engagement with various moral philosophers, I turn to Hannah Arendt's work on agency which argues that an agent is one who acts in the public sphere and whose actions contribute to the continuous construction of that sphere. I draw upon Arendt's idea of a public sphere and some of her work on responsibility to argue that a political agent is one who not only has the capacity for morally significant action, but whose actions are significant enough to alter the public sphere radically. At the global level, only agents who are political agents, that is only those who are capable of altering the global public sphere, should be subject to punishment at the global level. This conception of political agency does not replace domestic ideas of moral and legal responsibility, but rather supplements them with a different kind of agency, one that is necessary when conceptualizing responsibility and punishment at the global level.

Agency[133]

What does it mean to be an agent? At its core, agency is the capacity to change the world. This capacity, however, is not simply a physical characteristic; a hurricane changes the world, but we do not conventionally describe a hurricane as having agency.[134] Rather, agency connects the physical capacity to change with either an analytical or evaluative dimension. The predominant understandings of agency in the social sciences tend to focus on the relationship between agents and structures. The question driving these debates is whether or not behaviour can be explained as the result of properties internal to the units within a system or the properties of the system as a whole.

These sociological debates about agency achieved prominence in the study of international relations with the publication of Kenneth Waltz's *Theory of International Politics* in 1979.[135] Waltz argued – in response to the classical realist tradition that sought explanations of behaviour in assumptions about human nature – that explanations of international relations are best located at the level of the "system," or the structure of the system to be more precise. For Waltz, the anarchic character of international relations produced agents who pursue the same goal, survival, leading to strategies of war, balance of power and alliance. His rather parsimonious explanation led to a large-scale shift in American international relations, creating what is now called neorealism.

Most initial responses to Waltz did not focus on his conceptualization of agency, but on other dimensions of his analysis.[136] The publication of

Alexander Wendt's "The Agent-Structure Problem in International Relations Theory" in 1987 launched a new engagement with the concept of agency in the study of international relations.[137] Wendt linked Waltz's work with Marxist-inspired critical theory, arguing that both shared a conception of agency that assumed the preferences of agents. Wendt, along with other constructivist theorists, argues that neorealists fail to provide a theory that fully appreciates how the intentions, preferences, values and ideas that agents promote result not just from their internal properties but also from the social structures within which they operate. Constructivists have argued that agents do exist independently of structures in which they operate, but that they are partly constituted by those structures.[138]

While useful in understanding how the interests of states arise from factors both internal and external, these insights do not fully appreciate how a theory of agency has relevance not only for explaining behaviour but for grasping the role of rules and norms. Indeed, the sociologically derived debates about agents and structures have relevance primarily in so far as they provide some taxonomic rigour to theoretical explanations.[139] Moral and political conceptions of agency, however, are more central to the arguments of this book. These conceptions of agency – which remain largely absent from IR debates – provide important insights on how to evaluate international relations and foreign policy.[140] In the remainder of this chapter, I develop an account of moral and political agency that gives us an alternative means of understanding punishment at the international level.

Moral (and legal) agency

Moral agency begins with the capacity to change the world, but moves our attention in two directions. Internally, moral agency requires that the individual act in a way that is intentional. This means actions must be oriented towards a particular purpose, one that the agent can clearly articulate. The centrality of intentions is sometimes conceptualized as the existence of a will or, in older accounts, a soul. Intentions are not the same as motives, which can be understood as the dispositions that create certain intentions. Importantly, moral agency focuses first and foremost on the intentions and only secondarily on the motives of the agent. Some philosophers argue that not only is moral agency dependent on intentions, it also includes the requirement that an individual be responsible for the effects of his actions that he might not have intended, but that could have been predicted. Externally, moral agency is the capacity to change the world in the context of a body of norms or rules in accordance with (or against) which the agent makes such changes. These two dimensions of moral agency, the internal and the external, require some further explanation.

Intentions and the will have long been a subject of analysis by philosophers. Its centrality to accounts of moral agency is the focus of recent analytical work on responsibility. Harry Frankfurt's essay "Freedom of the Will and the Concept of a Person" provides one important explanation of the importance of the will.[141] Frankfurt argues that not just any kind of a will is important for attributions of agency and responsibility, but a special kind of will, one that can reflect upon its own desires. This second-order reflection, or the ability to create oneself as a particular type of person who wants some things and not others, constitutes the person as a moral agent. Charles Taylor builds upon Frankfurt's account of responsibility in his essay "What is Human Agency?" Taylor argues that to be an agent is to be able to reflect upon and make judgements about our desires.[142] Taylor takes Frankfurt's basic premise and extends it to argue that to be human is to evaluate actions, both one's own and those of others. Moral agency, in other words, defines what it means to be human.

Frankfurt and Taylor are largely concerned with the internal sources of moral agency, the capacity to will or intend actions and the capacity to reflect upon the desires that emanate from that will. But the capacity to intend actions is not the only element of moral agency, for intention alone tells us only that a person might be evaluated for certain behaviours, not what kinds of evaluations would be appropriate. This requires a consideration of what I would call the external dimension of moral agency. One might, in fact, completely avoid the internal element of moral agency by focusing on its external elements alone, something undertaken in a famous essay by Peter Strawson. Strawson argues that rather than seek to answer whether or not individuals have a free will, we need to understand how responsibility functions *in spite* of the existence of free will.[143] He begins by identifying the pessimist and optimist as two sides in the free will/determinism debate. The pessimist believes that because there is no free will, there is no such thing as responsibility, and our entire structure of ethics collapses. The optimist believes that even if there is no free will, responsibility is still an important concept and should not be abandoned. He adopts an optimist view and presents an argument as to why it does not matter whether or not free will and/or determinism exists. It does not matter because of what he calls a key "commonplace" that philosophers have tended to ignore:

> The central commonplace that I want to insist on is the very great importance that we attach to the attitudes and intentions towards us of other human beings, and the great extent to which our personal feelings and reactions depend upon, or involve, our beliefs about these attitudes and assumptions.[144]

Those attitudes, beliefs and reactions to others are in a fundamental way dependent on the assumption that individuals can be held responsible for what they do. For example, if I assume that my wife loves me, it matters a great deal to me that the actions that constitute our relationship can be in some sense attributed to her and not to some outside force. Without that assumption, my life would lose a great deal of its meaning. Strawson calls this an example of the "non-detached" feelings that are essential for life; attitudes like gratitude, resentment, forgiveness, love and hurt feelings. All these attitudes and feelings rely on the fact that they are attributable to fully responsible agents. Without that concept of responsibility – the connection between persons and actions/attitudes – the entire structure of our personal, social, legal and even political interactions would simply collapse for want of meaning. In other words, without the concept of responsibility, the communities within which we live and act would simply make no sense.

Strawson's essay is not on agency directly but on responsibility. But, underlying his argument is the assumption that individuals should be considered agents capable of formulating and undertaking plans of action for which they can be held responsible. His argument is useful in that it clarifies the external rather than the internal dimensions of responsibility. Rather than a metaphysical determination of whether or not our lives are controlled by internal factors, Strawson's article points us to the importance of our assumption that individuals are connected to actions in a morally significant way.

Strawson's article helpfully emphasizes the external realm in conceptualizing moral agency. But, by completely evading the internal realm, he leaves us with something of a puzzle. In Strawson's world, agents have a generalized responsibility no matter what realm they are in, for he focuses on emotional reactions that structure our reactions to each other in almost every setting. Clearly, however, our actions and our agency changes depending on the situations in which we find ourselves; that is, while there may be a few general emotional reactions that depend on shared assumptions about responsibility, different social settings demand different kinds of behaviours. Alasdair MacIntyre addresses this point and links internal and external accounts of moral agency in his article "Social Structures and their Threats to Moral Agency."[145] MacIntyre begins with a problem that crosses both domestic and international notions of responsibility – whether an individual can be held responsible for actions that might well be attributed to his or her position in a certain social structure. He uses the fictional story of J, who is an upstanding member of a community and who works for the railways. In that position, J ensures that trains run on time and timetables are kept, trains that are transporting individuals to concentration camps. His behaviour is perfectly acceptable within the social and political structures of his particular community – but, they do not seem at all acceptable when looked at from outside that community.

The fact that behaviour may be acceptable in one context but not in another indicates that social settings structure the ways in which moral agency functions. Importantly, however, MacIntyre does not end here with the conclusion that all moral evaluation arises from the specific social relation in which we find ourselves, for, as the case of J indicates, we are expected to be able to move between different social settings and be judged differently in accordance with the setting we are in. Imagine, for instance, that I walk into a room that is somewhat messy and find an individual reading a book. I ask that individual to stop and clean up his room. When he fails to respond, because he is so engrossed in his book, I take the book from him forcibly and say to him again that he needs to clean up his room. If that individual is my seven-year-old son reading a Harry Potter novel in his messy bedroom, then such behaviour would be considered morally appropriate. If that individual were my colleague reading Aristotle's *Politics* in her messy office, my behaviour would be considered morally wrong. The determining factor, of course, is that in the first situation I am a father and in the second I am an academic colleague. The moral evaluation of my behaviour, which is exactly the same in both situations, would be evaluated very differently.

MacIntyre calls the different roles into which I have divided myself – father, husband, academic, brother, son, golfer – a process of compartmentalization, a tendency in modern life to play different roles in different social settings. Moral agency according to MacIntyre is not simply the capacity to act intentionally in these different contexts, but the additional capacity to shift from one context to the other. Not only should one be able to shift from one role to the other, but one should be able to make judgements about the appropriate behaviour in these different contexts and keep them straight. The failure of the ticket collector J in his original example is his inability to see that while he may have been behaving properly in a "normal" social context, when trains are being used to transport people to concentration camps, the same behaviour becomes morally wrong.

Moral agency, then, includes both an internal element – the ability to intend certain types of actions – and an external element – the social setting in which certain moral norms create expected kinds of behaviours. MacIntyre's article suggests one way in which they might be combined; a moral agent is one who intends to act in certain ways in certain situations and who also knows how to adjudicate between those different situations and knows the criteria by which she will be evaluated in various situations.

The internal and external conceptions of moral agency map onto legal agency and responsibility in most domestic political contexts. We make judgements about the legal behaviour of individuals first on the basis of whether or not they can be said to have intended their actions, something upon which a criminal trial focuses. The plea of insanity is an argument that an individual cannot be held responsible for his behaviour because he, in some sense, did not intend to do that thing. Instead, the malfunction of his brain, will, ego or what have you led to the action that took place. In Anglo-American criminal law this criterion of legal responsibility is known as *mens rea*. Also, the external element or context in which an action is undertaken is important for determining criminal responsibility. In the previous example, I would not be legally at fault for taking my child's book out of his hands, but I might be legally at fault for taking my colleague's book out of her hands (if she accused me of assault, for instance). Legal responsibility, of course, includes a much wider array of dimensions, not all of which I will explore. I only want to highlight that there is a rough parallel between the way in which I have described moral agency and the most important dimensions of legal agency.

So what is wrong with moral and legal agency as they apply at the global level? First, as I mentioned at the outset of this chapter, the existence of different types of agents in the international system suggests that a simple description of moral agency will not be adequate to capture the entirety of the global realm. Second, the types of wrongs that we wish to address at the global level appear to be different than those at the domestic level. The difference, I would argue, has not to do with the number of people harmed (although this is related to the reason). Rather, the difference has to do with the fact that the political sphere at the global level is much more contested and fragile than at the domestic level (at least in Western democratic systems). What I mean is that wrongs committed at the global level do something much more dangerous than the wrongs committed at the domestic level – they have a tendency to destroy the entire political order through violence and exploitation. All political orders are subject to the dangers of violence and exploitation. The international level, however, has normalized violence through normative structures such as the "laws of war." While violence will not soon disappear from the international order, the argument here is that some violations so egregiously destroy the international order that they require special attention and are worthy of being punished. This fragility of the international sphere suggests that a different kind of agency and responsibility needs to be taken into account when theorizing international wrongs and the proper response to those wrongs. It is to this type of agency that I turn next.

Political agency

Political agency is the status of individuals in a community as being able to participate in the life of that community. That status sometimes results from an official body conferring it, such as in determinations of citizenship. At the same time, political agency does not stop with that official conferment. Rather, it must be continually re-inscribed by engagement in the political, by working with and sometimes against others in the political community. Agency then results not just from the actions of others giving one an official status but from one's own political activity.

The importance of an individual engaging in politics as a means to attain political agency is one I have borrowed from Hannah Arendt's *The Human Condition*.[146] Arendt argues in this book that the active life, or *via activa*, can be divided into three realms: labour, work and action. Labour is that which we do to stay alive, the daily activities that provide food, clothes and shelter. Work is that activity which results in goods that outlive us; creations of buildings, art and crafts that are not consumed but remain after individual human lives pass away. Because labour creates goods that we consume, it is only through work that the material objectivity of human existence is created.

The final category is action. Action is the most important realm in terms of politics, for action is that human activity in which human persons reveal themselves in moments of interactions with others. It is the way in which we assert who we are, in which we create ourselves by presenting ourselves in public. Politics, which provides the constructed stage of a parliament or town meeting, provides the paradigmatic instance of moments in which the human person can be revealed. Arendt develops this concept of action in an engagement with Greek and Roman philosophers who sought to define the realm of the political. That realm, combining a Homeric agonal spirit with an Aristotelian notion of speech as the quintessentially human characteristic, results in a public space that allows for competition and conflict.

According to Arendt, the public realm is the place where persons distinguish themselves, the arena in which "everybody had to constantly distinguish himself from all others, to show through unique deeds or achievements that he was best of all."[147] Indeed, it is this ability to act publicly that defines the human person:

> A life without speech and without action, on the other hand – and this is the only way of life that in earnest has renounced all appearance and all vanity in the biblical sense of the word – is literally dead to the world; it has ceased to be a human life because it is no longer lived among men.... With word and deed we insert ourselves into the human world and this insertion is like a second birth, in which we confirm and take upon ourselves the naked fact of our original physical appearance.[148]

Public political action puts us into the world and reveals the "who" of our existence in a way that no other practice can.

Furthermore, since Arendt believes that political action is a public presentation of the self, there must be a community to whom this presentation is made. She notes that action occurs within a "web of human relationships," a place composed both of other people acting and speaking and of the "common world" that surrounds and anchors human interaction: "...most words and deeds are about some worldly objective reality in addition to being a disclosure of the acting and speaking self."[149] Politics thus requires a public realm, one composed of fellow humans with an agreed upon equality, not one of merit but one of agency.

Arendt's understanding of political agency provides a starting point for me, but I do not end with her formulation. Most importantly for the purposes of this chapter, Arendt's idea of political agency highlights a key element of global politics: when they act, political agents change the sphere within which they are interacting. That is, the space within which they are granted political agency is not a static one but one that constantly shifts and changes as a result of the political actions undertaken by its members. This gives a great deal of power to political agents, for they can, in effect, recreate the public sphere every time they act in it.

Arendt's views on the political impacted her understanding of responsibility as well. She has a number of works that address guilt and responsibility, most famously *Eichmann in Jerusalem*, her report of the trial of Adolph Eichmann for the *New Yorker*.[150] That work is most known for its coinage of the phrase the "banality of evil" a description of the motives and intentions of Eichmann rather than a description of the actions themselves. That is, she argued that Eichmann demonstrates the complete thoughtlessness of those who commit evil, especially those working within a modern bureaucratic structure. Their capacity to avoid critical reflection on what they were doing suggests a need to avoid conceptualizing evil as somehow a radically demonic concept, which makes those undertaking it into monsters or even heroes (depending on one's perspective). Instead, they should be seen as the banal bureaucrats that they are.

In that book, and in a series of essays published after her death, Arendt explores the concepts of responsibility and guilt. She distinguishes the two, pointing out that guilt is a personal concept, something that can be attributed only to individuals, while responsibility is a political concept and, as a result, can be attributed to groups.[151] She argues that a courtroom and a trial are designed to pinpoint individual guilt, so it cannot be used to create a sense of collective guilt. She argued that David Ben Gurion, the Israeli statesman, tried to use the Eichmann trial to remind Israelis that they were the victims of a wider history of anti-Semitism, thus reinforcing the need for the state of Israel to be vigilant. For Arendt, this was a dangerous misuse of the trial and courtroom procedure.

At the same time, certain types of actions do not seem to fit into the courtroom process reflecting, as it does, notions of guilt and innocence.[152] For Arendt, one reason they seem not to fit into that procedure is that their evil extends beyond what can be captured in a normal judicial procedure; as she noted in a letter to Karl Jaspers,

> This guilt [of the Nazis] in contrast to all criminal guilt, oversteps and shatters any and all legal systems.... We are simply not equipped to deal, on a human political level, with a guilt that is beyond crime and an innocence that is beyond goodness and virtue.[153]

But to reduce her critique to one about evil is to simplify it radically; indeed, her ideas about evil and their relation to the political evolved over time, culminating in her analysis of the Eichmann trial. Another reason why such crimes may not fit into the normal judicial structure can be found in her conception of political responsibility. Her understanding of this kind of responsibility can be found in her rather complex article "Collective Responsibility." Because we cannot leave political community altogether, only exchange one for another, we are always responsible for some political outcomes that are undertaken in our name, i.e. by our state. She argues that political responsibility is for "things we have not done," i.e. only for things that are done in our name.[154] This is meant to differentiate it from her conception of guilt that is ultimately about what we do.

I find her idea of political responsibility somewhat confusing here.[155] She argues, on the one hand, that political agency is about changing the world, and even ends her essay on collective responsibility by returning to a form of this argument:

> This vicarious responsibility for things we have not done, this taking upon ourselves the consequences for things we are entirely innocent of, is the price we pay for the fact that we live our lives not by ourselves but among our fellow men, and that the faculty of action which, after all, is the political faculty par excellence, can be actualized only in one of the many and manifold forms of human community.[156]

But this kind of political action, whether it is for good or bad reasons, does not fit into a courtroom procedure, for such actions actually recreate the foundations upon which a court is based. That is, when true political actions take place they fall outside of normal political structures because they are recreating those structures. At another point, Arendt laments the fact that war crimes cannot really be punished:

> Thus, here we are [in a war crimes tribunal], demanding and meting out punishment in accordance with our sense of justice, while, on the other hand, this same sense of justice informs us that all our previous notions about punishment and its justifications have failed us.[157]

I would interpret Arendt here as failing to recognize that her conception of political agency, as she develops it in *The Human Condition* is what prevents us from punishing war crimes tribunals and fitting certain types of actions into a courtroom process. It is not because they are somehow more evil than other actions or that they undermine our notions of justice; rather, it is because they are the types of actions that recreate the world anew, the quintessential acts of political agency.

Although there may be a tension in Arendt's work on this point (or perhaps just a tension in my interpretation of her), I find in her understanding of political agency a way to think differently about responsibility and punishment at the global level. Many have interpreted war crimes and war crimes trials as incapable of capturing the enormity of evil that had been undertaken, a point to which I return in Chapter 7. My point is different. I would argue that war crimes trials fail to capture certain types of actions because those actions call into question the very structures upon which the trial system is built. Moreover, it is not just that particular state or particular trial system that is called into question – it is the very plurality of human existence. When one group of people tries to destroy another group of people simply on the basis that their existence is perceived to be some sort of threat to them or others, such actions simply do not fit into the normal trial structure. Arendt identifies the nature of this kind of crime: "Perhaps what is behind it all is only that individual human beings did not kill other individual human beings for human reasons, but that an organized attempt was made to eradicate the concept of the human being."[158]

What does this mean for responding to those types of actions? Are we left without recourse in certain situations? We might be, but let me offer an alternative suggestion. When certain types of actions undertake the destruction of the public sphere through the creation of policies of genocide, colonialism, slavery, economic exploitation or environmental degradation, such crimes need to be understood as a special type of norm violation. It is not simply that bad things are being done; it is that such actions are destroying the particularly fragile international political space. Such actions result from a particular type of agency, international political agency, which is the capacity to act in such a way that an agent does not only change a small feature of the world, but that agent fundamentally recreates the space in which other agents can present themselves and interact in a peaceful and just way.

Punishment at the international level, then, should be directed specifically to those crimes that destroy the global political sphere. Other kinds of norm violations should be punished at the domestic level, in which the more traditional notions of moral and legal agency operate. It is when an agent acts in a way that destroys the global public space that they deserve a special kind of punishment. Such types of norm violations may be undertaken by individual persons, but they will also be undertaken by corporate agents, including states, non-state groups and multinational corporations. In order to punish at the global level, then, we need a judicial structure that can adjudicate which type of agent should be held responsible.

International criminal courts have been constructed as an attempt to deal with the questions I have identified here. While such courts have been immensely important in holding individuals responsible for international crime, they have failed to address the kind of agency and responsibility that I have identified here. This should not be seen as a fault of those who designed or work within such judicial institutions. Rather, the problem is with the way in which those institutions fail to nest within a larger constitutional structure. In the final chapter of this book, I provide an alternative model for how such courts might fit into a global constitutional order.

Conclusion

This chapter has explored the ideas of agency and responsibility as part of a theory of punishment at the international level. I have pointed out that there are certain kinds of actions that do not correspond well with our standard notions of agency that underline domestic legal arguments about punishment. I have proposed that an alternative account of agency, what I have called political agency, needs to be incorporated into our normative evaluations and responses at the global level. This form of agency allows us to develop a different category of crime, one that is more specifically focused on the fragility of the global public sphere. One response to this fragility is to respond to these particular types of crimes by trying and punishing collectives.

In concluding this part of the analysis, let me emphasize two points. First, this argument should not be seen as an abandonment of individual criminal responsibility and the international criminal regime that has developed in the current international system. Rather, I have proposed an alternative understanding of agency and responsibility in order to account for the role of enforcement at the global level, a level that remains fragile because of the acceptance of violence and injustice that is, in some ways, built into the very nature of the system.

Second, I do not stipulate here what kinds of sentences should be imposed upon those agents, whether individual or collective, that are found guilty. There are immense amounts of difficulties in punishing collectives, ones that I have briefly addressed elsewhere.[159] But, the dangers of this process should not blind us to the fact that certain kinds of crime, particularly those that occur at the international level, can only really be undertaken by groups. If this is the case, then a judicial structure is necessary to account for those crimes. If these proposals at least generate a dialogue about how to create a more rule-governed order, I will have succeeded in my aims.

4 Punitive intervention

The previous three chapters have set out some conceptual clarifications about punishment at the global level.[160] In Chapter 1, I argued that punishment is necessary for a just political order, but only if the institutions that engage in punishment exist within a constitutional international order. Chapter 2 took on the claim that punishment cannot take place at the global level because of a lack of a single sovereign authority. In response to this critique, I drew on the works of John Locke and Hugo Grotius to argue that punishment can take place without a single sovereign but only if judicial institutions of a sort can play some role in adjudicating violations of norms. Chapter 3 pointed to the tension that arises at the global level when punitive practices do not target the proper agent. This raised questions of the relationship between agency and responsibility, especially in an international system in which there are different types of agents operating. I explore some of those tensions by developing the idea of political agency as an alternative to moral and legal agency, a concept I draw from Hannah Arendt.

I have through these three chapters begun to develop an institutional framework within which punishment makes sense at the global level. Now that this framework has been painted in broad brush strokes, the next three chapters will provide more detail through an exploration of three ongoing practices in the international order that have distinctly punitive elements: military intervention, economic sanctions and counter-terrorism policy. By examining these practices, I do three things. One, I identify their punitive dimensions. Two, I argue that they have become a central part of the current international order. Three, I argue that as constitutive elements of the current international order, these practices contribute to an unjust and violent international order. I conclude each chapter with suggestions for how revisions to the current practice might produce a more just international order.

This chapter will focus on military intervention. I have engaged with this topic in a number of different contexts, exploring questions of agency and ethics in some of my earlier work.[161] I begin the chapter by clarifying the concept of punitive intervention, particularly in opposition to humanitarian intervention. I argue that while humanitarian interventions continue to take place, changes in the international order since the end of the Cold War, particularly attempts to promote a more muscular liberalism, have resulted in more punitive intentions underlying intervention. I have compiled a database of interventions undertaken over the past 50 years that demonstrates punitive interventions have increased since the end of the Cold War. I link this increase to structural features of the current order, demonstrating how punitive intervention has become a more central dimension of international affairs.

Subsequently, I evaluate punitive interventions in accordance with the three concepts provided in the first part of the book. First, I argue that punitive intervention will not lead to a just system until such military actions better embody the two purposes of punishment, deterrence and retribution. Second, the question of the proper authority to undertake punitive intervention is explored. Finally, the question of which agent gets punished in a punitive intervention requires further analysis. These conceptual evaluations lead to some suggestions for how a revised constitutional order might better encompass the use of intervention for punitive purposes.

Punitive and humanitarian intervention

To distinguish punitive and humanitarian interventions, consider the following two cases. In December 1991, US forces began landing on the beaches of Somalia to prevent warring factions from disrupting the provision of food aid to the beleaguered population. After handing the mission over to the UN in 1992, US forces remained as part of the overall mission, partly under a UN command structure but also operating unilaterally. On 3 October 1993, US forces were attacked in an attempt to capture one of the warlords, Mohammed Farah Aideed, a mission that resulted in part from a UN decision to hold Aideed responsible for an attack on Pakistani peacekeepers in June 1993. Seeing Aideed as a central figure in attempts to disrupt the mission of UNOSOM II, both US and UN officials decided more actively to pursue and punish him and those who supported him. While stopping the activities of warlords like Aideed was important for the continued provision of humanitarian aid and creation of civil society, the purpose of the intervention grew to include the punishment of those hindering the peacekeeping operation. Not only did the US support a more punitive intervention; UN Secretary General Boutros Boutros-Ghali also saw the punishment of Aideed as a way to ensure future humanitarian interventions could contribute to peace and development.[162]

Security Council Resolution 1590, passed on 24 March 2005, put in place a multilateral intervention in Sudan in response to the ongoing atrocities being committed in the Darfur region of that country. The mission is designed not only to provide aid and observe combatants; it has an important criminal law function as well. As stipulated in section 4 of the resolution, the mission is to restructure the police, assist in the rule of law and "combat impunity."[163] Reports of the Secretary General, Kofi Annan, following upon this resolution, further emphasized these criminal law provisions, making them even more explicit. Report S/2005/467 of 18 July 2005 welcomed efforts at reconciliation, but noted that such efforts "should not be a substitute for the prosecution of war crimes cases." Annan also argued that the special courts set up by the Sudanese government to prosecute violators of human rights norms may not be enough, and that the international community needs to be involved in the process of ensuring that none escape punishment. These sentiments reflected the decision of the Security Council on 31 March 2005 that the International Criminal Court begins an investigation and possible prosecution of war crimes violations.[164] At the time of this writing, United Nations Mission in Sudan (UNMIS) includes over 700 international police officers, who both contribute to general law and order tasks and train Sudanese police forces. The mission mandate also includes a strong emphasis on the "rule of law."[165]

Most commentators and even those involved in these interventions identify them as humanitarian. Somalia was one of the first humanitarian interventions of the post-Cold War era, leading to numerous studies exploring both this case and broader questions about international order.[166] Intervening in Sudan has become central to those interested in ensuring that humanitarianism is not overwhelmed by the war on terror.[167] In what sense, then, can these interventions be called punitive rather than humanitarian?

Just as a definition of humanitarian intervention is not a simple matter, so the definition of punitive intervention raises conceptual difficulties.[168] One of the primary ones concerns the very act of defining a practice that is constitutive of the international normative structure, which intervention clearly is. Intervention in international affairs had long been considered a problem, something that violated the core principles of the international system. At the same time, because violations often help to define more clearly what that norm is, the fact that intervention violated sovereignty made it central for understanding what constitutes the international order.[169] When humanitarian interventions increased in frequency in the post-Cold War period, they also began to constitute the international normative order (although there were certainly interventions during the Cold War that were humanitarian).[170] Humanitarian intervention generated a larger discourse about rights and responsibilities at the global level, structuring the way we think about international order more broadly. Intervention, whether humanitarian or not, helped define the international order by highlighting core constitutive ideas of sovereignty and human rights.

Terry Nardin defines intervention as "the exercise of authority by one state within the jurisdiction of another state, but without its permission."

Intervention is humanitarian when "its aim is to protect innocent people who are not nationals of the intervening state from violence perpetrated or permitted by the government of the target state."[171] Jeff Holzgrefe defines it as such:

> [Humanitarian intervention is] the threat or use of force across state borders by a state (or group of states) aimed at preventing or ending widespread and grave violations of the fundamental human rights of individuals other than its own citizens, without the permission of the state within whose territory force is applied.[172]

Alternatively, I define a punitive intervention as follows:

> Punitive intervention is the use of force across state borders by a state or group of states aimed at inflicting harm on one or more agents that are responsible for violating the rules or norms governing international society.

Note some important distinctions between humanitarian and punitive intervention. First, while a humanitarian intervention is designed to halt the violations of human rights, a punitive intervention is designed to inflict harm in response to a violation already having been committed. Importantly, punitive interventions may halt the ongoing violation, but it has the additional purpose of inflicting a harm on those who caused the violation in the first place. This can come about through either a direct attack on the offending agent, such as killing a person or destroying a government, or through the creation of penal institutions within a sovereign state that can be used to try and then incarcerate non-state agents within a community who continue to violate human rights norms. The first type of intervention would be one designed to create a regime change, while the second would be one organized by the United Nations to create judicial and penal institutions within a failed state. Importantly, both are punitive in that both are designed to inflict harm of a sort on those who violated the norms in the first place.

A second distinction is that a punitive intervention is committed against an undefined agent. This point will be explored in more depth below, but for now it is important to emphasize that those who are the target of a punitive intervention may be the state, the government, a particular regime, a non-state terrorist group or specific individuals. The fact that a wide variety of agents might be targeted in this type of intervention raises a number of difficulties in whether or not this punitive practice contributes to a just political order, a fact addressed in the final section of this chapter. Both definitions of humanitarian intervention emphasize the violation of the target state's sovereignty, which would also happen in a punitive intervention. The difference is that a punitive intervention may be directed at the target state or an agent within that state.

A third distinction is that punitive interventions are undertaken in response to a broadly defined set of norms, not simply to protect against violence as in Nardin's definition or protect human rights as in Holzgrefe's definition. This is not an objection to the centrality of peace or human rights in constituting right and wrong in the international system, but rather that there are a wide range of norms and rules that may not fall within the purview of human rights norms that could prompt a punitive intervention.

One further point of clarification is relevant for both humanitarian intervention and punitive intervention. This is the matter of intentions. Nicholas Wheeler has argued that humanitarian intervention should not be defined solely by the intentions of the interveners.[173] Similarly, punitive interventions should not be defined solely by the intentions of the intervener. As I have argued in Chapter 1, if punitive intervention is a "practice" in the sense explained by Foucault, the intentions of the agents undertaking the intervention are not primary. What is relevant is the discursive space constructed by an intervention, a space that might include an emphasis on crimes, punishment, accountability and ensuring justice. These discourses help to construct certain types of intervention as punitive rather than simply humanitarian.

Some recent works have gestured towards the idea of punitive intervention, although not in the same sense as I explore here. In introducing his co-edited volume on humanitarian intervention, Terry Nardin points to the close association between protection and enforcement, noting that "the responsibility to protect includes responsibility to help change the conditions that allowed crimes against humanity to be committed in the first place,"[174] an idea that links to the potential for creating penal institutions in states and in the international society that can prevent such events from recurring. In the same volume, both Joseph Boyle and Kok-Chor Tan argue that punishment is not a viable justification for humanitarian intervention, with Boyle relying on the just war tradition and Tan relying on the idea of the responsibility to protect to make their arguments.[175] C. A. J. Coady hints at the fact that punitive intervention may become more popular after 9/11, but does not pursue this line of thought further.[176] These brief references to punitive intervention in some recent works on intervention suggest it is becoming an important issue but has not been addressed at great length.

Having provided a broad definition of punitive intervention and compared it with humanitarian intervention, I will now further clarify what punitive interventions might entail. I classify punitive interventions in three ways:

1   P1, when the intention is inflicting harm upon – usually killing – a particular individual leader or group of leaders without any trial or judicial procedure. Examples of this type of intervention include Aideed in Somalia, the Taliban in 2001, and Saddam Hussein in 2003.

2 P2, when the intention is the capture and trial of a particular individual or group of individuals. Examples of this type include the Panamanian intervention to capture Manuel Noriega in 1989 and the NATO interventions in Bosnia in the late 1990s to capture certain Bosnian Serb leaders. P2 interventions can be further divided,

- P2a interventions are defined by the intervening military forces engaging in the pursuit and capture of individual violators of human rights.
- P2b interventions are when intervening forces, both military and civil, engage in state-building actions focused in particular on the criminal justice system. This would include helping states to create a national police force, court system and penal institutions, i.e. jails.

3 P3, which involves inflicting harm on an entire political community, usually in order to convince them to change a regime, which is sometimes called coercive diplomacy. Examples here would include the bombing raid on Iraq in December 1998 and the air war against Serbia in 1999.

Table 4.1 lays out the distinguishing characteristics of these different forms of punitive intervention. These punitive interventions, however, could be simply military actions with specific short-term goals. That is, there is nothing in the above that makes these actions particularly punitive. Military conflicts have, especially in the twentieth century, sought to impose some sanction on the leaders of the losing state.[177] And what is called here P3 has a well-developed literature explaining its purpose as part of a military strategy to coerce change in opponents.[178] How can these really be punitive interventions rather than simply uses of military force to accomplish specific political objectives?

Table 4.1 Punitive intervention A

Punishment/ characteristics	Agent being punished	Action taken	Desired goal
P1	Persons	Targeted killing, assassination	Death of individual or group of individuals
P2a	Persons/groups	Capture and arrest	Trial of individual or group of individuals
P2b	Persons/groups	Creation of criminal justice institutions	Trial of individuals or group of individuals
P3	State	Aerial bombing, military campaign	Change in regime policy or complete regime change

Here the concept of a punitive practice as defined in Chapter 1 comes to our aid. Recall that punitive practices are the intentions, justifications, events and outcomes that result in the infliction of harm in response to a previous violation of a norm. There need not be a single intention articulated by a sovereign authority in order to describe these actions as punishments. Moreover, the intentions (and there are always more than one intention when states use military force) can include self-defence or the pursuit of national self-interest; indeed, punishment can be self-interested in part.

Recalling the importance of legitimate institutions for just punishment also helps to clarify the distinctions between these different types of military action. In particular, John Rawls' distinction between punitive institutions and punitive actions can help here. Drawing on the ideas of retribution and deterrence to further clarify the purpose of a punitive intervention, I add another characteristic in Table 4.2, which will help in clarifying the concept of a punitive intervention.

Table 4.2 demonstrates how certain types of military actions map onto the justifications of punishment offered in the philosophical literature. In the case of P1, the goal is primarily retributive, with little connection to a wider utilitarian or deterrent goal. While such a goal may be partly intended by the interveners, the failure to link that action to an institution makes such actions appear closer to revenge than to retribution. In the case of P2a, when the use of force is intended not only to inflict harm but also provide judgement, there is a link to an institutional structure. This

Table 4.2 Punitive intervention B

Punishment/ characteristics	Agent being punished	Harm inflicted	Short-term goal	Long-term goal
P1	Persons	Targeted killing, assassination	Death of individual or group of individuals	Retribution (or revenge)
P2a	Persons	Capture and arrest	Trial of individual or group of individuals	Deterrence and retribution
P2b	Persons	Creation of criminal justice institutions	Trial of individual or group of individuals	Deterrence and retribution
P3	State	Aerial bombing, military campaign	Change in regime policy or complete regime change	Retribution

link makes these actions appear to be more legitimate, although their legitimacy certainly remains questionable without a fully functioning international judicial system. P2b is more firmly linked to an institutional structure, for its purpose is the creation of such institutions in the future. Yet, it may also not be clearly linked to a global institution, unless an international institution is involved in the formulation of local criminal justice institutions. Finally, P3 is largely retributive and also close to revenge, primarily because it is not connected to any institutional order. As I have argued elsewhere,[179] it may be possible to construct an institutional framework for punishing states, but the current international legal order does not allow for this. Questions about the ability to attribute crimes to states might make some question the description of this action as retributive (which means, in part, that the correct agent is harmed), but since I believe states can commit crimes, I will label it as retributive.

Punitive intervention as a constitutive practice

Punitive interventions also appear to be increasing, both in actual numbers and in constituting a particular type of international order. To examine whether or not there has been an increase in punitive intervention, I have constructed a rough database of interventions undertaken from 1950 through 2005, listed in Appendix 1.[180] In some cases, such as the interventions in the former Yugoslavia, what is sometimes called a single intervention is split into more than one. These distinctions result from the differing specified missions, especially if those distinctions relate to the differing punitive purposes described above. So, for example, UNPROFOR (1992–1996) is listed as separate from SFOR (1996–2004).

Out of these 122 military interventions, I have interpreted 22 as being punitive. Of those 22, 16, or 72 per cent, have taken place since the end of the Cold War (1989). Table 4.3 lists all punitive interventions. While punitive interventions make up only 18 per cent of the total interventions undertaken in the entire time frame, they constitute roughly 33 per cent of the interventions undertaken since the end of the Cold War. That may not seem like a high percentage, but compared with the percentage of punitive interventions undertaken during the Cold War, 0.07 per cent, this does constitute a significant increase.

Appendix 2 displays the number of interventions undertaken from 1950 through 2005. Each data point is the beginning year of the intervention rather than intervention as a whole. In those cases where an intervention changed in its midst to adopting a new mandate or when an intervention is undertaken by states or institutions with very different mandates, these were listed as separate data points. Interventions were classified in four ways: non-punitive interventions, P1, P2 and P3 interventions. The graph does not distinguish P2a from P2b interventions.

The evidence suggests that there has been an increase in interventions

Table 4.3 Punitive interventions, 1946–2005

Intervener	Target	Dates	Purpose	Punishment type
US/UN	North Korea	1950–1953	Respond to NK attack on SK	P3
Belgium	Rwanda/Burundi	1959–1962	Control Hutu attacks on Tutsi	P2a
India	Pakistan	1971	Violations of Hindu rights	P3
Vietnam	Cambodia	1977–1989	Khmer Rouge human rights violations	P3
Israel	Lebanon	1978	Capture/kill PLO leaders	P1
Israel	Lebanon	1982–1983	Capture/kill PLO leaders	P1
US	Panama	1989–1991	Capture Noriega	P2a
US/UN	Somalia	1992–1993	Capture/kill Aideed	P1
UN/NATO	Former Yugoslavia	1992–1996	Coerce Serbs to stop attacks/assist capture of war criminals	P3/P2a
UN	Croatia	1995–1998	Assist in capture of war criminals/ create judicial institutions	P2a/P2b
UN	Bosnia	1995–2002	Create judicial institutions	P2b
NATO	Bosnia	1996–2004	Create judicial institutions/ capture war criminals	P2a/P2b
UN	Haiti	1997–2000	Professionalize police forces	P2b
UN	Central African Republic	1998–2000	Judicial and rule of law institution building	P2b
NATO	Serbia (Kosovo)	1999	Coerce Serbian behaviour in Kosovo	P3
UN	East Timor	2000–2003	Create judicial institutions	P2b
US	Afghanistan	2001–	Regime change, capture al-Qaeda leaders	P1/P3
UN/NATO	Afghanistan	2002–	Create judicial institutions	P2b
US	Iraq	2003	Regime change, capture/kill leadership	P1/P3
Australia	Solomon Islands	2003–	Create judicial institutions/ policing	P2b
EU/UN	Bosnia	2004–	Capture war criminals	P2a
UN	Sudan	2005	Halt genocide	P2a/P2b

undertaken for punitive purposes since 1990. Appendix 2 indicates the number of all interventions undertaken in a single year for the different reasons, with the percentage undertaken for punitive purposes dramatically increasing since 1995. P2 interventions in particular – which are attempts to either capture individuals for trial in international courts or create domestic court and policing structures – have seen the most dramatic increase. This could be explained by a combination of UN-led state-building efforts along with the growth in international criminal tribunals and forms of prosecution over the last 15 years.

The evidence from this data indicates that there has been a marked increase in punitive interventions, particularly in interventions intended to capture and try individuals for prosecution for violating human rights norms or interventions designed to create institutions for punishing those who commit violations of international norms. In other words, there appears to be a trend towards using military force to enforce norms of human rights, particularly through punitive means.

This increase in punitive interventions is not an isolated trend; rather, it is part of a shift in the international order towards a more aggressive, punitive approach to protecting human rights. Importantly, this does not mean human rights will always and everywhere be protected. Instead, in instances where the protection of human rights is deemed worth undertaking, states and international organizations seem more inclined to use punitive interventions to force that change.[181] This change has resulted from a combination of increasing American power, with its attendant liberal militarism, a greater emphasis on using force to protect human rights, the criminalization of war, and the employment of more punitive responses to violations of war crimes.

A part of this normative change is the use of military force to protect human rights, either by inflicting direct harm on those who violate them or creating judicial institutions in contexts where human rights violations are rampant. An example of the first trend would be the intervention against Yugoslavia over the violation of rights in Kosovo, while an example of the second would be the renewed emphasis on "rule of law" institutions in peacebuilding situations. It is because human rights are so central to the international order that there are more advocates for using force to defend them.

Since the end of the Second World War, human rights have become more integrated into the normative structure of the international system. The literature on human rights is voluminous, although certain authors have linked the discourses of rights to broader normative structures. Kurt Mills sees the emergence of human rights as a force in global politics as a "new sovereignty." As part of his argument, Mills explores how humanitarian intervention is being undertaken in response to human rights violations, admitting that such actions have not attained consistency. Yet, as he notes, "human rights has won the struggle with sovereignty but does not know what to do with the victory."[182] Mervyn Frost has made a powerful argument as well, focusing on how human rights have become a constitutive factor in the international system.[183] For Frost, and other constructivist theorists, human rights no longer act as simple constraints on the behaviour of states and leaders. Instead, they have become part of the very structure by which we understand and interpret the world around us. Frost makes this claim by focusing on the practices of global civil society and democratic states – which he claims are two of the most powerful forces in the international system. He demonstrates that the very meaning of these practices results from discourses of human rights.[184]

The publication of *The Responsibility to Protect* in 2001, the product of a series of investigations by a panel convened by the Canadian government at the request of Secretary-General Kofi Annan, puts intervention squarely in terms of human rights. They state quite clearly the link between protecting human rights and the need to intervene in situations where states have abandoned their "responsibility" to protect their own citizens. The report notes "What has been gradually emerging is a parallel transition from a culture of sovereign impunity to a culture of national and international accountability."[185] The report gestures towards some of the themes developed in this chapter when it notes that of the operational tasks an intervention should undertake, the pursuit of war criminals will likely grow in the future.[186]

The United Nations has also begun to emphasize the importance of creating judicial institutions within countries after interventions. In a report commissioned by the UN Department of Peacekeeping, Scott Carlson argues the United Nations and other international actors need to establish the "rule of law as a core priority of mission planning."[187] The report argues that from the issuing of mandates by the Security Council to the operations of soldiers on the ground, the reconstruction of judicial institutions should be central to peacekeeping operations, especially in situations of past violent conflict. The report, and other documents from the United Nations,[188] emphasize that the creation of a rule of law structure is not just about creating democracy but about the creation of institutions designed to investigate, try and prosecute those guilty of war crimes.

From a more critical perspective, David Chandler has linked the evolution of a human rights discourse to punitive interventions. He argues that not only are governments engaging in more punitive tactics to protect human rights, aid workers and NGO activists have also moved away from traditions of neutrality to more aggressive attempts to punish those who violate human rights norms:

> Through the human rights discourse, humanitarian action has become transformed from relying on empathy with suffering victims, in support of emergency aid, to mobilizing misanthropy to legitimize the politics of international condemnation, sanctions and bombings.[189]

Chandler links this emerging discourse to the rise of the British Labour government's "ethical foreign policy" agenda that helped make possible the intervention in Kosovo in 1999. Chandler is critical of this development, seeing the erosion of sovereignty that it entails a means by which the more powerful states in the system can continue to exert their influence over the whole. Chandler's linking of various agents in the system – NGOs, individual theorists and governments – demonstrates the wide-ranging influence of human rights and, importantly for this chapter, how that discourse leads to military interventions.

One could argue that rather than a larger constitutive norm emanating from the United Nations system, this trend is the result of American political culture being transposed to the international level. As its power has grown in the international system, norms emerging from American political culture may become more prominent. Is American political culture more punitive than others? To argue that one country is more "punitive" than another does not necessarily make sense; all states employ punishment to deter crimes. But, it might be that some states employ certain forms of punitive measures that are more violent. Here, evidence would suggest that the United States is distinct from other countries, certainly from European ones with which it is most often compared on other metrics. The death penalty is a punishment that few other states in Europe employ as a form of punishment, but it is one that is very much part of American criminal justice. Peter Lieberman has recently demonstrated a link between the use of force by the United States and various aspects of its criminal and legal culture concerning the death penalty.[190]

Moreover, of the punitive interventions listed above, eight out of 22, or 36 per cent, involved the United States. This suggests that the trend towards punitive intervention might be partly led by the United States. If so, and if American political culture has a more violent punitive ethos, than perhaps the trends towards punitive intervention can be explained by increasing American power and influence in the international system.

While the rise in punitive interventions may have resulted in part from American influence, the role of great powers in structuring the international system is not a surprise.[191] For example, the United States had a key role in constructing the International Criminal Court, but then backed out of signing on to the Rome Statute because of various political objections to the final structure. Punishment as a way to enforce human rights and create a more just intervention, particularly in military interventions in post-conflict and failing states, has increasingly become the norm in the international system. While the evidence provided here of an increase in number and linking those numbers to various normative trends in the system may not be definitive, I would argue that they provide strong evidence for the growth of a constitutive norm in the international system. Whether it be called the rule of law or punishment, the increasing use of military force to punish perpetrators of human rights abuses and the creation of judicial institutions to punish future violators suggests that punitive intervention is fast becoming a central part of the international system.

Evaluating punitive intervention: justice

Chapter 1 suggested how punishment can contribute to a just order. Punitive interventions might fulfil this goal by ending impunity, as Kofi Annan suggested. To reiterate what has already been suggested, justice is the proper distribution of goods. Proper, however, is the key word here. Proper could mean an equal distribution of goods, but equality depends on needs and status in a community. Proper might also refer not to the final outcome of a process but to the process itself. Because politics is an ongoing process, not one that has a single end point, many theorists of justice focus on the process more than the final outcome. How does punishment more generally, and punitive intervention more particularly, relate to these standards of justice? The "good" punishment seeks to distribute is not wealth, even though in some cases punishments take wealth from one and give it to the state. Rather, the good that punishment seeks to promote is protection from harm.[192] Harm can be defined in terms of human rights, i.e. harm is inflicted when one's human rights are violated, but it need not be defined in such a way. By ensuring that individuals obey the rules and laws of a system, punishment ensures that those rules and laws continue to provide the good of protection. One could take this point even further and argue that the infliction of harm that punishment entails cannot conceptually be called punishment unless it is intended to protect others. That is, inflicting harm is simply violence unless it is connected to ensuring punitive justice, i.e. protecting persons from harm.

This description of just punishment, however, focuses on how specific acts can be considered just. What of the justice of an entire punitive system, or what might be called criminal justice more broadly defined? For a system to be just, it must protect the society or group as a whole from harm, not just individuals in specific cases. This would mean including those who are potential criminals; i.e. the system should be designed not simply to inflict harm after a violation has occurred, but to construct a system in which individuals will not be put into a position to violate the rules in the first place.

This point returns us to Rawls' essay on the two concepts of rules described in Chapter 1. If we wish to construct a criminal justice system that is truly just, it is important that the system include within it forms of punishment that both inflict harm on those who violate the rules (the retributive function) but also convince others not to undertake such violations (the deterrent function). Does punitive intervention accomplish this objective? As noted in Table 2, only two forms of punitive intervention include both dimensions, what I have called P2a and P2b. P2b adds a further dimension to punishment, however, in that it includes a kind of rehabilitation. Rehabilitation is often included as one of the purposes of punishment, one that differs slightly from retribution and deterrence. It is part of both, however, in that a properly functioning criminal justice system would seek to deter by changing the character of the agent that violated the norm. P2b suggests a way in which a punishment might be deterrent, retributive and rehabilitative. That is, when force is used to help in the creation of a new set of institutions designed to try individuals, punitive intervention contributes to a just system. Such an intervention may involve the capture of suspected war criminals, but it cannot end there. Rather, there must be a clearly defined project by which those individuals who are captured will be tried before courts, either domestic or international.

This conclusion raises the question as to whether or not the capture and prosecution of individuals before the International Criminal Court, or other similar courts, might accomplish the same objectives, a point I return to in Chapter 7. It might, but it is not guaranteed to do so. The problem with the ICC is that while it may seem to construct a global system of international justice, too often individuals in specific locales are not aware of its existence or function. The best assurance that specific retributive punishments will be connected to larger punitive institutions of deterrence is to create such institutions in specific locales where the violations have occurred. A Human Rights Watch report from 1994 notes a similar point about the intervention in Somalia:

> The absence of a basis in law through which to prosecute those responsible for grave abuses may have also contributed to the U. N.'s myopic passivity concerning abuses of Somalis by Somalis. So long as it had no clear legal framework to prosecute Somalis for abuses committed against U. N. personnel, there was even less prospect of holding Somali authorities accountable for atrocities against their own people. There was, and is, no international criminal court to which the U. N. could readily turn in such scenarios, and the U. N.'s peacekeeping machinery offered no alternative legal mechanism.[193]

This quote suggests a link between punishment and justice that does not appear as readily in humanitarian actions. Humanitarian actions need not be motivated out of a desire for justice, but rather come from the virtue of charity. An important distinction between charity and justice is that the former can be practised towards those outside of one's political community and need not even result in an expansion of that community. For example, the story of the Good Samaritan in the Christian scriptures does not result in the lesson that the Samaritan and Hebrew suddenly become part of the same community. The story has resonance because the two communities remain distinct.

What does this mean for punitive intervention? It means that humanitarian interventions can be conducted without assumptions about what constitutes a right political community. Punitive interventions, however, must have underlying them a clearer notion of justice. Nor are these notions about international or global communities; rather, they must be about the specific order that a particular individual or group has violated. The problem with a military intervention is that it is the attempt by an outside power to impose an order on a community, but without explicitly defining what that order is. We assume that a punishment responds to the objective fact of a crime, but the "objective" nature of a crime does not make sense unless some legal provisions exist within a society.

The resistance to punitive intervention that arises from target populations can be found in this grey area where justice, authority and military force exist in an uneasy relationship. Populations resist because they intuitively grasp the failure of the intervener to articulate a clear notion of justice that would support their actions. Because the intervener cannot fall back on the majesty of sovereignty to justify its actions, the idea of what is just is all the intervening state has to rely upon. Without clearly defining justice, punitive interventions reveal themselves to be bereft of legitimacy. This leads me to the points raised in Chapter 2 concerning punishment and authority.

Evaluating punitive intervention: authority

Chapter 2 explored authority by engaging the works of John Locke and Hugo Grotius. The conclusion of that chapter was that agents in a state of nature can conceivably punish each other, although there is great danger that self-interested agents can allow their punitive actions to slip into vengeance. I argued in that chapter that the assumption by many scholars of international affairs that punishment has to emanate from a sovereign authority to avoid this danger results from a Hobbesian conception of political order. Locke's emphasis on the need for a judicial power to adjudicate the guilt and sentence to be meted out is developed by Hans Kelsen, whose idea of collective security relies upon an international judicial structure to make such decisions. The combination of Locke, Grotius and Kelsen suggests the need for a global constitutional order in which a judicial function is more clearly integrated into the international system.

Intervention, both humanitarian and punitive, raises important questions about authority. Many studies of humanitarian intervention, especially those focusing on the legal and ethical dilemmas that arise from it, address the question of authority. Because intervention violates a core principle of international society – the sovereignty and equality of the state – there are very few instances in which it can be justified.[194] But, just as in domestic society where harming individuals is never justified except when sanctioned by the authorities, so in international society, a "harm" imposed on a sovereign state can only be justified by the authority of the UN Security Council.[195] This authorization process has given the Security Council the role of a quasi-authority when it comes to this particular practice, a role that various international legal theorists have defended quite strenuously.[196]

The post-Cold War era has challenged the status of the Security Council as the primary authority when it comes to intervention. There were interventions undertaken throughout the Cold War not authorized by the Security Council, but these were not followed by arguments for radically changing the international legal structure that includes this provision. The no-fly zones over Iraq following the first Gulf War, the intervention in Kosovo, and the wars in Afghanistan and Iraq following 9/11 were undertaken either with no or limited Security Council involvement. As a result, some legal and moral theorists have challenged the status of the Security Council as the ultimate authority.[197] Even as these challenges appeared, however, others argued that undermining this authority would create chaos in the international system and lead to the powerful overriding the weak.[198] Some sought a middle ground; for instance, in 2001, the International Commission on Intervention and State Sovereignty published its important study *The Responsibility to Protect*, which argued that criteria for intervention need to be reconfigured. While the report raised important questions about the Security Council's role, it also reaffirmed that institution should remain the primary one for authorizing international interventions.[199] The United Nations built upon the ideas of this report, prompted by the encouragement of the Secretary General Kofi Annan, to argue for the continued centrality of the Security Council in authorizing the use of military force, particularly in cases of humanitarian intervention.[200]

These debates about the role of the Security Council in humanitarian interventions are even more relevant when it comes to punitive intervention. The role of authority in punitive intervention is central, for such interventions are much more directly linked to the political structure of the target state. While a humanitarian intervention may simply halt an ongoing conflict or provide aid in a situation of famine, a punitive intervention will decisively shape the political structure by altering the distribution of goods and order in the state. While not focused on punitive interventions, Robert Keohane and Michael Ignatieff both argue that an intervention will reshape the political order of the state targeted by restructuring the internal dynamics of the target state.[201] In a series of reports, the United Nations has also begun to recognize that intervention will decisively alter the legal structures within states and, as a result, has begun to construct frameworks for promoting the "rule of law" in states subject to intervention.[202]

If punitive interventions are increasing, and if they have a decisive impact on the political order within states, relying purely on the Security Council to authorize such interventions can no longer be the default position of the international community. Punishment, unlike humanitarianism, is a profoundly political action, one that raises questions of power and justice. As a result, to protect against both the abuse of power but also ensure that punitive actions are undertaken when necessary, punitive interventions must arise from an international political structure more balanced and constitutional in nature. Hans Kelsen's suggestions about the importance of the judiciary described in Chapter 2 are directly relevant here. A reformed International Court of Justice, one that could more quickly make judgements about whether or not a political agent has violated the rules of the system, could balance the powers of the Security Council, which currently is both the judicial and executive power (and even legislative, if one considers how regulations issued from the Council turn into law). The power given to this one institution needs to be disaggregated in order to construct a more truly constitutional order.

As noted in Chapter 2, the proposal that the ICJ and Security Council share the power to punish in a revised conception of collective security will not be happening soon. The proposal, however, reflects not only an idealistic attempt to radically alter the system; it is an attempt to create a political order in which power is respected and utilized for the pursuit of justice, but in which a constitutional structure can limit the capacity of any single institution to dominate the process. Increasing the role of the ICJ will contribute towards a more just global constitutional structure, one that can more fruitfully engage in punitive interventions.

Evaluating punitive intervention: agency

As described in Chapter 3, punishment raises important questions about agency, especially at the global level. Punitive intervention raises questions of agency in three different ways, some related to the broader issues of agency and intervention and others more specific to the relation of punishment to agency.

The first level at which agency is relevant to understanding punitive intervention concerns the way in which interventions more generally construct both the intervening state and the target state. The question of agency swirls around intervention more generally, as I have described in my previous work. In *Agency and Ethics*, I argued that intervention plays an important role in constructing the agency of the intervening state, which utilizes its history and political ideology to construct a particular self that can intervene and then project that self on to other political contexts. This results in powerful states constructing their identities through interventions.[203]

In that same book, I argued that the resistance that arises to an intervention results from an assertion of agency. Partly as a result of mid-twentieth-century decolonization movements in Africa, Asia and Latin America, people in states that are most often subject to intervention see them as a violation of something deeper than simple political borders. Sovereignty, while also a constructed concept, remains an important part of the political agency of many around the world. Robert Jackson's argument that some states deserve the term sovereignty more than others ignores this fundamental feature of the international political order.[204] The political agency of both the intervener and the target state play a central role in the success or failure of military interventions.

Punitive interventions give agency an even more central role. While a humanitarian intervention might be accepted by the target state because of dire need, a punitive intervention will be a direct challenge to the state's capacity to abide by certain norms or construct a criminal justice framework for addressing human rights issues in its own territory. Punitive interventions challenge a state's political agency by raising questions about its very status as a sovereign state in ways that a humanitarian intervention may not.

Punitive interventions will also arise in part from the political agency of the intervening state, and even regional or international organization, leading the intervention.[205] States and other organizations that undertake punitive interventions see their actions as not simply the irrational infliction of harm upon innocent civilians and infrastructure, but a measured response to a previous violation of international norms. Their role in enforcing those norms gives them the impression that they are playing an important role in constructing an international order that is more law governed and rule based. The discourses that surround punitive interventions highlight the way these normative concerns motivate and shape interventions.

The point to emphasize here is that punitive interventions construct a particular type of international order. This order is one that appears to be leading towards a more law-governed system in which norms are enforced through the infliction of harm upon those who violate those norms. Instead, what happens is that such interventions construct certain agents as "sheriffs" and others as "outlaws," mirroring the Wild West political order in which violence is used to punish individual violations but fails to create a global order in which agents adopt norms and follow rules designed to protect human rights. The political agency that results from various forms of punitive intervention is a violent, aggressive one with a patina of norm enforcement but which really undermines a rule-governed order. This is not to say that punitive intervention requires a single sovereign authority; rather, without a clear institutional structure from which such interventions emanate, they will lead to the construction of an unjust political order.

The second level at which agency needs consideration in a punitive intervention is the actual target of military action. As the description of the three different types of intervention demonstrates, a punitive intervention can target individual leaders, institutional structures or entire political communities. Fundamentally, the tripartite description is about agency, the agents who deserve punishment.

Outside of the first issue of agency addressed above, this second level in which agency matters needs careful consideration. Certainly, individual leaders violate international norms and deserve punishment, thus justifying P1 interventions. And, as I have described elsewhere, there may be situations in which the entire political community, particularly its status as a sovereign state, deserves punishment. The lack of clarity, however, about which agent – the state or leader – can commit crimes, be held responsible for crimes and be punished makes the practice of punitive intervention even less justified. Without a judicial structure at the global level that can make judgements about different kinds of agents, rather than the current structure in which the ICC judges individuals and the ICJ judges states, we need a judicial system that makes choices about which agents deserve punishment at which times. Both will certainly be deserving of punishment, but the randomness with which those choices are made, or perhaps the fact that the Security Council seems to make the final judgement in both cases, makes them less justifiable.

As the current international order stands, the only justifiable punitive interventions seem to be P2 types, ones in which the international community plays a role in creating domestic political institutions that can make judgements and punish violators of rights. The efforts by the United Nations to create a greater respect for the "rule of law" in post-conflict interventions are a positive move in this direction.

In truth, all three types of punitive intervention could be justified according to the criteria I have developed in the first chapter. My argument here is that P1 and P3 interventions might be justified in a constitutional order in which an international judicial system could make judgements about individuals and states in particular contexts. Such a system is not impossible to create, for there are already moves towards cooperation between various international institutions in certain situations, such as the UN intervention in Sudan. But, as recently argued by Adam March in the case of Uganda,[206] the role of the ICC can disrupt other efforts by the international community to bring some resolution to a conflict. While March argues that this is the result of punishment getting in the way of diplomatic efforts, I would argue that the ICC should have a role to play, but only within a larger judicial context in which the role of individual leaders, non-state actors and the political structure of the state can all be judged in terms of the violations taking place. While such a structure might be complex and politically infeasible at the moment, such concerns should not prevent the international community from developing a clearer judicial framework through which punitive military actions might be better conceived and executed.

Conclusions

This chapter has identified a military practice in the current international order that is punitive, military intervention. I have explained how a punitive intervention differs from other forms of intervention, particularly humanitarian. I have identified three different types of intervention that can be called punitive: P1, or attempts to capture or kill individual leaders; P2, attempts to construct judicial institutions in a target state in order to improve protection of human rights; and P3, uses of military force designed to punish entire states, what are sometimes called instances of coercive diplomacy. I have collected data that suggest punitive interventions are increasing in frequency since the end of the Cold War, an increase that arises from both the increased power of the United States and its more punitive approach to international affairs, and also a wider shift in the international normative order that has placed a heavy emphasis on the role of military means to enforce human rights. These changes in the international order are making it more punitive.

While this increase in punitive interventions has increased, it has not made the international political order more just, despite the intentions and/or hopes of those undertaking them. To make this more clear, I have drawn upon the three central points from part one of this book concerning justice, authority and agency and used them to critique this punitive practice. Because these interventions do not arise from a constitutional order that includes both a deterrent and retributive function, they fail to provide justice. Questions of authority remain unresolved in these interventions, undermining their legitimacy. The political agency that both motivates and is reinforced by punitive interventions creates a Wild West culture in which individual violations may be punished but respect for the rule of law remains weak. And, the confusion about which agents deserve punishment, states, non-state actors or individual leaders, leads to a political order in which attempts by institutions like the ICC in Uganda to prosecute war criminals is perceived to be political and detrimental to the larger goals of ensuring the protection of human rights.

Throughout this chapter, I have pointed to the lack of a judicial structure nested within a larger constitutional order as one of the central problems with the practice of punitive intervention. This emphasis on the importance of the judiciary for the proper exercise of punishment will continue throughout the remaining chapters as well. In the concluding chapter, I suggest how such a revised constitutional order might look; this chapter has, hopefully, demonstrated how what look like military interventions designed to create more respect for human rights are actually contributing to the creation of an unjust and violent international order.

5   Punitive sanctions

In the last chapter, I explored the practice of punitive intervention, identifying its increased frequency in the post-Cold War era and evaluating it in terms of justice, agency and authority. This chapter turns to a second international practice, economic sanctions, which I again describe, identify in the current system and evaluate according to these three criteria. The very word itself, sanctions, implies a punitive dimension, but strangely enough, many analysts argue that they need not be punitive, but could be simply strategic or coercive. One concern that seems to animate these proposals is that "punitive" implies retributive or vengeful, something to be avoided. Especially because sanctions have been presented as an alternative to war and have been embraced by those advocating non-violent means of conflict resolution and the protection of human rights, there is a strong resistance to claiming that sanctions are designed to cause harm.

Not all economic sanctions policies are punitive, although many have strong punitive elements. As with punitive intervention, punitive sanctions are defined not through the intentions of the sanctioning parties alone, but through a larger complex of intentions, actions and consequences. The primary criterion that differentiates punitive sanctions from other forms of sanctions is that they must be the infliction of harm in response to a violation of a norm or rule in the international system. This means that some forms of sanctions, such as US unilateral sanctions against Cuba to force a regime change in that country, do not count as punitive. Importantly, other sanctions that have as a side benefit the change of a regime, such as the sanctions during the 1990s directed against Iraq, can be defined as punitive in that they were imposed in response to Iraqi violations of various norms such as aggression and failure to abide by UN resolutions concerning weapons of mass destruction.

I begin the chapter by clarifying the meaning of sanctions, primarily by differentiating the strategic and punitive. The next section of the chapter explores how sanctions have become a constitutive feature of the current international political order. Unlike in the case of punitive intervention, where my evidence to support its constitutive nature was the construction of a database, in the case of punitive sanctions I review four sanctions episodes to demonstrate how they each contributed to a different kind of political order (1) League of Nations sanctions against Italy; (2) UN sanctions against Rhodesia; (3) UN sanctions against Iraq; and (4) UN/US sanctions in support of the "war on terror."

I then evaluate economic sanctions by means of the three concepts of justice, authority and agency. Overall, I argue that economic sanctions could be a just form of punishment in the international system. As with punitive intervention, however, the way in which they are currently being deployed, particularly in terms of the authority imposing them and the assumptions about the proper agents to be sanctioned, are undermining the potential for this tool to be used as a means to enforce international norms. As with punitive intervention, I again point to the need to construct a more constitutional global order.[207]

Strategic and punitive economic sanctions

Economic sanctions have long been a part of economic statecraft; Thucydides' description of the Athenian boycott of Megara during the Peloponnesian War provides an early example.[208] Sanctions can be understood as part of a toolkit of options open to states in their strategic interactions with each other.[209] As a result, much of the literature on sanctions has focused on the effectiveness of this tool and explanations for why states continue to employ it when it does not seem to work.[210] The general consensus on effectiveness appears to be that sanctions work only about 30 per cent of the time.[211]

Since most definitions focus on the strategic dimension of sanctions, clarifying punitive sanctions requires an engagement with definitions that focus on the strategic. As with intervention, the definition of sanctions more broadly has generated its own set of debates. For some, such as Hufbauer, Schott and Elliott, the definition of sanctions is quite broad: "the deliberate government-inspired withdrawal, or threat of withdrawal, of 'customary' trade of financial relations. 'Customary' does not mean 'contractual'; it simply means levels that would probably have occurred in the absence of sanctions."[212] Meghan L. O'Sullivan provides a similar definition: "the deliberate withdrawal of normal trade or financial relations for foreign policy purposes."[213] Daniel Drezner expands the concept in his exploration of economic coercion: "the threat or act by a nation-state or coalition of nation-states, called the sender, to disrupt economic exchange with another nation-state, called the target, unless the targeted country acquiesces to an articulated political demand."[214]

Those interested in sanctions imposed by international organizations, primarily the League of Nations or the United Nations, tend to focus on the normative dimension of sanctions. A pamphlet from the interwar period describes sanctions as follows:

> A "Sanction" is the name which legal writers give to measures for
> securing obedience to law. Sanctions can take the form of the infliction
> of penalties for a breach of law that has been committed, or they may
> consist in measures taken for the actual prevention of a threatened
> breach. Sanctions operate in two ways: negatively, in that the know-
> ledge of the will and power to apply them may deter a would-be
> wrongdoer from transgressing the law; positively, in that their applica-
> tion checks a wrongdoer in the act of transgression or compels him,
> after a transgression has been committed, to submit to the law and
> deprives him of the fruits of his transgression.[215]

This approach links sanctions more closely to international law and
conceptualizes them as a means to enforce that law. Although the League
and the liberal theorists who promoted it made this link with enforcement,
they were fully aware that sanctions were not part of a legal system as
existed in a nation-state; the authors of the above pamphlet noted that
"care must be taken not to press the analogy between individuals and
States too far."[216]

It is safe to say, however, that sanctions imposed by an international
organization are designed to enforce international law rather than simply
coerce another state in a bilateral relationship. Margaret Doxey describes
such sanctions in the following:

> When economic measures are used as sanctions the objectives should
> be to deter or dissuade states from pursuing policies which do not
> conform to accepted norms of international conduct. Compliance is
> considered to be in the general interest and sanctions are penalties
> which relate specifically to acts which the international society
> condemns.[217]

Writing from the perspective of the United Nations, James C. Ngobi
states that "Sanctions (in the modern sense of the word) take the form of
punishment at the international level."[218] In opposition to this view, David
Cortright and George Lopez have argued that sanctions imposed by the
United Nations should not be understood as punitive, but rather as part of
a bargaining process with renegade states. Drawing on coercive diplomacy
literature usually applied to foreign policy, Cortright and Lopez note that
when sanctions are "punitive" they are less effective because they do not
give the target state any incentive to stop its behaviour. Instead, they argue
that a bargaining approach to sanctions will make them both effective and
less harmful to innocent populations.[219]

In opposition to this view, Kim Richard Nossal argues that sanctions
are necessarily punitive.[220] Nossal argues that sanctions from both international organizations and states are punitive, using the case of US sanctions imposed on the Soviet Union for its invasion of Afghanistan in 1980

as a case study. According to Nossal, the decision to impose sanctions does not make sense if it is understood in the means–ends calculus that defines much of the coercive diplomacy literature. Rather, sanctions should be understood as punitive in all cases, with the success not necessarily based on a change in behaviour, since punishment does not necessarily change behaviour (although it hopefully should). As described in Chapter 1 of this book, punishment is deterrent and retributive, neither of which should be judged successful solely on the basis of whether or not a target (or criminal) changes behaviour. Examining retributive sanctions, Nossal points out that "Because it is imposed without regard to future behaviour, such punishment is immediately effective – as soon as, and to the extent that, the offender is harmed by the punishment. In short, retributive punishment, by its very nature, always 'works'."[221]

Nossal's analysis is closer to what I would describe as punitive sanctions. I differ from his argument, however, in that I do not see *all* instances of sanctions as punitive. Nossal's definition of sanctions is that they are (1) imposed in response to wrongdoing and (2) punitive in intent. I have argued already that intentionality should not be the defining feature of how we define punitive practices, although it certainly plays a key role. More importantly, however, Nossal's understanding of "wrongdoing" accepts a certain moral relativism. This means that any state definition of wrongdoing, even if it is a violation simply of that state's national interests, can be invoked to justify sanctions. For Nossal, this means that every sanctions episode can be defined as punitive.

Such an approach fails to acknowledge that we can rationally argue for right and wrong in a political system, even when a sovereign authority does not exist to determine what those rights and wrongs may be. Nossal draws upon the Hobbesian critique of moral norms by returning to the intention of the sanctioner, noting that even if moral norms do not exist, if a sanctioning party claims they are responding to a wrongdoing, this should be good enough.[222] One reason I draw upon Locke and Grotius rather than Hobbes is that they accept that morality arises from our shared understanding of the human condition, and that identifying those norms does not necessarily rely on a sovereign authority.[223] Moreover, recent work in constructivist IR theory has demonstrated how widely shared conceptions of right and wrong do exist and play an important role in the construction of the international system. Nossal's argument is important for identifying the punitive element of sanctions. But, he fails to accept that some sanctions are not punitive, specifically those that do not arise from a shared understanding of wrongdoing.

In light of these definitional debates, I propose that punitive sanctions should be defined as "the halting of normal economic activity with agents in response to a violation of a generally accepted rule or norm of international society." "Normal economic activity" does not mean in accordance with a particular norm, but only in relation to that agent's previous economic activity. "Generally accepted rule or norm of international society" however does mean exactly what it says; sanctions are understood as punitive only if they are imposed in response to a violation of widely accepted international norms. This point is important, for sanctions might be imposed by a state in response to violations of that state's particular rights or in violation of a particular ideological norm.

The distinction between punitive and strategic sanctions is certainly not hard and fast, for a number of episodes have both dimensions. For instance, in 1960, the United States imposed sanctions on Cuba because the government of Fidel Castro moved closer to the Soviet orbit. These sanctions were ideologically oriented but also in response to specific actions undertaken by the Castro government that violated international norms. Castro had nationalized the oil industry in Cuba, an action that fell afoul of the norm that states expropriating the goods of foreign corporations should fully reimburse them. Although this was a violation of a norm, one could argue that an emerging norm connected to decolonization was that the resources of states could be taken back from foreign companies, something demonstrated by the Iranian nationalization of its oil industry in 1951 and the Egyptian nationalization of the Suez Canal in 1956.[224] Yet, in all three cases, and particularly in the case of Cuba, the ideological dimension of sanctions seems most prominent. The goal was less to harm in response to a past violation but instead to change strategically the behaviour of the Cuban government.

The purpose of punitive sanctions is retributive and deterrent; retributive in that it is an infliction of harm in response to a past violation and deterrent in that it is intended to send a message to a wider community of individuals. Punitive sanctions are most often imposed by international organizations, but may also be imposed by individual states in their interactions with other states. The target of sanctions might be states, non-state groups and even individual leaders of states or groups.

Punitive sanctions as a constitutive practice

Since the beginning of the twentieth century, sanctions have played an important role in different international systems. Because they have been conceptualized as a way to enforce international law without using military force, individuals from across the political spectrum have been enthusiastic about their potential. But the role of sanctions versus other forms of ensuring compliance with international law has not always been shared across the Great Powers or throughout the international system.

The following cases demonstrate how sanctions become progressively more punitive during the twentieth and twenty-first centuries. At the same time, the episodes reveal the centrality of authority and agency in understanding how sanctions can or cannot contribute to a more just international order, one in which the rule of law is enforced through punitive enforcement mechanisms.

League sanctions on Italy, 1935–1936

The international order at the time of the League sanctions on Italy could be labelled as idealist and utopian, although it is perhaps better described as internationalist.[225] Internationalism has a series of overlapping meanings, all of which revolve around an attempt to regulate political life at the global level in the hopes of constructing a more peaceful order. Its most common meaning is that of a political ideology that advocates greater cooperation among nation-states in the pursuit of peace through the creation of international law and institutions. Internationalism is premised on the assumption that peace will only result from programmatic attempts at organizing international affairs. Internationalism was, and remains, closely linked to international law. Indeed, one could say that international law became the primary focus of attempts to promote internationalism, with its insistence that states remain the central agents but limit their ability to launch war. Internationalism arose as a political project from these legal attempts to align an unwillingness to give up on the nation-state with a desire for peace.

This link between law and internationalism can be found in the analysis of the League by Alfred Zimmern, although he was sceptical that law alone would ensure the success of the League.[226] A central point of disagreement among those advocating internationalism was how to enforce international law. Zimmern described the League as originating from various proposals of the early twentieth century, including the Hague Conference system of the late nineteenth century, peace plans developed by the American President William Howard Taft, and British efforts to organize its colonies and allies for a stronger war effort during the First World War. These diverse sources – particularly the differences between the American effort to create enforcement mechanisms through sanctions and collective security and the British efforts to organize states in a common purpose through more traditional diplomatic means but in a new setting – created very different perceptions of the role of enforcement in the League structure.

Out of these diverse origins, the League Covenant that eventually appeared did have a strong enforcement mechanism, as embodied in Article 16, which stated quite clearly that once a state had violated the norms against war the League members would

> immediately subject it to the severance of all trade and financial relations, the prohibition of all intercourse between their nationals and the nationals of the covenant-breaking State, and the prevention of all financial, commercial or personal intercourse between the nationals of

the covenant-breaking State and the nationals of any other State, whether a Member of the League or not.

Sanctions were to be used to punish those states that violated the norms of the system. This system of sanctions came into effect with the Italian invasion of Ethiopia in October 1935.

The origins of the conflict between Italy and Ethiopia lay in the dynamics of the colonial era. In 1889, Italy and Ethiopia concluded a treaty concerning Italian rights in the region. The treaty stated that Ethiopia would conduct its foreign relations through Italian control, which the Italians claimed gave them a protectorate over Ethiopia, an interpretation on which the two states did not see eye to eye, to put it mildly. The conflicting interpretations of this treaty led to a military engagement at Aduwa in 1896, where the Ethiopian army defeated a force of 20,000 Italian troops. In 1908, another treaty was concluded between the two states, one that gave Ethiopia control over water rights in the Wal Wal region. These sites were occupied by the Italians in the mid-1920s, a situation that Ethiopia never formally accepted. In November 1934, Ethiopia sent troops to the Wal Wal region to take it back. The troops were stationed near the Italian forces, but neither side acted aggressively at first. Eventually, however, shots were fired and the incident became a focus of attention for the international community.[227] While the Wal Wal incident was the immediate cause of the conflict, many have argued that Mussolini had been planning to take over Ethiopia since early 1933.[228] Italy invaded Ethiopia on 3 October 1935, and a few days later the League Council voted to impose economic sanctions on Italy.

Ethiopia had been accepted into the League as a full member in 1923 (sponsored by Italy, of all countries), a fact that made the conflict between the two states more central to the international order than it might otherwise have been.[229] But the sanctions imposed on Italy were eviscerated by events both internal to the League and events outside its confines. The League had created a Committee to investigate sanctions against Italy in the spring of 1935, prior to the invasion. After deliberating about the dangers to the civilian population in Italy of sanctioning too much, the committee proposed a list of very weak sanctions. As one author notes,

> By concentrating on the sufferings and misery of the civilian population in the aggressor country they forgot the greater sufferings and misery that would be inflicted on the fighting men and civilians of all the warring nations, more particularly in the territories where military operations would develop.[230]

Moreover, the League Secretary-General at the time, Joseph Avenol, tried to keep the issue of Italy and Ethiopia off the agenda, in that he did not believe in the centrality of sanctions as a way to enforce the peace.[231]

Outside the confines of the League, policies of the Great Powers, particularly France and Great Britain, severely undermined the League sanctions. At the Stressa Conference in April 1935, Mussolini was able to exclude Africa from a statement about respect for borders issued at the end of the conference.[232] The most decisive blow to the sanctions regime, however, was the meeting of the British Foreign Minister, Samuel Hoare and the French Prime Minister, Pierre Laval. Their agreement, the Hoare–Laval plan of December 1935, partitioned Ethiopia and gave a large portion to Italy. This plan was immediately denounced by the British public, which was much more aggressively in favour of sanctions than its leaders, as evidenced by the famous Peace Ballot of June 1935.[233] Neville Chamberlain, then Chancellor of the Exchequer, declared on 10 June 1936 that continuing sanctions was the very "midsummer of madness." The League ended all sanctions against Italy on 15 July 1936.

Because the Great Powers were willing to sacrifice the League and its enforcement mechanisms to appease Italy, many saw this episode as the moment when the League structure as a whole collapsed.[234] The concern with Germany and its rearmament may well have been a justified reason for appeasing Italy, but the perception of the French and British that League sanctions were a hindrance to the conduct of proper diplomacy suggests that they saw the relationship of sanctions, the League and world order in a much different way than those who supported the League agenda. These conflicting visions of what role sanctions and the League's constitutional structures should play reveals the importance of international order for understanding the function of sanctions as a punitive measure.

According to the Covenant of the League of Nations, sanctions on Italy were to be punitive; they constituted the international political order in that they were to be a non-violent way to enforce the primary norm of preventing war. The sanctions imposed a harm on Italian society and the Mussolini regime. That punitive dimension, however, was greatly weakened by the actions of the Great Powers, particularly Great Britain and France. The legitimacy of the League as a constitutional structure designed to enforce international law through the imposition of sanctions could not function with the competing vision of international order embodied in actions such as the Hoare–Laval plan. The punitive dimensions of the sanctions against Italy were decisively weakened by the lack of legitimacy of the League structure.

United Nations sanctions on Rhodesia, 1966–1980

The imposition of sanctions by the United Nations on Rhodesia in 1966, as with the previous case, demonstrates the interrelationship of the international normative order and punishment. In this case, the conflict was not simply one of Africa versus Europe; instead, it was about conflicting visions of the United Nations, with those in the developing world seeing it as a source for norms supporting self-determination and equality, and those in Europe and the developed world seeing it as an institution to promote those same norms, but in a much more conservative and measured fashion. This conflict meant that the sanctions were seen in the United Kingdom as a means to bring Rhodesia back to the fold of the Commonwealth and in African states as a way to topple a racist government.

As with the League, the United Nations embodied the spirit of internationalism. At the same time, it was created in part to rectify the problems of the League. The two problems identified in the Italian case were the differing perceptions of the Great Powers concerning the role of the institution and the lack of an effective enforcement mechanism. In response to the first problem, the United Nations was significantly different from its predecessor. The Security Council and the veto power of the five permanent members were designed to ensure that the Great Powers would not dissent radically from the purposes of the institution. One analyst suggested that the veto power was not designed simply to keep the Great Powers great and the small powers small, but rather to balance the powers of the five against each other.[235] No matter its purpose, this provision in the UN Charter was designed to prevent the type of conflicting interpretations of the role of the Great Powers that plagued the League during the Italian crisis.

The second problem, enforcement, was also addressed in the new institution. The League had included a strong enforcement mechanism in Article 16. But, as described above, the implementation of sanctions under Article 16, while technically "automatic," certainly did not exhibit this characteristic. Moreover, because the League was a "league" with a weak central agency, its ability to judge clearly that a violation of international norms had taken place was not very effective. The UN system was designed to rectify this problem by creating a Security Council that would both determine when breaches of peace and security had taken place and make its decisions obligatory on all member states. This strengthening of the institution gave it the ability to punish states that violated the rules of the international system, with economic sanctions being a central part of that enforcement mechanism.[236] Provisions for enforcing international law, particularly laws dealing with the use of force, can be found in Chapter VII of the UN Charter (Articles 39–51). Article 41 concerns itself with "measures not involving the use of armed force" or economic sanctions and the severance of diplomatic relations.

The sanctions against Rhodesia were not initially from the United Nations but were unilaterally imposed by the United Kingdom. The violation that prompted the sanctions was Rhodesia's Unilateral Declaration of Independence, or UDI as it became known in public debate and the literature surrounding it. Rhodesia's declaration, however, needs some historical context in that practically it was an independent country when it issued the UDI in 1965. Rhodesia was founded not by the British government but by Cecil Rhodes the entrepreneur, whose company governed the territory that became Rhodesia from 1890 through 1923.[237] In 1923, company rule ended and Rhodesia became a "self-governing colony with a constitution in which Great Britain had the right to intervene in the affairs of the country in certain exceptional circumstances." One of the issues over which it could intervene was "Native Administration," or the rights of the native black population.[238] While it was given this right, the government in London never used these powers, leaving the white Rhodesian population with the impression that it was a sovereign state member of the British Commonwealth.

In 1964 Ian Smith became Prime Minister of Rhodesia. He was seen as just the right person to stand up to both the black nationalists and the British, who were strongly resisting Rhodesian moves towards independence. Despite a last minute visit from the newly elected Labour Prime Minister, Harold Wilson, Smith declared independence on 11 November 1965. One day later the United Nations Security Council issued Resolution 216 condemning the UDI. Soon thereafter, it issued Resolution 217.[239] The resolution did not impose sanctions, but instead requested that states "refrain from any action that would assist and encourage the illegal regime ... and to do their utmost to break all economic relations with Southern Rhodesia, including an embargo on oil and petroleum products." This request for sanctions was not enforcement, as found in Article 41 of the Charter, but something less demanding. Harold Wilson claimed the resolution was located between Chapters VI and VII rather than a clear instance of either type of action.

The sanctions foundered on the fact that they sought to support two distinct normative visions. These differing norms can be found in two articles from the period published in *The Round Table*, the journal of the Commonwealth. In "Britain and the United Nations: A Demand for Results"[240] the author argues that the United Nations is a place where British interests, or the interests of other great powers, can be more easily pursued. In terms of Rhodesia, the United Nations should be used as a tool to reinforce British control rather than a source for authorizing collective sanctions. An alternative perspective is found in an article written by an anonymous representative of "black Rhodesia."[241] This author argues that "the wishes of the world as expressed through the UN are frustrated by the unwillingness of Great Britain to hand over settlement of the problem to them." This author sees the United Nations as a source for authoritative action to support the norm of racial equality, self-determination and sovereign equality – that is, support for emerging human rights norms.

Following Resolution 217, certain states, particularly South Africa and Portugal, resisted the imposition of sanctions and worked to violate them. When a ship carrying oil was able to dock at the port of Beira in

Mozambique in April 1966, with the clear intention of sending oil to Rhodesia, the Security Council acted again. The debate preceding that resolution revealed the differing normative visions surrounding the sanctions regime. Lord Caradon, the British representative to the UN, called for limited actions to be taken against Portugal and any state violating the provisions of Resolution 217. The African states, however, demanded that the resolution result in a wider debate so that, as the delegate to Uganda stated, the Council could "go to the root of the matter."[242] Precisely what the root of the matter was, however, was quite different from the British and African perspectives. For the British, the Smith government had violated the sovereignty of the British Parliament and its right to release countries from colonial status. For the African states, the Smith government represented a racist state in the heart of Africa. As the sanctions were not intended to create a majority rule situation in Rhodesia but only support the British efforts to bring them back in line, it would seem that the former norm was the one being enforced. And yet, the sanctions were not yet mandatory, but only requested, so the punitive dimensions of the sanctions were weak.

In the summer and autumn of 1966, the Wilson government hinted at the potential for negotiations with the Smith government. Wilson had to fight off the leaders of African states who were insistent on toppling the Smith regime and giving power to the native populations, along with the more liberal members of his own Labour Party. Yet, Wilson did not want to alienate the opposition Conservatives or cut off the potential for talks by alienating white Rhodesians.[243] In July 1966, the leaders of Zambia, Tanzania, Uganda and Kenya issued the famous NIBMAR statement, which stipulated that there would be "no independence before majority rule." This statement was reaffirmed by the majority of the African delegates in the Commonwealth prior to their meeting in September 1966, thus hardening their position and preventing any real progress. Wilson's decision to meet with Smith on board the *HMS Tiger* in December 1966 frustrated the African leaders, who believed that the British really wanted white rule in Africa.

Although Wilson tried to negotiate with Smith, the Rhodesian government refused his overtures, and the negotiations led nowhere. As a result, the British government turned to the United Nations Security Council, where, on 16 December 1966, it proposed a resolution to impose mandatory sanctions on Rhodesia. As a result, the Security Council passed its first ever resolution to enforce international law through a Chapter VII provision.[244] Resolution 232 stated that there was a threat to international peace and security and set up a strong economic sanctions regime against Rhodesia. The resolution banned important exports from Rhodesia and prevented various goods from being imported into the country. It was passed by 11 states with four abstentions (Soviet Union, Bulgaria, Mali and France).

The second declaratory clause of the resolution stated that the aim of the sanctions was to "bring the rebellion in Southern Rhodesia to an end." At the same time, in declarative clause 4, the resolution reaffirmed the rights of the people of Southern Rhodesia

> to freedom and independence in accordance with the Declaration on the Granting of Independence to Colonial countries and Peoples contained in General Assembly Resolution 1514(XV) of 14 December 1960, and recognizes the legitimacy of their struggle to secure the enjoyment of their rights as set forth in the Charter of the United Nations.

These two elements of the resolution, one stating the Rhodesian violation was one of rebelling against the British crown and the other suggesting that it was about the rights of the majority black population, reflect conflicting visions of normative order. The place of sanctions in this order could be to create a world in which colonial powers controlled recalcitrant states or could be one designed to support norms of racial equality and human rights. The fact that both norms were found within the text of the resolution suggests that the international community was unclear on what role sanctions were to play – or, perhaps more accurately, were unwilling to decide which norms were more central to the emerging international order.

The debate over the resolution also reveals the contrast between these visions. The British proposed draft did not include an embargo on oil and, connected to this, refused to stipulate penalties for countries that violated the sanctions. The African countries on the Council introduced an amendment to the resolution that included oil as part of the sanctions package, but the British resisted this. In the end, rather than preventing the import of oil as with other products, the resolution prevented "participation in their territories or territories under their administration or in land or air transport facilities or by their national or vessels of their registration in the supply of oil or oil products to Southern Rhodesia." As one author notes, this formulation was "less direct, simply obliging members not to participate in supplying oil to Rhodesia."[245]

The sanctions were reinforced in 1968, but the same tensions persisted between the differing visions of what role sanctions could play. Negotiations with the Smith government continued, and military conflict between the white government and black opposition movements eventually eroded the Smith government. Sanctions were formally ended in 1979 when it became clear that a black majority government would take over, creating the country of Zimbabwe in 1980.

Analyses have focused on the reasons for the failure of sanctions, which have stressed the effectiveness debate. The "leakages" in the sanctions structure, particularly the ability of Portuguese-controlled Mozambique and South Africa to continue to supply Rhodesia were decisive in their collapse.[246] The analysis I have presented here does not demonstrate that sanctions failed because of a conflict between world views (although I believe this contributed to their failure); rather, my point is that sanctions constituted an international political order that reflected tensions about the authority of the United Nations. One analyst of sanctions, Margaret Doxey, argued that the norms that sanctions were intended to support were clear, but the legitimacy of the United Nations to impose them was lacking.[247] I would agree in part with Doxey here, although I would argue that the conflict over legitimacy produced and generated a conflict over norms as well. Overall, sanctions played a role in constituting a particular political order, but it was an order that failed to define clearly the norms that the order was to promote, a lack of clarity found in the conflicting purposes of sanctions.

Sanctions against Iraq, 1990–2003

The end of the Cold War radically changed the international order. As detailed in the previous chapter, one of the changes was an increase in punitive interventions, part of a larger trend towards more multilateral enforcement mechanisms undertaken by the United Nations. The role of the United Nations in this new order was largely celebratory about the potential for the institution finally to achieve its aims of bringing peace and security. One way in which the United Nations could achieve those aims was through the use of economic sanctions in accordance with Article 41 of the Charter.

At this moment, in other words, the problem of legitimacy that plagued the sanctions episodes in 1935 and 1965 seemed to be solved. Rather than an institution riven by conflicting normative visions and thus weakened as an effective agent of punishment, the United Nations Security Council suddenly appeared to be the institution it was designed to be. As a result, the imposition of sanctions upon Iraq following its invasion of Kuwait came swiftly and firmly. The punitive dimension of the sanctions soon became central to their effectiveness, as the discourse surrounding them focused on the evils of the regime of Saddam Hussein. The sanctions, of course, soon became controversial, primarily because of the suffering that was imposed upon the civilian population in Iraq. For many, this suffering rendered the sanctions unjust. As a result, while they remained punitive, their contribution to creating a just international order was severely undermined.

What I will argue here is that this episode demonstrates how confusion over agency makes punitive measures unjust. Rather than focus on the suffering imposed on the Iraqi population and attempt to distinguish the correct agent from the incorrect one, I want to highlight how from the very first Security Council resolution, UN actions constructed a particular form of agency. This agency, what might be called state agency, is so much part of the international order that it is difficult to identify. In the case of Iraq, the way in which the reparations regime and sanctions focused on the responsibility of the Iraqi state produced a regime that harmed civilians rather than coerced a leadership into changing its behaviour. To uncover the role of state agency in the Iraqi sanctions episode, I focus on the discourses of responsibility that located Iraq in a particular moral and legal structure in which the regime could not really be separated from the state as a whole. This structure can be seen as productive of the devastating humanitarian impact on the Iraqi civilian population.

The sanctions on Iraq resulted from its attack on Kuwait in 1990. Within eight hours of the Iraqi invasion of Kuwait on 2 August 1990, the Security Council issued Resolution 660, condemning the invasion and demanding that Iraq withdraw. But it was Security Council Resolution 661, passed on 6 August, that began the process of formally imposing sanctions on Iraq. While neither resolution explicitly mentions the word responsibility in their texts, they do assume that Iraq deserves punishment for its actions. This construction of Iraqi agency was an important factor in the way in which sanctions were understood to serve as a tool of enforcement. Despite the fact that Iraq was a dictatorship in which the citizens who would be subject to sanctions would have very little capacity to change the policy of their government, the discourse that surrounded the imposition of sanctions assumed "Iraq" was the responsible agent.

During the early part of August Iraq sought to eliminate Kuwait as a separate state,[248] a process that required the elimination of any diplomatic representation to Kuwait as a separate entity. This meant denying any special privileges to members of the diplomatic community stationed in Kuwait. On 18 August 1990 the Security Council passed Resolution 664, which emphasized that Iraq had an "obligation" to the well being of third country nationals in Kuwait. That Iraq was responsible for the diplomats and third country nationals in both Iraq and Kuwait found its fullest expression in Resolution 666 passed on 13 September. That resolution stated, *inter alia*,

> *Deeply concerned* that Iraq has failed to comply with its obligations under Security Council resolution 664 (1990) in respect to the safety and well-being of third State nationals, and reaffirming that Iraq retains full responsibility in this regard under international humanitarian law including, where, applicable, the Fourth Geneva Convention...

Resolution 667, passed on 16 September also established Iraqi responsibility:

> *Recalling that* Iraq is fully responsible for any use of violence against foreign nationals or against any diplomatic or consular missions in Kuwait or its personnel...

The foreign ministers meeting of the Security Council, held on 25 September, further constructed the Iraqi state as the responsible agent. In his remarks before the council, the Kuwaiti foreign minister argued for Iraqi responsibility in these strong words:

> [Iraq is] fully responsible for the behaviour of its forces and all its policies in Kuwait directed against the people of Kuwait under occupation. Therefore the government of Iraq is bound to bear full responsibility for the destruction and pillage being inflicted on the economic and social infrastructure of Kuwait, both public and private. The Iraqi government is also legally bound to pay full reparations for the destruction it has inflicted on Kuwait.[249]

Finally, Resolution 674, passed on 29 October 1990, brought together many of these claims into a single, concisely worded accusation levelled against Iraq:

> 8. *Reminds* Iraq that under international law it is liable for any loss, damage, or injury arising in regard to Kuwait and third States, and their nationals and corporations, as a result of the invasion and illegal occupation of Kuwait and Iraq.

At one level, this process simply reflects the normal diplomatic language of UN Security Council resolutions. At the same time, the construction of Iraqi agency cannot be limited to debates within the Security Council (although these debates do have a special significance), nor should it be summarized so quickly. The texts of the resolutions and the comments made in the chambers of the Security Council reveal some confusion in the public discourse concerning the responsibility of either Saddam Hussein or the state of Iraq.

In fact, the choice need not even be between the state and the leader alone. Other agents, including multinational corporations and other states, can be seen as sharing some of that responsibility. David Campbell argues that the construction of Iraq's war-making capability could be read as the responsibility of a US national security policy that favoured Iraq over Iran. Nor are the possible agents limited to other states; international financial and industrial corporations can also be included; as Campbell notes "The question of agency and responsibility in the West's relationship with Iraq becomes even more complex when one considers that many of these commercial transactions were financed by banks operating in gray areas."[250] That is, the responsibility for funding the Iraqi military build-up cannot even be clearly pinned on the US government, for it occurred through a diverse network of international banks and industries, none of which can in any way be clearly identified as responsible for the Iraqi build-up. Of course, the Iraqi leadership had to put those resources into action against

Kuwait. Nevertheless, the "responsible agent" here seems to include numerous agents, not limited to governments alone.

But despite these other agents, the state of Iraq continued to be the responsible agent. Why Iraq became the responsible agent and not Saddam Hussein's regime or the international corporations that funded his build-up relies on a set of overlapping discourses in international relations and international law, all of which contribute to the moral structure of global politics. That moral structure demands that there be responsible agents (as most moral structures require) but it also demands that the most important responsible agent be the state.

Constructing Iraq as the responsible agent, however, was not simply a theoretical process. It made the imposition of economic sanctions a justifiable and logical policy response. At first, that regime was designed largely to reverse the Iraqi invasion of Kuwait; that is, it was not seen at first as a means by which to punish Iraq. But perhaps because of the process by which Iraq was constructed as the responsible agent, the notion of punishment began to enter more into the construction of the sanctions regime.

As noted above, sanctions were imposed on Iraq in the very first days of the crisis, with the passage of Resolution 661 on 6 August 1991. But the initial sanctions regime did not mention punishment explicitly, nor did its machinery emphasize this aspect. The initial UN debates and decisions on sanctions were designed largely to force a return to the *status quo ante*. They sought explicitly to reverse the Iraqi invasion, and much of the debate focused on this element. When the sanctions were the primary means to end the Iraqi intervention, notions of punishment were not in the forefront of the resolutions. For example, Resolution 661 states explicitly in its prologue that one of its intentions is to "bring the invasion and occupation of Kuwait by Iraq to an end and to restore the sovereignty and territorial integrity of Kuwait." There was very little in these early resolutions, either in their prologues or in their demands that could be seen as punishment; the language emphasized an attempt to reverse the action.

But, along with the US decision to move from sanctions to military force, the language of the Security Council resolutions slowly changed to emphasize punishment. Troop levels increased throughout October, and President Bush addressed the United Nations in a speech that could have been read as supportive of continuing sanctions or as a prelude to a more aggressive US military reaction. Soon the resolutions began to reflect a more aggressive approach. Even more importantly, the resolutions contained the beginnings of a sanctions regime that could be directly tied to a reparations regime. On 29 October the Security Council passed Resolution 674, which, after explicitly reminding Iraq of its responsibilities, began the process of formally creating a reparations regime:

> 9. Invites States to collect relevant information regarding their claims, and those of their nationals and corporations, for restitution or

financial compensation by Iraq with a view to such arrangements as may be established in accordance with international law.[251]

While this phrase did not actually create a reparations regime, it suggests that the Council intended a combination of sanctions and reparations.

Little progress in terms of sanctions and reparations occurred during the course of the war. But Resolution 687, passed on 3 April 1991, linked the sanctions regime much more clearly to a reparations regime. After a number of points concerning the disarmament of Iraq, the resolution turns to the responsibilities of Iraq and the means to provide compensation. Section E first "reaffirms" that Iraq is "liable ... for any direct loss, damage, including environmental damage and the depletion of natural resources, or injury to foreign governments, national and corporations, as a result of Iraq's unlawful invasion and occupation of Kuwait." The resolution goes on to create a reparations structure that clearly holds Iraq as a state responsible for the invasion of Kuwait. This led to Resolution 692, passed on 20 May 1991, which created the Compensation Fund and Commission to administer the fund, including mechanisms for Iraqi payments to the Fund and mechanisms for distribution of moneys from it to the various countries and corporations that could make claims.[252]

Based on Resolutions 687 and 692, on 31 May 1991 the Secretary-General submitted a report to the Security Council outlining the specific mechanisms of the Fund and the Commission.[253] The report establishes that Iraq will pay into the fund from monies generated by its oil sales, and not by use of "frozen assets" held in third countries. This point had been a matter of some debate after the war, with the United States seeking to use those assets to finance the fund, but they were overruled on this matter.[254] The United States also sought to have 50 per cent of the Iraqi finances from oil sales sent to the fund, but the Secretary-General opted for 30 per cent instead.[255] The administrative body established by the Security Council and Secretary-General published its report on the process by which the Fund would handle claims. The Secretary-General's report had noted that while the Council would not be a judicial organ, it would be performing a "quasi-judicial function" in the adjudication of claims.[256] The Council's report of 2 August 1991 created different categories of claimants and the procedures by which those claimants could be satisfied.[257]

A number of elements of the process by which claims could be made deserve special attention. First, only governments could bring claims before the Council. They were expected to consolidate the claims of all their nationals, corporations and any state claims into a single claim and present these to the Council. This decision, while logical from the perspective of time and bureaucracy, also reinforces the status of the state in international law and relations. Since states are the main agents, it is only states that can be harmed, a fact reinforced by the reparations and sanctions regime.

Second, paragraph 16 of the Council report states that "Compensation will not be provided for losses suffered as a result of the trade embargo." This means that, in effect, the actions of the Allied coalition were removed from possible consideration as having caused any destruction or harm during the prelude to the war. Paragraph 18 does point out that claims can be made on the basis of actions undertaken by "either side" in the war. Nevertheless, the Fund was financed mostly by Iraqi contributions, thus making it the responsible agent. Also, no claims could be made on the basis of harms resulting from the sanctions regime. This legal distinction between harm caused by military action and harm caused by economic sanctions creates a moral distinction that is hardly tenable. It does, however, reinforce the practice of economic sanctions as the better means by which to enforce international norms.

The third element of the Council report that demands attention is perhaps the most important in understanding how the construction of Iraq agency related to sanctions. Paragraph 17 of the Council report explicitly states, "Claims will not be considered on behalf of Iraqi nationals who do not have bona fide nationality of any other State."[258] The assumption here is that because Iraq as a whole is responsible for the conduct of the war, all parts of Iraq, including all of its citizens, are responsible; since they are responsible for the war they cannot claim compensation from the Fund. Although this may not have been the intention behind the creation of the Fund and its functions, it is a result of its operation. Moreover, the operation of the fund results from the discourse of state agency that I have been emphasizing all along. This automatically rules out the possibility that an Iraqi citizen could make a claim against the Allied coalition or against his own government. Iraqi citizens suffered as much as Kuwaiti, Egyptian or any other citizens. But, once again, because of the language and concepts of international law and international relations, states cannot be divided in the creation of a sanctions regime. Instead, sanctions are imposed on a whole community, none of whose members can distinguish themselves from the state.

Furthermore, the inability of Iraqis to claim compensation for the consequences of the sanctions regime effectively undermined their legal agency vis-à-vis the international community. The reparations regime, however, did provide some sort of quasi-legal status in the international legal realm to some individuals, i.e. Egyptians, Kuwaitis, Qataris, etc. By allowing them to make claims against Iraq (admittedly through a government), they attained a form of legal agency. Iraqis, however, were unable to demand that same status. Because their state became responsible, usually through no actions to which they can even be remotely connected, Iraqi citizens lost any sort of legal standing in the international community. Hence, they suffered because of the imposition of state responsibility not simply in a humanitarian sense, but in a political and legal one as well.

This brief review has focused on the initial set of resolutions, those arising in the immediate aftermath of the war. Sanctions, of course, continued through 2003, with various attempts to revise them and their punitive dimensions becoming a core concern of the United Nations bureaucracy in the 1990s. The "oil for food" resolutions, specifically 986 passed on 14 April 1995, sought to lessen the negative humanitarian consequences of the sanctions regime.[259] As these policy efforts continued, the sanctions regime generated a widespread moral debate about the consequences of this tool. Authors drew upon the just war tradition, utilitarian logics and other sources to assess critically the sanctions regime.[260] While these critiques of sanctions arise from different normative traditions, they are united in their emphasis on the issue of agency (although they do not name it as such); that is, they are all reflecting the fact that the sanctions harmed the civilian population rather than the regime. As the above analysis of the reparations regime demonstrates, however, the fact that the discourses of international affairs focus on states as the primary agents hindered the United Nations and other states from framing sanctions in such a way that they might not impose such harms. Many critiques of the sanctions avoided this idea by assuming that the United Nations, led by the United States, intended to harm Iraqi citizens in order to weaken the Arab world. I would argue, instead, that assumptions about agency created a sanctions regime that could only hold Iraq responsible.

This brief review of the Iraqi sanctions regime leaves much out.[261] The point I want to emphasize is how important agency is in understanding the punitive dimensions of economic sanctions. As I will argue in the concluding sections of this chapter, our assumptions about agency can be revised so that punishment can more clearly target those responsible. More importantly, by rethinking agency we can see the ways in which punishment not only imposes a harm, it also constructs responsible agents in particular ways.

Sanctions in the war on terror

One of the consequences of the debacle of Iraqi sanctions was the idea of "smart sanctions." These were intended to be tools that could more clearly target the responsible agents in states such as Iraq by imposing harms on the assets that a regime holds dear, ranging from bank accounts to travel privileges. Designing these sanctions regimes has become an important part of how the international community responds to violence and seeks to enforce international law in the current international order.

Perhaps because they were a response to the humanitarian disasters of the Iraqi sanctions regime, smart sanctions did not originate with state leaders or even civil servants in the United Nations. Instead, they arose in large part from the advocacy of scholars and activists who wanted to enforce international norms but avoid the sufferings that had become so much a part of the Iraq episode. Human Rights Watch played a key role in prompting the Clinton administration to reconsider its policies on Iraq. Research projects at the University of Notre Dame,[262] Brown University, the University of Uppsala, and the Brookings Institute[263] all generated new thinking in response to the Iraq war.[264] Scholars such as David Cortright, George Lopez and Meghan O'Sullivan developed alternative approaches to sanctions that sought to target the individuals guilty of committing violations rather than whole communities. The Swedish Ministry of Foreign Affairs, in cooperation with the University of Uppsala, played an important role in bringing together experts and NGOs to study the importance of sanctions.[265]

Although the Bush administration in 2001 seemed to be moving towards something like a smart sanctions approach to Iraq, the attacks of 11 September 2001 radically changed the agenda of the United States and, as a result, of the international community more broadly. Sanctions suddenly became a means for combating terrorism and punishing states that were hosting terrorist organizations. The move towards war with Iraq also moved attention more towards using sanctions for terrorism rather than countering Iraq.[266]

Using sanctions to combat terrorism resulted in part from the debates about Iraq, although targeted sanctions had already been used by the United Nations in some civil wars. Various sanctions regimes were employed in the 1990s, including sanctions on Somalia, Rwanda and Haiti. While these would seem to fall under the broader rubric of sanctions, the fact that they "targeted" certain individuals and companies within states differentiated them from the broader sanctions regimes imposed on Yugoslavia, Iraq and Libya. The first time targeted sanctions were used against a non-state entity was their employment against UNITA in the context of the conflict in Angola.[267]

The United Nations has largely embraced this approach to sanctions, with almost all of its sanctions regimes being targeted on specific individuals or groups within a country. The procedure for sanctions within the United Nations is to create a committee that monitors the sanctions regime, all of which have websites devoted to their activities. These websites are an invaluable source of data on targeted sanctions, providing useful insights into the ways in which the different regimes operate.

Rather than explore the general topic of targeted sanctions, in this section I will focus on one particular sanctions regime, those resulting from UN Security Council Resolution 1267 concerning al-Qaeda and the Taliban. This resolution, passed on 15 October 1999, predates the 9/11 attacks, but became a central component of the international community's response to the attacks. It has also been reinforced by a number of further resolutions and has resulted in the creation of not only a sanctions committee, the normal UN procedure, but a monitoring group that has sought to ensure that the sanctions both contribute to peace and security and yet also do not violate the rights of those who are its target.

The initial sanctions were quite limited, preventing air travel in and out of Afghanistan (except for humanitarian reasons, such as the *haj*) and the freezing of financial assets of the Taliban. The resolution explicitly uses the term "Taliban" rather than the regime of Afghanistan in order to target the sanctions specifically on them rather than the population as a whole. Of course, as the ruling regime, the sanctions imposed on the Taliban would inevitably impact the entire country. The primary demand of Resolution 1267 was that the Taliban stop supporting terrorism and hand over Osama bin Laden to a country where he has been indicted. The sanctions appear to have arisen as a result of the attacks on US embassies in Africa, although the resolution also notes the killing of Iranian diplomats, suggesting it had a wide acceptance in the international community.

Further resolutions both reinforced the sanctions and created a large-scale administrative structure to ensure that the sanctions were both effective and truly targeted. Resolution 1333, adopted on 18 December 2000, included a ban on military sales to Afghanistan and downgrading diplomatic relations with the Taliban. It also included sanctions specifically targeted on Osama bin Laden and al-Qaeda as an organization. Resolution 1390, passed on 16 January 2002, imposed a complete travel ban on al-Qaeda members and further reinforced previous measures. This resolution also moved the sanctions out of the territory of Afghanistan by lifting the ban on travel in and out of the country and also making the travel ban on al-Qaeda individuals and entities applicable to anywhere in the world. Resolution 1455, adopted on 17 January 2003, sought to clarify the process by which individuals are "listed" or put on a list that indicates that their movement and financial assets will be targeted. The Monitoring Team was created by Resolution 1526 on 30 January 2004 to produce independent reports on the performance of the sanctions procedures. Resolution 1617, adopted on 29 July 2005, sought to clarify what it means to be "associated" with al-Qaeda and clarified the role by which states put names on what had now become the "Consolidated List" or the list of those individuals subject to the various sanctions. The Council passed Resolution 1730 on 19 December 2006 to clarify how individuals and entities could be "de-listed" or removed from being sanctioned, followed soon thereafter by Resolution 1735 that sought to clarify further the process of listing and de-listing, along with specifying various exemptions from the sanctions.

The Committee's initial work, prior to the passage of Resolution 1390, focused primarily on determining which flights could move in and out of Afghanistan.[268] It first introduced a list of individuals to whom sanctions would apply on 25 January 2001.[269] This list became the central focus of the Committee's work. At the time of writing the list includes about 500 entries and is divided up by the Committee into four types of agents: individuals and entities associated with the Taliban and individuals and entities associated with al-Qaeda.[270]

These resolutions created an administrative bureaucracy designed to sanction those individuals who are associated in any way with al-Qaeda and the Taliban. Other sanctions regimes exist for other purposes that include similar targeted sanctions. But the 1267 structure has become one of the central tools of the United Nations in its response to terrorism.[271] As noted above, it is important to emphasize that this regime was created prior to 9/11, although it became much more central to the UN's efforts to respond to terrorism after that date. Moreover, such a regime could not have arisen from the Security Council without the impetus of the United States.

The creation of targeted and smart sanctions is clearly an improvement on the Iraqi sanctions model. By focusing directly on those who have committed norms violations, sanctions regimes such as the one created by Resolution 1267 have played a key role in rectifying the humanitarian dilemmas of the previous sanctions episodes. The role of scholars, universities and government–NGO collaboration to refine these instruments demonstrates real commitment and idealism in pursuit of making the international system both more peaceful and more just.

At the same time, these sanctions regimes remain punitive. The evidence for their punitive nature does not arise from the intentions of those implementing the sanctions, a point I have made in my description of a punitive practice in Chapter 1. Indeed, the UN Sanctions Committee has stated explicitly that "A criminal charge or conviction is not necessary for inclusion on the Consolidated List as the sanctions are intended to be preventive in nature."[272] Summarizing the work of the 1267 Monitoring Team, a report from the Watson Institute states that the sanctions are designed to prevent acts of terrorism rather than punish; "the fact that there may be a criminal law connotation does not mean that the sanctions should be characterized as criminal sanctions."[273] UN Secretary General Ban Ki-Moon at a recent workshop on targeted sanctions emphasized that sanctions work best when used as a means of persuasion and not punishment.[274] The process of de-listing also suggests a non-punitive intent to the sanctions strategy. Because individuals are not put on the list for a specific period of time and then "released" – a method that might be employed if the sanctions were to be seen as a form of punishment – but instead can be taken off the list if they change their behaviour, they seem to correspond to the bargaining model advocated by Cortright, Lopez and others.

At the same time, three other elements of the sanctions regime point to a more punitive dimension. First, the Security Council Resolutions that created the sanctions regime read as if they are imposing a punishment for the violation of a norm. For instance, Resolution 1390, from 16 January 2002, notes the indictment of Osama bin Laden and his associates and condemns them for "the multiple criminal, terrorist acts" that they have committed. Moreover, the operative clause that specifies the funds to be frozen (paragraph 2(a)) does not specify funds to be used only for terrorist activities, but all funds. In other words, the harm to be imposed is not simply preventive but retributive; an action intended to inflict harm on those who have violated norms.

Second, the fact that individuals are placed on a list after being identified as a terrorist or associated with terrorists implies that they have violated a norm and are being harmed in response to this – the definition of punishment in Chapter 1. The purpose of putting them on the list may well prevent their engaging in future acts of terrorism, but incarceration does the same thing. Another purpose might be to deter others from engaging in such actions, but this would also be part of a punitive strategy. While the committee insists that being placed on the list does not require a criminal conviction, those identified become, in effect, international criminals. As one author notes, "Certainly, being put on the list (either travel sanctions or financial sanctions) now involves a social stigma, which can be particularly damaging for businesspersons who live on their reputation/cash flow."[275]

Ironically, attempts to protect individuals on the list from violations of their human rights reveal this punitive dimension of the process. It soon became clear that being put on the list violated an individual's human rights.[276] Two ways of responding to those human rights issues have been the question of judicial review and the question of due process. In terms of judicial review, the Watson Institute project has provided a useful summary of the different options that range from a panel of experts to review each decision to an arbitration hearing on disputed cases to a full-fledged judicial review process.[277] These proposals suggest that the consequences of listing and de-listing have a criminal and punitive dimension to them, for why else would there be a need for such protections? Judicial review of decisions impacting individuals generally implies that the practice has a punitive element to it. In terms of due process, the Office of Legal Council in the United Nations itself commissioned a report on this subject.[278] Due process is something only needed in situations where individuals are to be punished by the state through some sort of legal procedure; in other words, by commissioning such a report, the UN bureaucracy tacitly admits that its sanctioning procedures are punitive.

Third, and perhaps most importantly, the process by which states place individuals on the list reveals a punitive dimension to the regime. UN sanctions cannot come into effect without national country legislation that enables those resolutions. The 1267 Committee website includes a list of reports by countries on their activities to enable the resolutions. In looking through three different countries' actions – the United States, United Kingdom and Egypt – the punitive dimensions of the sanctions list become more obvious.

In the case of the United States, the enabling legislation is Executive Order 13224 issued on 23 September 2001. This order blocks the financial resources of any individual who has committed terrorist activities or is associated with those entities that promote terrorism. The order explicitly mentions Resolution 1267. Moreover, in announcing the Order, President George W. Bush made the following statement about the creation of the US list of Specially Designated Global Terrorists: "We have developed the international financial equivalent of law enforcement's 'Most Wanted List'." While such statements could be attributed to Bush's personality, at the same press conference, Secretary of the Treasury Paul O'Neil stated "we will punish you for providing the resources that make these evil acts possible."[279]

The American proclivity to punish, addressed in previous chapters, might explain these punitive dimensions of their enabling legislation. Yet, similar punitive elements appear in other countries' legislation and statements. The United Kingdom's statement to the UN 1267 Committee states that its ability to list individuals and entities comes from The Terrorism 2000 Act which

> contains provisions to proscribe, or ban, organisations connected with terrorism. Proscription means than an organisation is outlawed in the UK and that it is illegal for it to operate here. The Terrorism 2000 Act makes it a criminal offence to belong to, support, or display support for a proscribed organisation.[280]

In other words, being put on the list by the United Kingdom results from being branded a criminal, i.e. it is a punitive measure.

Egypt, the last country considered here, states quite clearly that its implementing legislation is punitive in nature. In its report to the UN 1267 Committee, the Egyptian government states the following:

> The Egyptian legislature introduced Act No. 97 of 1992, known as the Terrorism Act, which is incorporated within section II, articles 86–102 of the Penal Code. Under these articles, all forms of terrorism and the financing thereof are criminalized, as are all forms of assisting, instigating and acquiescing in the perpetration or attempted perpetration of such acts. In that regard, it is worthy of note, under Article 30 of the Penal Code, a court which hands down a punishment for felony or misdemeanour is permitted to order the confiscation of items derived from or used in the crime. Article 98 of the same code also requires the confiscation of assets which prove to be earmarked for expenditure on terrorist organisations and groups.[281]

Clearly, for the Egyptian government, listing individuals and freezing their assets is directly connected to a criminal violation, the commission of acts of terrorism or support of those who commit such acts.

These three countries' implementation procedures suggest that as much as the UN Committee seeks to make the Consolidated List non-punitive, it will inevitably have punitive dimensions to it. This is not to say that efforts to make the sanctions more in accordance with the bargaining model advocated by Cortight, Lopez and others will not be possible; as noted above, the de-listing procedure clearly makes such activities less punitive and more strategic. But, the result of being put on the list and the procedure by which states name individuals for the List has clear punitive elements to it.

The targeted sanctions regime in trying to correct the problems of agency that arose in the Iraqi sanctions regime has certainly provided some relief from the humanitarian dilemmas identified above. But, in so doing, it has made sanctions even more punitive than when they were targeted at entire states. This is particularly true in the case of the counter-terrorism sanctions as found in the 1267 sanctions regime. The punitive nature of these sanctions, however, has not been accompanied by the proper legal structures necessary to make the process more just. Proposals to make the regime less punitive have really been designed to avoid harming innocent civilians; the regime itself remains punitive by labelling individuals as terrorists or in association with terrorism, a stigma which is unlikely to be removed by simply being taken off a list. In the final section, I suggest that these targeted sanctions are perhaps one of the best ways to enforce international law *precisely because they are punitive*. They still require modifications along the lines of the Watson Institute's report, but their punitive nature is not necessarily something to be avoided, but is perhaps a necessary element of their function.

Evaluating punitive sanctions: justice

As with the previous chapter, the conclusion of this chapter is an attempt to evaluate this punitive practice. The four sanctions episodes explored here reveal a wide range of issues to consider in evaluating this practice. First, do punitive sanctions create a more just international order? Recall that in Chapter 1, I argued that a just punitive regime would be one that is both deterrent and retributive, following the argument made by Rawls. Moreover, accomplishing this objective requires a separation of powers between a legislative and judicial agency so that the deterrent function of the legislature is not confused with the retributive function of the judiciary.

Rather than justice being a victim of a failure to implement both a retributive and deterrent function at the same time, the cases display a more fundamental problem – a failure to clarify which norms justified the harm being imposed. In both the Italian and Rhodesian sanctions episode, the primary problem with the sanctions was competing normative visions animating the sanctions regime. In both cases, sanctions regimes were imposed by institutions in which great powers sought to use those sanctions regimes for their own purposes. In the Italian sanctions case, the norm was supposedly clear – the Italian regime had undertaken an act of aggression against Ethiopia and sanctions were imposed in response. But, the British and French saw the need to protect norm violations from a different source – Germany – as being more important. As a result, these great powers effectively undermined the justness of the sanctions regime.

A related problem plagued the Rhodesian sanctions episode. Here, it was unclear which norm had been violated that would justify sanctions. For the British and other colonial powers such as the French, the Rhodesian regime had acted "unconstitutionally," or outside the boundaries of acceptable behaviour in a centre–periphery relationship. For African states, the norm the Rhodesians were violating was the equality of citizens. The vacillation between these two normative concerns severely undermined the sanctions regime.

A lack of clear norms seems less of a problem in the second two cases. Almost every state agreed that Iraq had committed an act of aggression in invading Kuwait. Some problems arose, however, from the fact that the norm of responding to aggression was interpreted as a cover for the fact that the United States was simply protecting its interests, particularly access to oil. This is perhaps more a case of clarifying intentions and motives rather than the underlying justness of the cause. At the same time, it does raise questions about whether or not a normative ideal can be enforced by individual agents who may have their own self-interests for enforcing those norms, especially when force is used.

In the case of the counter-terrorism sanctions, again the norm seems less contested. Almost everyone sees terrorism as a violation of core norms in the international system. I return to this point in the next chapter, however, for there are problems arising from the failure to define terrorism clearly, problems that might be informing some of the tensions arising from other counter-terrorism policies.

In sum, then, the use of economic sanctions in the international order reveals a tension in which norms are being protected. Perhaps because much of the sanctions literature is focused on refining the tool itself rather than clarifying the norms it is being used to enforce, there has been a lack of attention to this issue. But, as these cases demonstrate, if those normative goals are not clarified, the tool itself will not work, as displayed most clearly in the cases of the League and early United Nations sanctions episodes.

Evaluating punitive sanctions: authority

The problem of authority has plagued the practice of economic sanctions throughout the twentieth and twenty-first centuries. As argued in Chapter 2, we normally associate just punishment with a legitimate authority. But many assume that a legitimate authority needs to be a single Hobbesian sovereign that can clearly define the norms being violated and impose punishments to deter others from violating those norms. As I argued, however, a better model for the international system may be a combination of Locke and Grotius, both of whom argued that in a state of nature, individuals can punish each other if they are careful to avoid vengeance. While Grotius relied on Christian charity to discipline those urges, Locke pointed to the importance of a constitutional structure in which the judiciary has a central role. The idea of collective security as found in the work of Hans Kelsen embodies this idea.

In both the Italian and Rhodesian sanctions episodes, the fact that a single body – the League Council in the first and the UN Security Council in the second – combined the judicial and legislative functions undermined separation of powers element that I identified in Chapter 2 as being important for a just authority structure to function. In the case of Iraq, the justice of the punishment imposed by the Security Council again violated the provision of having the judiciary and legislative contexts kept separate. This became even more important because of the power of the United States in turning the Security Council towards its own interests. Because there was no judicial structure in place to interpret the actions of the Council, the United States was able to claim that its actions were enforcing the will of the international community. Its position in the early post-Cold War system of being the most powerful state left standing eliminated the balance of power that had kept a check on excessive normative impulses. So, while the justice of punishing Iraq may be clear in one sense, its actual practice became yoked to the interests of the United States creating a situation in which its policies were left unquestioned for too long.

The last case of targeted sanctions still suffers from the lack of a distinction between the legislative and judicial functions. But the advocacy of various groups and the discussions in the United Nations and elsewhere about judicial review and due process suggest that this may be changing. Ironically, the increased punitive nature of the targeted sanctions regime has moved the international community towards the consideration of more constitutional measures. So, in terms of authority, while targeted sanctions still violate the provisions set out in this book, they at least move us closer to a structure that is more constitutional and thus more just.

In all three cases, then, the authority seemed at first glance to be a just one. But, as the imposition of sanctions was undertaken by a single agent without any grounds for judicial review, a situation most clearly revealed in the sanctions imposed in response to terrorism, the authority structures can be called into question. Especially when sanctions regimes progress for a long period of time, it is important to ensure that the agents executing the sanctions are not necessarily the same ones making judgements about them.

Evaluating punitive sanctions: agency

Finally, how should we view punitive sanctions in terms of agency? The first two episodes tell us less about questions of agency, for they simply assume that states can be treated as singular agents that can be held responsible for the violations of norms. This is ironic in the first episode, for one could argue that it was precisely the assumptions of German guilt and attributions of responsibility to that state as a whole that were seen as the cause of the First World War. Perhaps because the League grew out of the post-war world in which this problem was not yet firmly identified, it remained hidden from view.

The sanctions on Iraq, however, revealed the dangers of assuming that states are singular agents that can be held responsible for specific outcomes. More accurately, the practice of imposing sanctions on Iraq helped to construct it as a violator of norms. Targeted sanctions, however, are an attempt to identify more correctly the proper agent to be punished. Thus, they seem closer to corresponding to a just form of punishment in terms of targeting the right agent than any of the others.

But, in recalling the arguments I made about political agency being central to punishment at the global level, it is worth hesitating here. I argued that the only type of crime at the global level that deserves international punishment – as opposed to normal domestic forms of punishment – is the type of violation that radically alters the international system. Major acts of international terrorism seem to fit into such a framework. Yet, the way in which the 1267 list is being used to include a wide range of "terrorists," including at times individuals engaged in political activities that are perfectly legal, suggests that the "crimes" for which individuals are being put on the list are becoming too expansive. This might also be the result of not wanting to call the targeted sanctions list a punitive measure – if it is not understood as punitive, then there is no need to specify clearly the crimes for which individuals should be put on the list.

These cases reveal, then, not only that sanctions raise questions about the proper agent to be punished, they also reveal how punitive actions construct agents of a particular type. In other words, in an international order in which agents are not clearly differentiated, punitive practices give certain agents more responsibilities than others. In so doing, however, it is important to recognize that punishment is a powerful practice, one that can actually create the world rather than simply enforce rules in the world. I return to this dilemma in the conclusion, offering some ideas for how we might reconceptualize punitive practices in light of the fact that punishment plays a key role in constructing our world.

Conclusion

One of the themes of this book is that punishment is necessary for political systems to function effectively, but that the current means of punishment in the international order are creating an unjust world. Ironically, one of the ways to make punitive sanctions more just is to clarify what has been called a strategic action as a punitive one. I make a similar argument in the next chapter, critiquing the claim that counter-terrorism policy should only be understood in terms of self-defence, but should be conceptualized as a punitive practice. This would require more clarity on what constitutes a crime that deserves punishment, an ongoing problem in the case of terrorism.

This proposal for admitting the punitive nature of sanctions needs to be balanced by the point explored above that sanctions not only force agents to obey rules, they actually create the agents themselves. This process of constructing agents needs to be kept in mind, especially as counter-terrorism efforts target both groups and individuals. It should not halt public policies from being implemented to target terrorists, only kept in mind as an issue that must constantly be recognized.

In light of these issues, my concluding thought is that in order for targeted sanctions to function effectively in the international order as a tool for combating international terrorism, they need to be clearly understood as punishments. Once this admission is made, individuals can be more clearly accused of a crime and protected by the kinds of legal provisions normally used to protect the rights of the accused. In other words, while the efforts of scholars and activists who have fought to create the targeted sanctions structure have been an important part of making sanctions more just, they can become even more just if they are understood to be punitive.

6 Punitive counter-terrorism policy

This chapter continues the exploration of punitive practices in the current international order by exploring counter-terrorism, or what has been called by the United States, the "war on terror."[282] Terrorism has long been a problem in the international system, and efforts to combat it have ranged from military actions to criminal justice procedures. This chapter addresses global terrorism, or terrorism undertaken by organizations or individuals not targeted at a single domestic context, but targeted at key players or institutions in the larger international order. This chapter will not seek to explain differences between old and new forms of terrorism, or even define terrorism itself, a project that has generated a vast amount of literature.[283]

Continuing with the variety of methods employed thus far in this book, this chapter will focus on counter-terrorism campaigns undertaken by a single state, the United States, while drawing to some extent on counter-terrorism actions of the United Kingdom and some policies emanating from the United Nations. Specifically, the chapter explores three particular types of counter-terrorism policy: military actions, detention and interrogation policies. These three policies, none of which are labelled as punitive by those undertaking them, each has punitive dimensions to it. In the first, the military action against Afghanistan was distinctly punitive, with strong similarities to the descriptions of punitive intervention from Chapter 4. In the second case, the practice of detaining suspects is framed as a simple means of preventing further terrorist activity, rather than imprisonment. But, as will be made clear in my analysis, the means by which individuals have challenged their detention has made the punitive nature of such practices more clear. Finally, the interrogation of suspects while in detention is also framed as a national security practice – something designed to extract information that can protect individuals in the future. But, as interrogation slides into torture, the practice appears more punitive.

As with the other chapters, this one begins by defining counter-terrorism and examining its punitive dimensions. To do this, I examine the terrorism studies literature, along with international legal writings. The next part of the chapter details these three practices, beginning with a brief historical overview of how counter-terrorism fits into broader US foreign policy goals. In these sections, I demonstrate the change in counter-terrorism to a more punitive approach and also suggest that the pervasiveness of these practices is contributing to the constitution of a particular type of international order. Finally, I conclude the chapter by evaluating counter-terrorism in terms of the three concepts of justice, authority and agency.

Defining punitive counter-terrorism

Counter-terrorism is the use of governmental policy to address the problem of terrorism, including (but not limited to) military action, covert action, administrative detention and financial sanctions. Such policies can be undertaken prior to an attack or in response to an attack. It differs from antiterrorism policy which tends to focus on defensive measures such as criminal investigations designed to uncover attacks, surveillance of borders and populations, and ensuring the readiness of "first responders."[284]

Not all forms of counter-terrorism are punitive, however. For a counter-terrorism policy to be punitive, it must have two elements. First, the policy must be framed as a response to a specific norm violation, i.e. it must be targeted at the agent (individual, group or state) that is purportedly responsible. Second, the policy must include a harm (broadly defined) inflicted upon the terrorist agent. Harm can range from military strikes against a state to targeted killing of individuals to prison time to torture. To recall arguments from previous chapters, it is important to emphasize what a counter-terrorist policy does *not* need to include to be defined as such: a specific intention to punish or a single sovereign authority. While such elements may also be present, it is important to emphasize that punitive counter-terrorism, like the other punitive practices defined in this book, does not require intentionality or authority as defining features.

Counter-terrorism methods fall into two general categories: the war model and the criminal justice model.[285] The war model treats terrorism as a threat to national security, and, as a result, terrorists are treated as enemies that need to be defeated. This leads to military actions in direct response to terrorism, ranging from missile strikes to full-scale war. It also includes the use of the military to capture and interrogate individual suspects, without regard for eventual prosecution. Instead, their capture is better defined as detention, with the primary goal to remove them from the "battlefield" and, usually in addition to this, to interrogate them for more information. An Israeli Supreme Court judge described detention as "intended to prevent and thwart a security danger from arising from actions which the prisoner is liable to carry out and which there is no reasonable possibility of preventing by regular legal means."[286]

The criminal justice model treats terrorism as a crime that needs to be addressed through legal structures and institutions. Any actions against terrorists will only be undertaken in response to an attack and will be designed to prosecute individuals in a court of law. It can criminalize the behaviour of groups, although prosecuting a group is more difficult than prosecuting an individual. The conflict between these two models has been a defining feature of public debate about counter-terrorism policy in the United States since the attacks of 9/11. Critics of the Bush administration argue that while a war might be a useful metaphor, it has resulted in faulty methods that only increase the potential for terrorist actions.[287]

The distinction between these two models of counter-terrorism raises important theoretical questions related to the issue of punishment. War can be understood in different ways, and the American discourse concerning the response to the attacks of 9/11 drew upon different meanings at different moments. According to the Clausewitzian ideal of a war, sides in a war do not punish, they pursue political ends.[288] Carl Schmitt's conception of friend/enemy as the defining feature of politics also supports this model of war as one in which no side is more just than the other, but in which the two sides are enemies that simply seek to destroy each other.[289] President Bush's statement to Congress on 20 September 2001 captured this model of war:

> Our response involves far more than instant retaliation and isolated strikes. Americans should not expect one battle, but a lengthy campaign, unlike any other we have ever seen. It may include dramatic strikes, visible on TV, and covert operations, secret even in success. We will starve terrorists of funding, turn them one against another, drive them from place to place, until there is no refuge or no rest. And we will pursue nations that provide aid or safe haven to terrorism. Every nation, in every region, now has a decision to make. Either you are with us, or you are with the terrorists. [Applause.] From this day forward, any nation that continues to harbor or support terrorism will be regarded by the United States as a hostile regime.[290]

War can also be understood in legalistic terms, as a contest that is governed by legal rules at both the *ad bellum* and *in bello* stages. This legalistic conception of war as it relates to counter-terrorism includes important protections of those captured, protections not provided to criminals but to combatants. Counter-terrorism according to this version of the war model should include the treatment of terrorists or suspected terrorists according to the laws of armed conflict. But even those who invoke the war model in this legalistic guise do not accept that terrorists deserve the protection of combatants or prisoners of war. Writing before the 9/11 attacks, US Air Force JAG (i.e. military lawyer) Richard J. Erickson argued that even if one adopts the war model for counter-terrorism policy, it does not mean that terrorists deserve the respect of being combatants. Erickson argues that

> the law of armed conflict would treat [terrorists] as criminals, would recognize them as engaging unlawfully in combatant activity, would consider them as unlawful combatants, and would deny them legitimacy by identifying them as perpetrators of acts contrary to the fundamental international humanitarian law that serves as a basis of the law of armed conflict.[291]

Erickson's analysis, while certainly in accordance with some interpretations of the laws of armed conflict, also moves the war model to a more punitive one. By identifying terrorists as individuals who have violated central norms of the international system, specifically the norm of noncombatant immunity, the legalistic war model moves from its Clausewitzian and Schmittian clarity of enemies engaging each other to a model in which one side is punishing the other. This idea may not sit easily in the current laws of armed conflict, but it has a rich heritage in the just war tradition, a tradition that has been the primary source for international law.[292] From Augustine through the medieval scholastics, just war included punishment as one of the just causes of war. Grotius, whose work is explored in Chapter 2, drew extensively upon these thinkers to develop his view that war can be justified as a form of punishment.

Punishment, then, can be part of the war model of counter-terrorism. The criminal justice model includes punishment more directly, although it is strangely absent from most analyses of this model.[293] Instead, advocates of the criminal justice model of counter-terrorism focus more on the legal protections of a domestic criminal law process. As one study emphasizes, the criminal justice model "prioritizes the preservation of democratic principles as being the fundamental premise in the fight against terrorism, even at the expense of reduced effectiveness."[294] International legal analyses of counter-terrorism tend to emphasize these elements of the criminal justice model.[295]

One leading theorist of terrorism studies adopts a version of the criminal justice model, arguing it fits best the traditions of a liberal and democratic state structure. In his *Terrorism and the Liberal State*, Paul Wilkinson introduced the idea of the "hard-line approach," which he summarized in his later work as

> A multi-pronged approach enabling a liberal democratic state to combat terrorism effectively without undermining or seriously damaging the democratic process and the rule of law, while providing sufficient flexibility to cope with the whole range of threats, from low-level spasmodic attacks to intensive bombing campaigns verging on a state of civil war.[296]

Wilkinson argues that combating terrorism need not undermine the liberal constitutional order, drawing upon the dilemmas created by counter-terrorism policies in the British response to the conflict in Northern Ireland. It is hard-line, though, in that the government of a liberal state needs to avoid "underreaction" – the danger of not supporting the full constitutional authority of the state to use all means necessary to combat terrorism. The policies that Wilkinson finds most useful, however, are those of crime and punishment, stressing that "war is a far greater evil [than terrorism] involving infinitely greater numbers of deaths and far greater destruction, with the attendant dangers of other states being drawn into the conflict."[297]

Wilkinson's approach points to some of the difficulties of punishing terrorists at the global level. While he argues that terrorism is inherently international, he also notes that the problem of a liberal response suffers from the lack of a global authority.[298] The dilemma that Wilkinson reveals here is one of direct relevance to understanding how counter-terrorism policy can be punitive. Without a sovereign authority to define an action as punitive, such actions appear to be nothing more than attempts to secure nation-states in a world of anarchy. This is precisely why analysts do not define counter-terrorism policy oriented towards international actors as punitive.

International lawyers who have explored terrorism have generally concluded that criminal justice can only be pursued in domestic contexts. One pre-9/11 legal analysis focused almost exclusively on questions of rendition, either extradition or deportation, as the only real international treaty-based response to terrorism.[299] Because terrorism is a political crime, one that either targets or is supported by states, there is a need to find some authority over and above the state level to respond to this inherently international crime. One scholar notes, "It is easy to understand the impulse to seek an authority above the State for the handling of terrorist offences when the alternative would be to rely on law enforcement on the very state that sponsored the terrorist act."[300] An opposite, albeit related problem, is that a terrorist suspect would find it difficult to receive a fair trial in a state against which he or she had committed a major attack.[301]

A different problem with the criminal justice model arises from the group nature of terrorism. Robert Pape has recently argued that suicide terrorism should be understood as a group phenomenon rather than an individual one.[302] If Pape is correct, then the individual-level approach to counter-terrorism found in the criminal justice model will not work. As the history of British attempts to deal with the IRA suggest, this has been a long-standing problem of the criminal justice model. For instance, the UK Terrorism Act of 2000 included a crime of "directing a terrorist organization" as a way to address this group nature of terrorism. As one commentator on the legislation notes, this provision would mean that even if a leader of a terrorist organization ordered his subordinates to lessen their terrorist activities, he would still be guilty under the act.[303] In other words, trying to use legal structures designed to prosecute individuals to stop group activities may lead to more problems than solutions.

An opposite problem arises when terrorism is understood as an individual-level phenomenon, as it is by those who take a psychological approach. Recent research has explored the issue of why individuals might join, participate in and eventually leave a terrorist organization. This approach suggests that punitive responses to terrorism will not actually do much, for they ignore the conditions that lead individuals to join or leave terrorist organizations. One analyst notes that individuals leave terrorist organizations primarily because of how the group dynamics of the organization play a role in their perceptions of their goals and ideals.[304] If this is the case, counter-terrorism campaigns need to be restructured to focus on how best to encourage individuals to leave such groups rather than punishing them for being part of them. Although theorists of this approach do not necessarily eschew punishment, the logic of their analyses would suggest that punitive measures will only exacerbate the proclivity to terrorism by reinforcing the group dynamics that draw individuals in and construct strong us/them attitudes among those in the group. A related approach to counter-terrorism that draws upon economic logic rather than psychological analyses results in a similar conclusion. A utility model would lead one to the conclusion that carrots rather than sticks would change terrorist behaviour.[305]

Some scholars have addressed the problem of agency (for this, indeed, is what the conflict between the group and individual level is) by exploring the potential for group punishment. Drawing primarily on the Israeli experience, Boaz Ganor reviews tactics such as home demolition and closure and curfew as models of corporate punishment. These tools may not result from a formal judicial hearing of individuals or groups, but according to Ganor, the administrative procedures put in place by Israel correspond to a criminal justice model.[306]

Finding within the counter-terrorism and international legal studies of terrorism the punitive dimensions of those policies thus reveals a number of normative and political tensions in these practices. These tensions in terms of authority and agency create the dilemma of unjust punitive counter-terrorism. Put simply, a just punitive response to terrorism should be both deterrent and retributive, helping to construct a world in which individuals are safe from the fear that terrorism generates, but also one in which individuals found guilty of terrorism are punished in accordance with clear sentencing guidelines.

In light of this review, I define punitive counter-terrorism policy as the infliction of harm on an individual, group or state through military or criminal justice procedures as a response to a specific act of terrorism. This means that surveillance techniques would not count as such a tool, nor would broader techniques used to prevent undefined actions in the future.

While the counter-terrorism policies I identify below have elements of punishment, they also are resulting in unjust and violent outcomes that are not, in fact, constructing a world in which agents both feel safe and are convinced not to engage in terrorism.

This is not to say that preventive acts of counter-terrorism may not halt specific terrorist actions. Punishment, however, should be designed not only to prevent specific crimes but create a more just and peaceful order to ensure compliance with rules more broadly. The problems are not simply with the implementation of US policies, but with broader dimensions of counter-terrorism policy. As this brief review of the terrorist studies literature suggests, the various counter-terrorism policies in place today fall into two black holes: between the domestic and international and between the individual and the group. These empty spaces are being filled with a diverse range of policies, most of which violate the norms that would sustain a just response to terrorism. Before suggesting some possible alternative ways to think about punitive counter-terrorism, let me now turn to the specific policies of the United States government in response to terrorism, demonstrating how efforts to place counter-terrorism policy in a non-punitive and purely strategic context fail to appreciate how the practice of counter-terrorism has become increasingly punitive.

Punitive counter-terrorism as a constitutive practice

Counter-terrorism appeared as a central part of American foreign policy in the Reagan Administration. In response to attacks on US forces in Lebanon, along with attacks on US forces in Europe, the administration undertook a military strike against Libya in 1986. This missile attack, along with various policies initiated by Secretary of State George Schultz, placed counter-terrorism policy in the centre of US national security doctrine.[307]

Although he chaired a commission on terrorism as vice president, President George H. W. Bush did not place counter-terrorism policy in as central a position as Reagan had. When he came to office in 1993, Bill Clinton was soon forced to deal with terrorism, as a result of the first attack on the World Trade Center in February 1993. In response to this attack, the administration made counter-terrorism a central focus of its foreign policy agenda. It adopted the criminal justice model, resulting perhaps from the fact that the planners of the 1993 bombing were arrested only one month after the attacks through the investigative work of the US Treasury's Bureau of Alcohol, Tobacco, and Firearms and the Federal Bureau of Investigation (FBI). From 1993 to 1999, the number of FBI officials devoted to counter-terrorism efforts rose from 550 to 1400 and the percentage of the FBI's budget devoted to counter-terrorism efforts rose from 4 per cent to 10 per cent over roughly the same period.[308]

Alongside the criminal justice model, a parallel war model also came to prominence. Clinton signed Presidential Decision Directive 39 in June

1995 which made terrorism "a national security concern as well as a matter for law enforcement."[309] The creation of the administrative structures was designed to ensure effective coordination at the highest levels of government. On 7 August 1998, American embassies in Kenya and Tanzania were bombed, resulting in a more militaristic counter-terrorism policy. On 20 August 1998, cruise missile strikes were launched at a pharmaceutical plant in Sudan and al-Qaeda training camps in Afghanistan. While justified as attempts to take out dangers, i.e. national security actions, these strikes had a strong retributive dimension.

These open military strikes were soon followed by the circulation of a plan within the Administration called Political-Military Plan Delenda. As the 9/11 Commission Staff Report reminds its readers, Delenda is from the famous Roman phrase, *Carthago delenda est* – Carthage must be destroyed.[310] This phrase was invoked by Cato the Elder in the Senate in the lead up to the Punic War in which the Romans completely destroyed Carthage, sowing salt in the ground to ensure it would never grow crops again. In other words, the invocation of a Plan Delenda reflected the view of the Administration that al-Qaeda should be destroyed; i.e. the plan was designed not simply to protect the United States but to punish al-Qaeda for the harms they had committed.

The Bush administration came to office retaining some of the individuals who had been key players in the Clinton Administration. Richard Clarke, the lead counter-terrorist analyst in the National Security Council, sought to continue the emphasis on counter-terrorism that had characterized the later stages of the Clinton Administration. As he details, however, the Bush administration failed to focus directly on the concerns that had animated the Clinton administration.[311] Largely as a result of the more realist nature of some of the key players in the administration, along with the need to deal with an Air Force plane being held hostage by China, the administration focused more on traditional great power politics such as the emergence of China and relations with Russia.

The attacks of 9/11 quite dramatically changed the Bush administration's focus. As Bob Woodward describes it, Bush and those surrounding him were at first in a state of shock concerning the attacks.[312] They soon found a focus, however, one that drew upon the war model of counter-terrorism quite directly. In the remainder of this section, I will examine that response in three specific contexts: the war on Afghanistan and the missile attack in Yemen against suspected terrorists; the creation and use of detention facilities in Guantanamo Bay, Cuba; and the slide from interrogation practices to the torture of suspected individuals. These three practices demonstrate how what the administration frames as an attempt to win a war and protect the American people includes strong punitive elements that fail to conform to any just notion of punishment.

The war model as real war[313]

The first responses to the attacks of 9/11 were military ones. After quickly determining that al-Qaeda was the responsible agent for the attacks,[314] American forces were sent to Afghanistan to dislodge the ruling Taliban and search for Osama bin Laden and the larger al-Qaeda infrastructure.[315] American actions in Afghanistan, while certainly an attempt to eliminate al-Qaeda, and thus a form of self-defence, took on a punitive character as the desire to avenge the attacks filtered through not only popular culture but the military as well (as evidenced by US soldiers there carrying American flags that were found at "ground zero" in New York City). The war against Afghanistan sought to punish not only al-Qaeda but also the Taliban, a regime that did not itself threaten the United States in any way. The only reason for using such force against it is to punish it for assisting terrorists.

Careful attempts were made to distinguish military actions that targeted civilians and those that targeted the regime. But, especially when war is justified as a form of punishment, and particularly when aerial warfare is used, such distinctions become blurred. As I have argued elsewhere, the very origins of coercive diplomacy, or the use of aerial power to change the policies of states, has a strongly punitive dimension. Early air power theorists argued that such uses of military force would, of necessity, need to hit civilians to punish them for supporting their leaders and thus change those leaders' policies.[316] Barry Buzan draws upon these assumptions about air power in his reflections on the air campaign in Afghanistan. While not using the term punishment, Buzan suggests that modern assumptions about civilians and warfare should not lead to a complete separation of governments and people when waging war. Such arguments hint at the fact that punishing the Taliban for harbouring al-Qaeda might well include punishing the population for supporting the Taliban.[317]

The public discourse surrounding the war took on a punitive dimension. In a public letter signed by a large number of scholars across the American intellectual spectrum, the war was seen first and foremost as a justified act of self-defence, but the opening statements of the text are not focused on harm to the United States.[318] Instead, they focus on basic values that are both American and universal. The implication is that while the war is being fought to protect the United States, the war is also being fought as a response to a violation of the "rules" of the system – i.e. a punishment.

The letter goes on to state that wars can only be fought in self-defence and should not be fought for purposes of retribution. But, it also draws upon the just war tradition, pointing to the Augustinian text that states protection of the innocent is the primary obligation of a just authority. One sentence by Augustine has been draw upon by various writers in the just war tradition to emphasize the centrality of punishment in the justification of war: "Just wars are defined as those which avenge injuries, if some nation or state against whom one is waging war has neglected to punish a wrong committed by its citizens."[319] To protect the innocent means stopping future attacks, but it also means ensuring that others do not act in the future through deterrence – a central justification of punishment. The letter, like much of the political discourse that arose in the aftermath of the attacks, focused on the principle of self-defence, but as the emphasis of the war moved away from simply stopping further attacks to ensuring that those who committed the attacks would suffer for their crime, the punitive dimension of the war became clearer. Individual theorists furthered this punitive justification; Jean Elshtain, who played a key role in drafting and publicizing the letter noted above, made a strong case for the justness of a punitive response to terrorism in some of her own scholarship.[320] Arguments such as these reinforced the punitive nature of the Afghanistan campaign.

In other words, the practices and discourses sustaining the initial military response to the terrorist attacks of 9/11 demonstrate an inchoate punitive impulse. As the American administration argued, however, Afghanistan was just a first step in a longer war. On 4 November 2002, a United States Predator unmanned aircraft launched a Hellfire air-to-ground missile at a car travelling through a remote region of Yemen. This strike killed six people, including Ali Qaed Senyan al-Harethi, who was a suspect in the attack on the USS Cole in 2000 and who had been a close associate of Osama bin Laden.[321] Most reports suggested that the Central Intelligence Agency (CIA) launched the strikes, a divergence from the fact that the war model should be conducted by the military. Although he refused to confirm the attacks had happened, Secretary of Defense Donald Rumsfeld noted about al-Harethi that "It would be a good thing if he were out of business."

Such attacks may be taking place more often than this one admission would suggest. The fact that it was admitted suggests a punitive logic at work. The descriptions of the attack focused particularly on the role of al-Harethi in the attack on the USS Cole, with only one news story out of the five that I surveyed indicating that there was any evidence that these individuals were intending a new terrorist action. In other words, rather than a national security strike to eliminate a future threat, this attack seemed to be about punishing someone for a past one. A deterrent logic was also in evidence, as Deputy Secretary of Defense Paul Wolfowitz stated that such attacks were not only about killing terrorists but about "forcing al-Qaeda to change its tactics."[322]

This punitive military strike has close parallels to the policy of targeted killing, a military strategy employed by Israel against the Palestinians. While it has been claimed that such strategies draw upon a judicial structure of sorts, they certainly do not include a trial before a court of law, the gathering of evidence or a clear set of guidelines about sentencing. Military and/or administrative bodies make determinations of potential future danger or past attacks and then strike to kill.[323] In a critical analysis of the Yemen attacks, Nyier Abdou highlights the similarities between the attack and the policy of targeted killing, nothing that the "US cannot be judge, jury and executioner at once and brand the strike noting short of an extra-judicial execution."[324] Abdou quotes a range of officials who point to the legal and moral dilemmas this kind of strike raises, especially as it fits neither comfortably into a war model or a criminal justice model. The article emphasizes that this kind of strategy not only challenges the type of counter-terrorism campaign being conducted, it also challenges our under-standing of the "rules" governing war and conflict:

> This point [about a lack of clarity about the rules] has been expressed in a number of different ways by administration officials, who argue that we are in uncharted waters. White House spokesman Ari Fleis-cher called it a "different kind of war, with a different kind of battle-field," and former senator and co-chair of the presidential commission on homeland security, Warren Rudman has stated, "I think in the war on terrorism there are no rules."[325]

The war in Afghanistan and attacks such as the one in Yemen do indeed challenge our understanding of not only counter-terrorism policy, but wider questions about the proper rules for conducting warfare. On one level, these problems might easily be solved by simply "following the rules" as many legal analysts suggest.[326] At the same time, counter-terrorism policy could be formulated as an attempt to "enforce the rules," i.e. the rules that make international terrorism a violation of so many of the central tenets of the international order.

The punitive dimension of the war on terrorism reveals an important dilemma for not only counter-terrorism policy but the wider international order as one defined by rules that need enforcement. If that order is becoming increasingly punitive, but the rules that punishment is suppos-edly enforcing are becoming less clear, then punishment becomes dis-connected from rules and law and becomes much closer to vengeance; recall from Chapter 1 that vengeance is designed to respond to an indi-vidual harm without any concern for the enforcement of broader rules or a rule-governed order. The war on Afghanistan and the attack in Yemen construct a world in which powerful agents simply lash out at those who have wronged them rather than an attempt to reinforce political and moral order through properly punishing those who break the rules.

Detaining or punishing terrorists

The second practice to be explored here is the detention of individuals captured in various contexts. The Bush administration has described

Guantanamo Bay as a facility to remove dangerous individuals and draw from them information to support further operations in the field. But, despite their explicit claims that these facilities are not designed to punish, their punitive nature soon came to light as the detainees used the American criminal justice system to demand the right of habeas corpus, or the right to challenge their detention. This fundamental right was used by the US Supreme Court to force the American administration to create a system of trials for those accused that turned into the Military Commissions Act of 2006.

Guantanamo Bay was not designed simply for the detention and inter-rogation of suspects in the war on terror. Rather, it was created in 1903 as a fuelling station for US naval vessels in Cuba. After the United States severed relations with Cuba in 1961, the base continued to operate, although for very different reasons. It took on a detention purpose in the mid-1990s with the housing of Haitian refugees there. With the attacks of 9/11, it became the location for Joint Task Force-Guantanamo, giving the US government a location for housing those identified as being involved in terrorism.[327]

On 13 November 2001, the President issued the Detention, Treatment and Trial of Certain Non-Citizens in the War against Terrorism Act. This act established the provisions by which individuals were to be detained at Guantanamo Bay and other locations (Guantanamo Bay not being identi-fied in the text of the act as the primary location). In its first section it states that individuals "subject to this order pursuant to Section 2 hereof to be detained, and, when tried, to be tried for violations of the laws of war and other applicable laws by military tribunals." At the same time, it goes on to state that "it is not practicable to apply ... the principles of law and rules of evidence recognized in the trial of criminal cases in United States district courts."

On one reading, then, the act suggests that individuals will be detained and then tried, a normal procedure for criminal trials and punishment. Even if the individuals under question were not tried according to strict US criminal law, it could still be argued that they will be subject to some form of trial procedure by which they might be justly punished. But, the act inserts a subtle change. In Section 2(b) it states that individuals are to be detained and "if the individual is to be tried, that such individual be tried only in accordance with section 4." The key word here is "if" – there is, in other words, no guarantee that individuals will be tried, but only a guaran-tee that they will be detained. While this could be explained by the fact that the US government had not worked out what the military commis-sions would be, it might also be explained by the fact that the overriding purpose of the facility was to interrogate individuals and not determine their guilt or innocence.

Statements from American legal and military officials reinforced the argument that the United States did not intend to try individuals at all, much less in accordance with standard rules and procedures. In a statement issued on 4 March 2005, Mario Mancuso, a special advisor to the Department of Defense's General Counsel stated that individuals at Guantanamo are being held for reasons of national security and not because they are being punished. His argument concerning the logic of detention was as follows:

> We want to try to shield civilians as much as we can from the horrors of war. We want to shorten war as much as we can. And so the laws of war recognize that combatants can detain the other side's soldiers, if you will, for the duration of hostilities, because we want to take them off the battlefield. We want to shield civilians from these unlawful enemy combatants, because in fact, they target civilians and we want to protect our troops."[328]

The logic of this statement might suggest that this means these individuals would receive POW status, in that they are not being punished but are being detained. The attorney goes on to argue that granting them the status of POWs would give them "too many privileges" and would decrease the incentives for them to follow the rules of war. In other words, if the "prize" of being labelled a POW is available, such individuals might perhaps continue in their fight for they would be granted the rights of POWs in detention.

The logic of keeping individuals detained without any prospect of trials remained central to US government justifications for Guantanamo Bay. In an article on the US Defense Department website of 10 January 2006, a spokesman claimed that the detention of suspects is keeping individuals in the US safe. The spokesman noted that these individuals "should not be let back on the streets." He went on to argue that the US military was trying to use the military commission system to try individuals, but they were being hampered by the attorneys for the defendants. He noted that the government would "continue to work through these legal challenges as they exist and to pursue justice through the military commission system."[329]

These "legal challenges" – things such as the right of habeas corpus and the rules of evidence – were not only products of pesky defence attorneys but of the US Supreme Court. The Court ruled in its 2004 decision, *Rasul v. Bush* that individuals detained at Guantanamo Bay could bring legal challenges against the US government concerning their unlawful detention. This reversed lower court rulings that had denied them that right. The Court's decision was based primarily on the right of habeas corpus, one of the oldest rights in the United States and, indeed, the entire common law tradition, which allows an individual to challenge the grounds on which he or she is detained.

Partly as a result of this ruling, the Bush administration began to formulate more clearly the military commissions that could be used to try individuals. Again, the Court ruled against the Bush administration, ruling on 29 June 2006 in *Hamdan* v. *Rumsfeld* that the Military Commissions established by the 13 November 2001 act were illegal. This decision prompted the Administration and Congress to negotiate and produce a compromise act, The Military Commissions Act of 2006 (MCA), signed into law on 17 October 2006.[330] This Act created a structure by which individuals could be tried for various crimes and, importantly, punished in a more formal manner rather than simply be detained without charge.

The act includes provisions about sentencing, including the death penalty in certain cases. Rather than explore these elements of the MCA in any detail, I wish to focus instead on one constitutional debate that surrounds the creation of the act. This is not because the sentencing procedures are irrelevant to the arguments of this book – rather, it is because a brief reading of this debate points to an important dimension of authority and constitutionality, a theme that has been running through my argument thus far.

The provisions of the MCA are an attempt to respond to the rulings of the Supreme Court about specific elements of the way in which individuals were detained. It is important to emphasize, however, that the larger reason for creating the Act was the Court's argument that the executive authority had abrogated to itself a right reserved to Congress in the US Constitution – the lifting of the provisions of habeas corpus. In Article 1, Section 9 of the Constitution, it states clearly that "The Privilege of the Writ of Habeas Corpus shall not be suspended, unless when in Cases of Rebellion or Invasion the public Safety may require it." The fact that this provision is listed in the sections defining the Congress' role clearly indicates that this is not a privilege that the Executive can lift, but only the Congress can.

Yet, even though the Court framed the illegality of the original provisions as resulting from a need to protect habeas corpus, the MCA prevents individuals from appealing to this right (Section 7(e)). The MCA declares that individuals determined to be enemy combatants or those awaiting that determination cannot appeal to any court, judge or justice on these grounds.

It is unclear whether the Court will make a further ruling on the MCA. Because the Congress passed the law, the Court's concern about the executive running roughshod over the authority of the Congress has been rectified. But the fact that the Congress has passed a law that still denies the right of habeas corpus to individuals suggests that the core issue may not have been rectified.

Recall from previous chapters that I have pointed to the possibility of a more constitutional order as being a potential means to avoid the unjust nature of punishment. The ongoing constitutional debate about the MCA reveals how such an order might function. Rather than simply being about the protection of the rights of individuals who are to be sentenced, a constitutional structure leads to punishment becoming a means by which courts can reinsure a structure of power and politics that constrains excesses. This may not necessarily help those in immediate danger of being unjustly punished. But, importantly, it does reveal how courts can play a key role in not only protecting individuals but protecting the larger political sphere.

Interrogation or torture

The final element of punitive counter-terrorism that I wish to explore here is the practice of interrogation. The ways in which interrogation of those being detained have become debates about torture has become a central element of the public discourse surrounding the war on terror. In this section, I want to draw upon these debates not simply to argue that torture is wrong (although I certainly believe it to be); rather, I want to use them as a window into the complexity of the rules governing interrogation, and how those rules can easily become a tool by which individuals justify their actions as part of a larger punitive response to the initial terrorist attacks that resulted in the need to interrogate.

Torture has long been part of political practice, but more often part of an investigative process. John H. Langbein describes the history of torture as a part of European medieval judicial structures. Rather than a punitive practice, or even the result of a feeling of vengeance, Langbein argues that torture as a form of evidence gathering resulted from the high standard of proof that reigned in the criminal justice system of medieval Europe. That structure demanded that at least two individuals were witness to the crime, or the individual accused had to confess. Since finding two witnesses was often difficult, extracting a confession from the individual became a common practice. "The law of torture grew up to regulate this process of generating confessions."[331]

Even further back historically, Jill Harries describes the role of torture in the Roman legal digest. While acknowledging that Roman law put torture squarely in the place of interrogation, her analysis also points to how its operation in different contexts reveals a punitive ethos. Roman law allowed for the torture of slaves, but not free citizens, in order to obtain information about crime. But, as distinctions between classes became more blurred, the protections afforded to citizens, especially poor citizens, were undermined. Social class clearly informed who could be tortured. Importantly for the purposes of this chapter, however, other changes in the practice demonstrated how torture moved from an investigatory practice to a punitive one. When Christians began to be a problem for the Roman Empire, they were routinely tortured. Rather than a tool to gather information, however, the torture of Christians served different purposes. Christians did not hesitate to admit being Christians, and so saw their admission as an important part of being a martyr. Instead, the practice of torturing Christians became a means to both force them to change their beliefs and also a demonstration to the wider Roman society of the power of the state in response to a rebellion. While the judicial function of torture still played a role in the practice inflicted on Christians, it became something more, an attempt to punish those who disrupted the political and moral order of the Roman system:

> Why did this change occur? Although the legal interpreters, and those modern writers who have analysed judicial torture, were clear that the infliction of pain for purposes of discovering the truth was distinctive and could be regulated as such, popular culture and usages were less scrupulous about such distinctions. People died under torture; it would not always be clear to the casual observer whether the torture was judicial or punitive, especially as the same judge presided over both. Moreover the public display of judicial torture blended with that of public punishment. Justice, Roman-style, had to be seen to be done. The infliction of pain in the arena made death a spectator sport and those aristocrats and emperors who financed the games went out of their way to invent new and bizarre distractions for the crowd.[332]

This dual interrogatory and punitive function of torture remains alive today. In an analysis of how Argentine soldiers looked to the moral author-ity of the Catholic hierarchy to justify their conduct in the "dirty war," Mark Osiel suggests some similar themes. The soldiers were not ordinary functionaries who did not see their conduct as problematic according to Osiel; rather, they were deeply troubled by what they had to do to defeat the guerrilla campaign. The advice from Church authorities was that the conduct of the war was a just one, one that demanded the infliction of harm on those who violated the norms of the political order.[333] There is not a spe-cific instance of a torturer stating clearly that he or she was engaging in this conduct to punish guerrillas; rather, the moral universe in which they were operating, one reinforced by the authority of not just the state but the Church, created a world in which the infliction of pain on the body could be justified as a punitive means to prevent future civil war.

A moral and political order was certainly disturbed by the attacks of 9/11. In response to that disturbance, one attempt to reinforce order was to detain and interrogate those who had refused to follow the rules. But the rules about how to conduct such a war soon made the counter-terrorism campaign more complicated. The UN Convention against Torture and Other Inhuman and Degrading Acts specifically states that torture can never be employed, a point made in the strongest terms pos-sible in Section 2 of Article 2:

> No exceptional circumstances whatsoever, whether a state of war or a threat of war, internal political stability or any other public emergency may be invoked as a justification for torture.

Sanford Levinson points out that this language is particularly forceful for a legal rule in that it shuts out the possibility that any circumstance could ever justify it.[334]

But while this strong condemnation exists in this clause, the definition of torture in the same convention is so open ended that it does not really specify what counts as torture and what does not:

> any act by which severe pain or suffering, whether physical or mental is intentionally inflicted upon a person for such purposes as obtaining from him or a third person information or a confession, punishing him for an act he or a third person has committed or is suspected of having committed, or intimidating or coercing him or third person, or for any reason based on discrimination of any kind, when such pain of suffering is inflicted by or at the instigation of or with the consent or acquiescence of a public official or other person acting in an official capacity. It does not include pain or suffering arising only from, inherent in or incidental to lawful sanctions.

This definition, which relies on the infliction of severe pain as the primary criteria, albeit qualified by the purposes of punishment, attaining information or intimidating others, does not give much clarity to what counts as torture. Moreover, the last sentence, in which the infliction of pain can be justified on the basis of "lawful sanction," might leave further space open for potential abuse.

And it is this opening in terms of a definition that has been exploited in the American counter-terrorism campaign. The most important moment in the American shift in what constitutes torture can be found in a memo written by Assistant Attorney General Jay Bybee to then Counsel to the President Alberto Gonzalez.[335] The memo, written on 1 August 2002, explored what interrogation techniques were allowable according to US law. Bybee argues that the

> Physical pain amounting to torture must be equivalent in intensity to the pain accompanying serious physical injury, such as organ failure, impairment of bodily function, or even death ... We conclude that the statute, taken as a whole, makes plain that it prohibits only extreme acts.[336]

Bybee goes on to examine what it means to be "extreme" – even turning to the dictionary to clarify its meaning – and examines the US ratification of the UN Convention, Israeli court decisions and European Human Rights court cases to determine what can be allowed. While not explaining specific practices, Bybee basically concludes that very coercive forms of interrogation can be employed.

This wide-open interpretation of the rules continued in the American context. After much criticism, the US Department of Justice declared in

December 2004 that torture was "abhorrent" and could not be used in any circumstance. But soon thereafter, the Justice Department issued a secret ruling to the CIA, justifying a number of extreme forms of interrogation, including "painful physical and psychological tactics, including head-slapping, simulated drowning, and frigid temperatures."[337] Lawyers throughout the US administration argued for the legality of different forms of interrogation. One line of argument begun by John Yoo, a Justice Department lawyer, relied upon the power of the executive office as having almost complete authority to wage war without interference from Congress or the Courts. This argument became a point of contention among individuals within and outside of the Administration, as for some it represented a protection of executive privilege to conduct operations, while for others it violated core principles of the constitutional order of the US political system.[338]

Almost all the arguments made in these legal briefings argue that these practices are to obtain information not to punish. But, the disturbance of the moral and political order prompted by the attacks of 9/11 might create a punitive response within the interrogation of suspects. As one interpretation of the post-9/11 practice of torture suggests,

> In other words, at times when social order is threatened, especially by people seen as outsiders or subordinates, torture may function as a method of individual or collective assertion that creates a perhaps illusionary sense of overcoming vulnerability by the thorough domination of others.

The result is a situation in which "torture mocks the law, using punishment to gather evidence to justify the punishment already inflicted, rather than using evidence already gathered to justify punishment."[339]

This section has not demonstrated that those ordering or engaging in interrogation practices specifically intended to punish. Rather, I have suggested that when interrogation takes place in response to a challenge to the larger political and moral order, the need to restore the certainty of that order may allow interrogation to become punitive torture. Despite the strict rules outlawing torture at both the international and domestic American levels, its practice seems to have increased in a post-9/11 world. The fact that torture rarely produces certain information, yet continues to be practiced, defies explanation. Perhaps the explanation can be found in the need to punish those who break the rule that terrorism can never be a part of the political order.

Evaluating punitive counter-terrorism: justice

In principle, punishing a terrorist does not need much justification – as an individual or group that violates a fundamental feature of the international normative structure, terrorists deserve punishment. But, the specific practices being employed to carry out that punishment seem to be creating more violence and injustice. Why is this? Connected to the arguments about the justice of punishment in Chapter 1, and building on some of the conclusions from Chapter 5, I would suggest that the first problem is a lack of clarity about the norm being violated. As noted in the review of terrorism studies literature, one of the long-standing problems with counter-terrorism is clarifying exactly what terrorism is. This is not simply an academic debate, but one that directly impacts the ability to hold individuals or groups responsible for a crime. That is, if the norm is not clear, there will be no capacity to define terrorism as a crime that deserves punishment.

At the same time, putting terrorism into a clear legal definition also raises problems. The review of the debate about torture reveals this as a broader problem than just in terms of terrorism; when practices that "everyone knows are wrong" are turned into rules without a larger authority context, individual interpreters will construct their own definitions to suit their own needs. This only reinforces the need for an acceptable judicial structure that can interpret contexts to explain what constitutes terrorism.

A second way in which counter-terrorism policy violates justice is the failure to define it as punitive rather than something else. In the previous chapter, the problem was that sanctions were defined as a means to coerce individuals into changing their behaviour, while in this case, the problem is that counter-terrorism policy is framed in terms of self-defence rather than punishment. One reason is that those carrying out these policies resist calling them punishments because to do so would be to violate another key norm of the international system – that states cannot punish but can only use force in self-defence. This norm is so constitutive of the international order that even the most powerful states are hesitant to violate it.

As a result, self-defence becomes a principle that justifies such a wide range of practices that it distorts the reality of what is happening. Importantly, it means that the normal protections of those who are punished in a domestic system are not available. The fact that the detainees had to turn to American criminal law demonstrates the necessity of these protections, especially when no such protections exist in a world in which self-defence is the only justification for the use of force. In other words, there is no protection available to those who are being attacked in self-defence, but there are defences available to those being harmed for purposes of punishment.

The three practices upon which I have focused in this chapter, war, detention and interrogation, have been justified as matters of self-defence. As a justification for counter-terrorism, however, self-defence allows these means to be employed forever, for terrorism will not disappear in the near future. Every terrorist action or threat of an action becomes reason to continue with the policies identified above. There is no need to respect the rights of individuals, for the worry that the next terrorist will soon appear justifies continuing to occupy rogue states and detain individuals without any sign of release.

How would a punitive justification differ? Punishment is not something that continues forever, but has a clear beginning and end point. If counter-terrorist measures are understood to be punitive, they will be oriented towards identifying the guilty, trying them and imposing a clear sentence. Once that sentence has been carried out, the guilty are released.

These suggestions about how terrorism might be confronted more centrally through a punitive response rather than a self-defence one should not be read to suggest that self-defence is not important. Indeed, the proactive measures employed by the international community should continue and will play an important role in the prevention of terrorism. Rather, by admitting that counter-terrorism policy contains a punitive dimension and making that punitive dimension more in conformity with the protection of the rights of those accused may go some distance to curtailing the tensions currently surrounding the international order as it relates to this practice.

Evaluating punitive counter-terrorism: authority

The proposal to define terrorism more clearly as a crime and then admit that counter-terrorism policy should be a punitive response to that crime may sound simple. But the review of how the rules governing detention and torture were twisted and turned by American lawyers suggests that a turn to rules may not be an easy answer. Rather, what seems more important is clarifying the authority structures that should be engaged in the practice of punitive counter-terrorism. As my brief review of some of the counter-terrorism literature suggests, there is a problem in framing an international response to terrorism because of the lack of a clear single authority to undertake such practices.

The two primary candidates for counter-terrorism authority at the global level are the United Nations and the International Criminal Court. The United Nations Security Council has undertaken a counter-terrorism policy of economic sanctions, as explored in Chapter 5. This approach, while approaching a just form of punishment, puts the executive and judicial authority in the hands of a single agent, a problem explored above.

The ICC convention considered terrorism as a possible crime under its jurisdiction, but this was rejected on the grounds of the political nature of defining terrorism (a similar problem arising with the definition of aggression). More importantly, as Madeline Morris explains, the complementarity element of the ICC militates against terrorism being justly prosecuted before it. Because all crimes should be dealt with first at the national level, and because of the reporting mechanisms of the ICC which allow all state parties involved to be informed of a prosecutor's decision to indict a suspect, it would be likely that a state sponsor of terrorism would effectively block it from being an issue before the court.[340]

The authority by which to undertake counter-terrorism measures, then, seems to be the state, whether it is through the war or criminal justice models. But state prosecution of terrorism does not seem to provide the right means to address this problem. Especially if there is to be a just punishment of those who commit terrorist actions, some alternative formulation of global authority will be necessary.

Rather than determine which authority is best suited to conduct counter-terrorism, I would suggest two alternatives to thinking about authority. First, the principle of collective security provides a way to think about proper authority for violating international norms. This might be undertaken through the Security Council, or it might arise from other sources. As noted in Chapter 2, Hans Kelsen argued that collective security responses to norm violations are justified. Collective security has long been a central part of the international order, and yet it does not seem to have been invoked as a conceptual tool for responding to terrorism. Instead, responses remain mired in the domestic context, except when it comes to sanctions. The Bush administration's use of "coalitions of the willing" rather than international institutions may have reflected a discouragement with the United Nations, but it should not mean an abandonment of the idea found in Grotius and other natural law theorists that a punishment of such a primary principle of the international order should arise from the community as a whole, even if this action is manifested through a delegated agent.

A second rethinking is the centrality of the judiciary as the best way to think about an international response. As Kelsen suggested, it is judiciaries that should be central in this global constitutional order. The example of how the US Supreme Court forced not only the respect of the rights of those detained but, even more importantly, an acknowledgement that the punitive practices being undertaken were violating the constitutional order, demonstrates how an international judicial authority might play a key role in constructing a more constitutional global order.

A judicial structure would play a key role in not only interpreting the current rules concerning terrorism, but also clarifying the rules governing the practices of interrogation and torture. Of course, such an order would need to work in conjunction with the domestic legal orders of those states most directly engaged in counter-terrorism, i.e. the United States. It is doubtful, to say the least, that convergence of the international and domestic legal systems is possible in the current international order. But perhaps by building upon rulings already made in the US courts, an international judiciary might be able to structure effectively a political order acceptable to the great powers and the wider global order.

One further thought on a judicial authority is that it need not rely solely on an international legal context. Judgement is a philosophical idea that informs a number of different traditions of political thought. The natural law tradition from which Grotius and Locke formulated their ideas drew upon the scholastic concept of casuistry, or the use of reasoned judgement to decide in situations where the rules alone may not be the best guides. This is not an argument for abandoning the rules, but a suggestion that alternative formulations of what it means to make a judgement might be useful here.

This turn to alternative forms of judicial reasoning points to political traditions outside of the secular and towards the religious. In the context of the current war on terror, there has been an attempt made to differentiate this conflict from the "clash of civilizations" that Samuel Huntington suggested was the new political structure of the international order.[341] What if an international judicial structure was designed that did not include just international legal jurists but scholars from Islamic, Christian and Jewish traditions? Such a "court" broadly defined might be better able to present its determinations about various aspects of the war on terror as truly representative of those engaged most directly in the conflict. Certainly, other traditions should be included as well, although much of the terrorism animating US policy arises from an extremist Islamic context. In other words, thinking about a constitutional order that included not just international law, but a wider range of religious and philosophical traditions that drew upon their traditions of judgement might be a step towards constructing an international order that could punish in a more just way.

Evaluating punitive counter-terrorism: agency

But even if such a court were structured, who would it punish? What would it mean to punish at the global level for crimes of terrorism? The debate identified in the literature about the group versus individual level of responding to terrorism reveals that there remains a core conceptual confusion about what or who is responsible for acts of terrorism. Is it individuals or groups?

The first point to emphasize is that it is the very counter-terrorist practices in play that construct the responsible agents. War punishes a group, despite attempts by technocrats in the military to claim that they are moving towards more precise forms of warfare that will discriminate civilians from combatants. Military responses will always punish groups, no matter how individuals seek to avoid this. The legal structures employed by the United States through the construction of military commissions construct individuals as the responsible agents. Indeed, the entire criminal justice model of counter-terrorism emphasizes the individual as the responsible agent.

But, as I hope I have demonstrated, the American response to terrorism has failed to clarify whether groups or individuals are responsible for terrorism. One interesting consequence of this conceptual confusion is the hesitancy to define terrorism because it is a political crime, i.e. one that is undertaken for public or group-related reasons rather than for individual reasons. Because groups are the ones using terrorism, it is difficult to respond to them through criminal justice methods, for our entire criminal justice structure is designed to respond to individuals.

The Israeli policy of responding to Palestinian acts of terrorism demonstrates the moral dilemmas of this conceptual confusion. The tactics of home demolition and curfew employed by the Israeli Defence Forces against Palestinians appear so unjust, no matter what one's view on the issues animating the conflict, because they punish groups for the actions of individuals. But, those who defend the Palestinians fail to acknowledge that the political claims animating the Palestinian cause do not justify the use of tactics such as suicide bombings. Some of the moral outrage on both sides of the conflict can be traced, in my view, to confusions about the proper agent to be held responsible for terrorist actions.

In Chapter 3, I argued that the agency that deserves punishment at the global level is political agency, or the capacity to inflict harm upon not only individuals but the order as a whole. In the next chapter, I suggest an institutional structure that would allow for the trial of both individuals and groups, with the ICJ serving as a final court of appeal. Such a structure would allow both non-governmental groups such as al-Qaeda and states to be tried and punished. Again, the construction of such a judicial order will not be easy. But, what it will allow is an alternative to the current order in which attempts to punish individuals for crimes of groups, or attempts to punish groups for the acts of lone individuals, might be prevented.

Conclusion

The review of American counter-terrorism policy I have provided in this chapter points to the problems that arise when counter-terrorism does not adequately address key questions of justice, authority and agency. This is not the result of power hungry state leaders or evil terrorists – rather, the problems I have identified are the result of conceptual complexities at the heart of violence and global political order. My suggestions for mitigating some of the confusions are less important than the interpretation and analysis of the source of the problems.

This chapter has explored counter-terrorism policy. It provides a useful segue to the final chapter, in which I address the conceptual difficulties of punishing evil. For almost everyone would admit that blowing up over 3,000 civilians by using aircraft is evil. Hopefully, we should admit that waging war, detaining individuals without hope of ever releasing them, and using torture to punish are also evil. Figuring out how to respond to evil in the current international order, evils which are perpetrated by both individuals and states, will be the subject of the final chapter.

7 Punishment or politics?
Responses to global evil

In this book, I have made two overarching arguments. First, that an illiberal order is being constructed at the global level by a series of punitive practices that neither reinforce justice nor create peace. Second, that by altering certain institutional arrangements at the global level, it is possible to employ punitive practices such that they construct an international order that is more just and peaceful. The practices I have explored are intervention, economic sanctions and counter-terrorism policy. The institutional change I have emphasized throughout the book is the construction of an integrated constitutional order in which a judiciary plays a more prominent role.

This chapter provides some critical reflections on these conclusions. I summarize the arguments in the following pages, but use that summary to examine whether or not punishment is the right response to global evil. I stand by the conclusions of the previous chapters but also recognize they deserve more critical scrutiny. My critique focuses primarily on how a focus on politics, broadly defined, might provide some alternatives to a focus on punishment.

The chapter proceeds as follows. The next section briefly reviews the arguments made in the specific chapters, arguments that lead up to the centrality of a judicial structure. Next, I examine the practice of inter-national criminal courts as they have responded to various crimes in the post-Cold War context. Drawing on some recent critical literature on the courts, I point to their successes and failures in constructing a punitive response to international crime, which leads to a proposal for the creation of a dual court structure for trying individuals and groups. I then turn to the idea of evil as the motivating force behind punishment. I suggest that our desire to see the world as evil may prompt punishment, and that responding to this world may require radical revisions in how we see the world and our role within it.

Punishment in international relations

This book began by identifying a problem in the international order – that punitive practices are taking place without being acknowledged as such.

This meant defining a punitive practice outside of the normal terms that tend to rely on sovereign authority and clear intentions as constituting punishment. Instead, I suggested that punitive practices could be understood as those that impose harm on agents in response to violations of shared rules.

I then argued that in order for punishment to be just it must conform to certain structures, drawing on John Rawls' two-tiered institutional framework of a legislature that enacts deterrent laws and a judiciary that interprets and punishes for retributive purposes. In reviewing the practices that I define as punitive, however, I have come to a further conclusion, one that is obvious at one level, but sometimes difficult to grasp when focusing on a practice designed to enforce rules – the problem of what norms merit protection through punishment.

There are in fact different problems here. There is the standard complaint of the moral relativist, that there are so many differing conceptions of norms in the international system that there can be no agreement. I do not think this is a serious problem, however. As of this writing there are a wide range of international legal norms that are broadly accepted in the international community concerning the use of military force. When powerful agents contest those norms or even ignore them, it is rarely because they begin from a completely different metaphysical or ontological starting point. Rather, as with current American efforts to dispute the rules governing the use of force, those efforts usually result from self-interested actors twisting the rules to their purpose. Even Chinese resistances to certain human rights norms are not placed in terms of a radically different cultural approach to politics, but in terms of sacrificing some norms (individual rights) for others (economic development). In other words, there is no real philosophical difference at the international level in terms of the issues being debated here. Instead, there are actors who ignore rules for their own interests. The best response to this refusal to comply with the rules is precisely what I have argued for here: punishment of those who break the rules.

A more serious problem is with the way in which punishments are used to enforce norms. This has been the point of this book. The punishments I have identified here help to construct the norms that shape the international order. I have proposed some institutional changes that might make punishment more possible. But, outside of this institutional issue, it is important to recognize that punishment cannot really be separated from the construction of the norms that structure our world. Constructivism as a theory of international relations has informed my approach to international affairs for some time. I am now realizing that this theoretical tradition in IR needs to be stretched to consider how enforcement mechanisms themselves actually create the world around us rather than focusing primarily on how the norms construct the world around us. These mechanisms, especially the punitive ones I have identified in this book, are creating a particular type of world. In other words, punishment constructs the norms that construct our world.

Connected to this point is the role of rules in making shared norms concrete.[342] Punishments in the legal model emanate from the violation of specific rules or laws. But putting certain political practices into the form of rules does not always solve the problems of safety and welfare. As I have argued elsewhere, rules can only do so much for us; they might provide guidelines for behaviour, but if we put all our hope in rules as the answer to political dilemmas, we will be disappointed.[343] In fact, one might argue that rules can impose violent outcomes on individuals and communities, outcomes that do not allow for change and evolution in response to new situations.[344] An institutional response to this dilemma is to encourage agents to not only "obey the rules" but to engage constantly in new fora through which rules and norms can be constructed. While I have argued that there are norms aplenty in the current international system, there is always the need for new conventions and multilateral initiatives to develop responses to new situations. The call for a new Geneva Convention to develop new laws of armed conflict relating to counter-terrorism would be such an example.

What I am suggesting is that when we see how norms and rules are actually constructed by practices of punishment, we need to recognize that norms and rules, and even laws, need constant attention. Norms, rules and laws do not appear from nowhere – they result from political practices. The obvious political practice that creates a law is a parliament, but norms and rules also result from political activism. At one level, then, we need to think critically about how to construct political realms within which individuals can engage in political actions that produce new norms, rules and laws. Such spaces can be the space of the parliament, but, as I have argued elsewhere, they can also be diverse spaces of political activism.[345] Movements of global political protest, for instance, are important sources from which new normative structures arise. Rather than rely on the UN General Assembly or various national parliamentary structures, citizens of the world should turn to a wider array of political practices to reconstruct a world that responds to their needs. This is not to discard punishment as a tool for creating a just world, only to recognize that the norms, rules and laws that punishments enforce need to be constantly tended and contested.

Punishment and authority

This leads to my conclusions about authority. In each of the practices identified here, I have suggested that the authority structure undertaking the practice needs to be judged according to which it can legitimately engage in punitive responses to norm violations. There are two kinds of authority structure that might punish in the current international order. One is the sovereign nation-state and the other is the United Nations or other international or regional organizations. My reading of Grotius and Locke suggests that individual agents in a state of nature might be justified in undertaking punishment. But, only if there exists some form of interpretation can those agents truly act in a way that conforms to some norms of legitimacy.

My suggestion throughout the chapters has been a global judicial one. Such a solution might be seen as nothing more than a "fluffy Leviathan" or the replacement of an executive with an all-powerful judicial structure.[346] Two responses to this are relevant. First, the reason I emphasize a judicial structure is that this is precisely what is missing in the current international order. Many legislative and executive institutions already play a role in the international order. While the growth of international criminal tribunals has certainly increased in the post-Cold War period, the problem is that these tribunals and the ICC remain disconnected from the wider international normative structure. They are positioned to enforce rules arising from conflicts and war, but they do not have a clear connection to the overall structure of the international system.

Second, I acknowledge that the creation of such a judicial order will not solve all the problems identified in this book. It may help to mitigate them, however, in that it will force a reconsideration of the punitive practices that have increased in the post-Cold War era. If progressives in the international elite wish to enforce norms of human rights, a goal I share, they need to work harder to develop structures that will integrate the various dimensions of international affairs into a cohesive order. This is not to create a world state, which I find to be highly problematic in terms of its potential to become a global Leviathan. Rather, if such institutions can not only work to enforce the rule of law but also balance each other, with the executive having a role in appointing the judiciary, the judiciary being able to rule against the legislature and executive, and the parts being able to govern outside of the powers of the centre, a more constitutional order will perhaps emerge.

A second problem concerns the willingness of strong members of the current international order to give up their powers and create such an institution. In other words, will the United States allow its counter-terrorism policies to be dictated by the whims of an international judiciary? Probably not at this particular moment. The point of this book, however, is not to convince powerful agents to change their behaviour (although it would be nice if they read this and did). Instead, the point is to draw on the real problems of the current international order and suggest some alternative ways of imagining it. I do think the emphasis on constitutionalism would appeal to American policymakers, as it did at the turn of the twentieth century when the US played a key role in turning international law into a set of new institutional arrangements. There is no guarantee that change will come about, only a set of proposals that might point in the direction of such change.

A further problem, however, is that creating authority structures will limit the freedom of agents to pursue their own interests and desires, agents ranging from individual persons to corporations to states. This is a long-standing problem of political authority, one that can be captured in the assumption that if individuals conform to authority they "surrender their individual judgement." As Richard Flathman has argued, however, such a concern avoids the fact that when individuals conform to an authority they make a judgement, the judgement that this authority is worthy of acceptance. Once the authority becomes so powerful that it is coercive and brutal, then it loses its authority. But, the very nature of authority is to be somewhere between pure coercion and pure anarchy.[347]

Negotiating this space between authority and anarchy is an ongoing problem of politics, one that this book (or any book) should not presume to be able to resolve. I have merely suggested some ways in which one practice of authority – punishment – might be better designed to take into account the particular dilemmas of authority at the global level.

Punishment and agency

The last conceptual issue I have addressed in this book is the problem of agency. As each practice has demonstrated, ensuring that punishment will be just depends not only on ensuring that those doing the punishing conform to certain criteria, but that the choice of who to punish also conforms to certain criteria. A central problem in the international system is that while states have a primary role as the agents who structure the system, individuals become the ones who are punished through formal legal procedures.

One response is to punish states, a proposal I have explored elsewhere.[348] In the next section, I suggest how such a model for punishing both states and individuals in the current order might be possible by redesigning certain international judicial institutions. But this institutional response can only take us so far. As demonstrated in Chapter 5, punitive practices not only punish agents they construct agents. I noted above that punishment creates norms, but it also creates the very agents who can be held responsible for such violations.

The recognition that it creates agents is central to understanding the power and dangers of punishment. This point is not new to those who see politics through a post-structural lens, particularly those who draw on Foucaultian themes to inform their understandings of the political.[349] Foucault argued that practices of punishment and surveillance construct the human person as an agent capable of being held responsible, participating in the political and, most importantly, being subjected to the disciplinary powers of the state.[350] Foucault's account reveals how specific punitive practices can result in a world in which freedom is lost to the needs of a disciplinary society.

As I noted in Chapter 1, while I have found Foucault's approach to be critically important for understanding the relationship of punishment to agency, I would resist some of his conclusions, such as all punishment is simply an exercise of power (albeit not the power of a single agent, but widely dispersed power relations). My response would be to acknowledge Foucault's point about the construction of agency, but continue to design institutions and undertake investigations that can hopefully mitigate some of the pernicious effects of this power. Instead, I think punishment can be undertaken as a result of a deliberative process that acknowledges there are different kinds of agents, but also acknowledges that those agents do violate the rules and norms that structure a system, and thus need to be brought to justice.

This is perhaps too cautionary for some, but, as in the previous section concerning authority, presuming that one can resolve the problem of agency and punishment is to presume to resolve a problem that is endemic to the political. Instead, we need to continue with punitive practices but keep in mind their capacity to change and construct agents in the international political order.

Punishment in international criminal justice

Having summarized and extended some of the conclusions of the book thus far, I want to turn to some practical and theoretical suggestions. Admitting the tensions and challenges that have arisen in the previous chapters, I still believe it is possible to propose alternative ways of implementing punitive measures and creating a more just international order. This section draws upon writing in international criminal justice to propose an alternative international criminal justice structure.

Along with punitive intervention, punitive sanctions and punitive counter-terrorism policy, there is one further punitive practice that has appeared in the post-Cold War order that warrants attention – international criminal justice. This emerging field of international law has existed for quite some time, but with the end of the Cold War, the creation of the ad hoc tribunals for Yugoslavia and Rwanda, and the creation of the International Criminal Court, the belief in prosecuting international crimes has taken on a greater urgency.

Underlying this emerging criminal justice structure, of course, is a set of political dynamics that privilege powerful actors. As Gary Bass has described, war crimes tribunals can be found in the early nineteenth century, such as in attempts to prosecute Napoleon for his "crime" of waging war on the European political order.[351] Bass' account reveals the politics of bringing individual leaders to trial and how those political dynamics do not always match the legal purism of scholars of international law. He claims that the legalism that prompts liberal states to put individuals on trial is counteracted by the selfishness of those same states to refuse to put their own citizens on trial. This failure to be fair represents a realist strain in the idealism of such court structures.

Steven Roach recounts the political history of the International Criminal Court in his work, arguing that it cannot be understood outside of the dynamics of the debates that constituted its structure.[352] Unlike Bass, however, Roach argues that these political dynamics should not be seen only as realism inserting its ugly head into the purity of law; rather, these political dynamics point to a constantly contested, but still hopeful, trajectory of the international political order as moving towards a form of cosmopolitan governance.

Gerry Simpson has also recently explored the political dynamics underlying the creation of international criminal courts.[353] His account addresses some of the same themes I have explored in this book, although not focused directly on punishment. What he does provide, though, is an insightful analysis of what international law can and cannot do in responding to crimes of war and genocide. In particular, his reflections on the dilemmas of agency in the construction of international justice parallel some of the points I have developed in Chapter 3, pointing to the tensions in trying to hold individuals responsible for crimes that can really only be committed by communities as a whole.

To say that international criminal justice reflects certain political dynamics, then, does not necessarily dictate what our response should be. Such dynamics can produce outcomes that advance justice, while they might also hinder justice. Scholars like Roach and Simpson demonstrate that rather than a pessimism about the potential for law to achieve justice at the global level, exploring the dilemmas that arise through the construction of courts and their practices reveals competing trends that cannot be easily captured in the dichotomy of liberalism and realism that characterizes so much of international relations scholarship.

Interestingly, many of these critical perspectives on international criminal law fail to address the element that I have been exploring in this book – punishment. Mark Drumbl's recent book on this subject fills this important lacuna in the literature on international criminal justice by providing an extensive empirical overview of how international and domestic courts sentence those found guilty of international crime. Drumbl, who served as a defence attorney in trials before the International Criminal Tribunal for Rwanda (ICTR) has examined a wide range of sentencing procedures and judgements in various international criminal tribunals and the proposals for such procedures in the International Criminal Court.

Drumbl's examination first points to the freedom of justices in their sentencing decisions. This freedom has resulted in a range of different sentences from the international to the local, none of which seem integrated. A second conclusion is that many sentencing decisions seem to reflect a retributive logic rather than a deterrent one. As Drumbl notes, "A survey of all the cases of ad hoc tribunals over time, though reveals a preference for retributive motivations, especially when it comes to the aggravating and mitigating factors the tribunals consider in sentencing."[354] This conclusion about international courts is mirrored in domestic and national courts that punish international atrocities.[355] Drumbl is not arguing here that a retributive purpose has been formally developed in law or that it is justified; rather, his analysis demonstrates that the sentencing procedures of justices in a wide range or contexts seem to result in retributive logics. He concludes with some important insights about how to reformulate international criminal justice such that it can better connect the local to the international (through the principle of subsidiarity) and capture the problem of collective responsibility.

The review of international criminal sentencing procedures in Drumbl's book points to some important tensions. Perhaps the most important is that the way in which punishment is actually being meted out at the international level, at least in the international criminal justice system, still requires a great deal of work. The fact that Drumbl's is the first book to appear on the subject in English although international tribunals have been in operation for some time now, suggests a lack of attention to this fundamental feature of the international justice system.

In the following, I offer some alternative formulations of the international criminal justice system. These build upon ideas like Drumbl's but suggest a much more radical reform of the system. Various institutions exist in the international system that can be revised to take into account these alternative ideas about agency, responsibility and punishment at the global level.[356] Three in particular might be restructured: the International Court of Justice, the UN Security Council and the International Criminal Court.[357]

As the judicial organ of the United Nations, the International Court of Justice's mandate is to make judgements on disputes between states and offer advisory opinions when states or other international organs request them. When a judgement is passed, states are obliged to abide by it, in that they have signed on to the treaty creating the Court (i.e. the UN Charter).[358] The Court has ruled that states need to pay compensation or reparations in certain cases, although there is some question as to whether or not it has "passed judgements" that amount to punishments. Moreover, it has never issued a sentence that directs one state to use military force against another.[359] The Court also takes quite a long time to deliberate on its cases, having made relatively few judgements in its years of existence.

As I have argued in the previous chapters, the Security Council currently functions as both a quasi-judicial institution and an executive one. That is, it makes judgements on issues in the international community and then imposes punishments (or sanctions) when it deems it necessary.[360] In fact, the combination of these two functions in one institution goes against the essence of constitutional government that protects unfair accusations of crime in other political systems. By combining judicial and executive functions in the Security Council, the current international order does not reflect a constitutionally legitimate structure.[361]

The International Criminal Court (ICC) is a more recent addition to the international judicial structure. Prompted by the advocacy of various NGOs and, to some extent, Western democratic states, the ICC was created with the passage of the Rome Charter in 1998, and then came into force with the ratification of the Treaty by 60 states in July 2002.[362] At the time of this writing (August 2007) the Court has four "situations" under consideration, which will, it is assumed, become cases soon. These situations all focus on African conflicts, although the Court will presumably have a wider range of cases as it develops. The Charter names four crimes as within the ambit of the Court: genocide, war crimes, crimes against humanity and the crime of aggression. The last crime cannot yet be tried, however, because an agreed upon definition of it has yet to be approved by the UN General Assembly.

There are two major problems with this structure. First, the two courts hear cases by two different institutions, neither of which are linked by any institutional structure. This means that determining whether an individual or a state is responsible, to say nothing of other kinds of agents, is never coherently addressed. Second, the quasi-judicial role of the Security Council, particularly when it comes to issuing punishments, is disconnected from the other two institutions. While the ICJ cannot really issue sentences, the ICC will be able to, but it is unclear how these will be carried out.

In response to the current order, I propose the following revision. First, there should be three International Criminal Courts, for Persons, Groups and States. The second category would include both non-state political groups (NGOs, terrorist organizations) and multinational corporations. These courts would hear only cases that fall into the category of international political crimes, or those crimes that violate the norms structuring the political order as a whole. Such crimes should be identified in a meeting of the UN General Assembly, drawn primarily from the UN human rights regime.[363]

Selecting the individuals who would serve on these courts would obviously be a matter of some controversy. Rather than assume they would come to the position through their knowledge of international law, integrating the process into a larger constitutional context might be a better idea. As suggested in Chapter 6, it might be wise to include individuals from non-international law backgrounds but who have some experience of "judgement" broadly defined. This might include religious scholars or experts from various technical fields. In order to make the structure more constitutional, the members of these courts would not be appointed for life, but would have fixed terms. The Security Council might make their appointment, but perhaps the UN General Assembly could confirm them, after sitting through a confirmation process in a specific committee context. Obviously, this idea draws upon the American judicial structure, although there are certainly other models that could be drawn upon as well.

The following agents could bring cases to this tripartite judicial structure in the international system: the UN Security Council, individual states or NGOs. The cases would be brought to the Office of the Prosecutor, whose role it would be to determine (1) if there exists an international political crime and (2) which court should hear the case. This would mean that the Prosecutor could not initiate cases on his/her own, but it would place a great deal of importance on this office, for its role would be not only to investigate potential violations but also determine which agents should be held responsible. Of course, the determination of whether or not they were responsible would result from the trial, but the determination by the Prosecutor would be an important first step in this process.

Once a trial has been heard, a separate sentencing procedure would take place. As with most criminal courts today, and with the International Criminal Tribunals for Yugoslavia and Rwanda, the sentencing processes would be kept separate. The same court that determined guilt or innocence would decide the sentence, but the procedures would be kept separate.

Finally, the ICJ would play the role of an appeals court. It could hear appeals from all three courts, including whether or not a court was wrongly identified as the proper one for a particular situation, i.e. if the wrong agent was being tried. This appeal concerning the proper court might come after the Prosecutor has determined which case, so that the appeal process can address both the proper court and also the determination of guilt and sentencing.

The UN Security Council would be authorized to carry out any punishments, particularly those directed at states. Using military force (as in collective security actions), economic sanctions against states, the incarceration or execution of individuals found guilty, military or economic actions against groups, and the liquidation of certain corporations would be the responsibility of the Security Council. Importantly, the Council would not have a role in changing the judgement, although it would have an initial role in being able to bring cases to the judicial structure.

This structure is, obviously, an ideal proposal. It is not completely removed from reality, however, in that it builds upon the current international system and retains some of the powers of the current system. For instance, this suggestion would substantially change the Security Council, for its judicial function would largely disappear and it would become an institution that simply carries out judgements. Another alternative would be to continue to allow the Security Council to function in the way it does, but add to its tasks the function of carrying out judgements passed by the ICJ. There is a parallel here in the construction of the ICC. The Security Council was given a new task when the ICC was created, which is to recommend cases for prosecution to the Court. It did not lose its other functions, but was simply given a new task. In a similar way, the Security Council could be given this additional task if the ICJ were reconstituted to pass judgements on states that include sentences.

Of course, constructing this new institutional relationship would require a great deal of political capital and is open to objections on grounds of feasibility and practicality. But, it is closer to a possible structure than the proposal for a world government would be. It is, I would argue, a possible world that can be constructed from within the current international system.

Punishment and evil

This judicial structure as a possible way to carry out punishment at the international level is only one possibility. It is not necessarily the solution for the problems this book has identified; indeed, it might create its own set of problems. For some, an overemphasis on the judiciary undermines the very constitutional order that I have been proposing throughout this book by undermining the capacity to engage in deliberative politics.[364] Moreover, while I have tried to add groups to the agents that can be punished, law presumes that it is individual agents that deserve punishment. A judicial structure does not allow a response to evils that arise from broader structural dynamics. In other words, to put so much hope into a judicial context may not be the only route to take.

In this final section, I want to propose two alternatives, both of which point to the importance of politics. By politics here, I do not have a single definition in mind. What I want to explore briefly here are a different set of responses to corporate life, responses that point to how individuals can engage each other with the hope of creating a new world.

Structural evil and politics

My concern in this book has been to create institutional responses to what most would call evil. The idea of evil has long been part of moral and political discourse. It structures the way we label certain events as extreme, as outside legitimate boundaries. For some, the turn to evil is a way to disenfranchise those with whom we disagree. I believe the discourse of evil does keep some individuals out of the boundaries of legitimate political life, but it also represents a reality. It would be difficult to deny that some events and actions are so far from acceptable that they cannot be called anything but evil.

It is how we respond to those events and outcomes, however, that is my concern. This book has been premised on the assumption that agency creates evil, that is the actions of individuals construct outcomes we label as evil. An alternative way to see evil is not as located in the individual person, whose agency and responsibility determine our punitive response.

It is not even to locate that evil in corporate agents such as the state. Instead, we can also see it in the social and political structures that constitute the international. Patrick Hayden has explored Hannah Arendt's understanding of evil in relation to a wide range of issues, including genocide and global poverty.[365] Hayden clarifies Arendt's conception of evil, and connects it to the theme of political agency, by identifying the importance of the evil of making humans superfluous in Arendt's philosophy. As Hayden notes:

> The logic of superfluity is not merely to kill people, but to completely dehumanise them, to strip them of all dignity, and to deny that they are anything more than manipulable and expendable matter. The core of Arendt's conception of political evil as a tragic feature of modernity is, then, that it "has to do with the following phenomenon: making human beings as human beings superfluous." For Arendt, the horrifying characteristic of political evil in late modernity is the fact that it can be "committed on a gigantic scale" on the basis of the most mundane, petty and all-too-human motivations. For this reason, the modern evil of making humanity superfluous is not only political in nature, it is also banal.[366]

Hayden develops this concept in an analysis of global poverty, pointing out how evil cannot be reduced to an individual demonic agent, but instead to the social and political constructs that structure our world.

I take from Hayden's analysis the importance of understanding political evil as intimately connected to political agency; that is, I do not wish to deny the link between agency and evil. For me, this means that individuals do commit evil, but their evil is, in part, the destruction of a political sphere that allows the free celebration of agency and difference. While Hayden is focused on how to link this concept of evil to the existence of global poverty, I would argue that the dehumanization of individuals that makes global poverty possible is the destruction of a political space within which individuals can assert themselves as unique and worthwhile persons.

This means that punishment can still be a response to global evil, although it is also important to stress that numerous different agents can be punished, as I have suggested above. Importantly, however, in order to prevent individuals from being rendered superfluous, we need to ensure that every individual can play a role in constructing the political realm. Not everyone will want this role, but ensuring that the political realm is not limited to the few but open to the many, and open in diverse formats and structures, may go some distance to ensuring the construction of a global realm in which individuals are not left out and thus dehumanized.

The evil within and the political

One response to evil and the international has been to focus on restorative justice and practices of forgiveness. I have found in these approaches much to be learned, although they do not appear much in the pages of this book. My primary concern with this literature is that forgiveness cannot be something that is dictated or institutionalized. Because it is a response to a personal evil it must be a personal response, one designed to reconstruct a specific relationship.[367]

But the call for forgiveness points to an alternative approach, one that requires a different kind of response. One of the concerns of this book has been to critique the punitive practices that do exist in the international order, practices that invoke the language of evil to justify their sometimes harsh terms. Indeed, many of the violations that do take place are indeed evil, ranging from mass terrorism to genocide.

The human condition seems to require some notion of responsibility to make sense of the world around us. In comprehending evil, this need seems even more apparent.[368] At the same time, when individuals are held responsible for evil, and not just for bad actions, the desire for vengeance arises. While the human condition needs to link the individual to evil through a discourse of responsibility, that link can lead to labelling the individual perpetrator as evil, a label that justifies not just a punitive but a vengeful response. Such responses are not oriented towards achieving justice or reintegrating the individual back into society, but to destroying the evil individual and cleansing the community of a disease.

This tendency towards vengeance and destruction of evil is heightened when the individual who is responsible for the evil action is outside the domestic political community. In other words, a foreigner who commits evil is even more liable to a vengeful response than a fellow member of a community. Consider, for instance, the response of the US polity to the attacks of 9/11. By locating the responsibility for the attacks outside of the American political community, the Bush administration has been able to employ the language of war and destruction in its response. As noted above, those held at Guantanamo Bay are not being punished, they are being held so that they can be used to obtain information. When they have been drained of all their information, they can be destroyed or forgotten (a form of destruction in the political sphere).

One of the clearest articulations of the dangers of locating responsibility for evil in the will/intentions/motives of individuals comes from the political theory of William Connolly. In *Identity/Difference*, Connolly explores the ways in which formulations of responsibility structure the late modern response to evil. The book seems to be building upon, but radically diverging from, Peter Strawson's point about the importance of responsibility that I explored in Chapter 3; indeed, the first chapter of Connolly's book is entitled "Freedom and Resentment." In a chapter entitled "Responsibility for Evil," Connolly confronts the themes I am exploring here. He begins by noting that while responsibility has had different resonances across different cultural contexts (using the Homeric notion as an alternative), nevertheless a version of it seems to structure much of our reactions to evil. For Connolly, unlike for Strawson, this commonplace is not something to be celebrated, but something that may contain within it the "problem of evil":

> Perhaps standards of responsibility are both indispensable to social practice and productive of injustices within it. Perhaps because every society demands some such standards, a problem of evil resides within any social practice that fulfils this demand relentlessly.[369]

Connolly argues that the demand for responsibility represents a kind of moral calculus that prevents any act of evil from slipping away unaccounted for. In our attempts to locate all evil in structures of responsibility, Connolly suggests that we force individuals into particular identities that do not accurately capture them.

An example of this process at the international level is the crime of aggression. The crime of aggression was a central element of the Nuremberg Trials. But an individual cannot really commit the crime of aggression; aggressive war is something that can only be undertaken by a state with a military. Of course, in some countries that are run by dictators it may be easier to locate responsibility in a single individual who could be tried. But, if a semi-democratic or democratic state waged an aggressive war, would it make sense to argue that specific individuals are responsible? One need only consider the responsibility of the American public for the war against Iraq – a case in which the US Congress voted to support the Bush administration and public opinion polls strongly favoured military action in the fall of 2002 – to see that a democracy might really be better held responsible than particular leaders. Reality overflows the demands of responsibility.

I find Connolly's critique of responsibility quite persuasive, for it reveals how responsibility is a constructed concept and how its construction does not always lead to justice. At the same time, I do not want to abandon responsibility because I think it can provide an important means through which punishment can function, a response to evil that, as I noted in the introduction, can prevent vengeance and hostility from being the only response. Indeed, Connolly's concern about the ways in which a discourse of responsibility lead to forcing individuals into particular boxes is exactly the kind of move I think punishment can help us avoid. This might seem ironic to argue, for one of the concerns motivating Connolly's argument is the need to punish, something he draws from Nietzsche, whose critique of punishment is well known.[370] While I would not suggest that we could avoid the ways in which identity/difference structures our ethical and political engagements, I would suggest that punishment properly conceived could avoid some of its worst excesses. The way in which this can take place is by focusing more on agency than on intentionality in understanding evil.

This book has suggested ways to rethink agency, although not necessarily in the ways that would conform to Connolly's critique. Rather, the point I want to emphasize from Connolly's formulation is the danger of relying on agency, responsibility and punishment as ways to respond to evil. These means can do something, and I have proposed some ways in which the international order might be made more constitutional in order to respond to evil.

If punishment is an attempt to locate responsibility for evil firmly in the individual, but it seeps out of that container into the larger political sphere, our response should be to reconstruct that sphere. One way to do that is what I have proposed above – an alternative institutional arrangement. An alternative might be to think about how to reconstruct ourselves, particularly the way we see our relationship between the self and other.

I want to conclude this book with a figure who does not appear in most international political theory – Jesus of Nazareth. Hannah Arendt argued that Jesus was the first thinker to propose forgiveness as a public issue, something that should play a role in constructing the public sphere.[371] Based upon the evidence that we have from the Christian scriptures, Jesus did indeed embrace a logic of forgiveness. He also engaged in something closer to anti-politics, in that he pushed his followers to think about the state of their souls rather than the state of their political arrangements. But, this focus on the self was not the same as being selfish, for it meant focusing on how individuals see each other. Jesus sought to find in individuals around him something worth valuing, even those whom everyone else would condemn, as evidenced by the story of the tax collector. Rather than accepting the norms of the society in which he lived, Jesus lived, preached and constructed a world in which responsibility for evil and punishment was not the first response to political injustice – instead, he sought to create a world in which our first response to each other was to reconstruct a world that promoted peace and justice. Importantly, that creation meant first looking to the self and being constantly critical of how that self engages the world around us.

This suggests that while punishment should be one response to evil, an alternative and perhaps more difficult one is to undertake the difficult task of political reconstruction. This means working towards alternative formulations of how we understand the political, not those that draw upon distinctions like friend and enemy but those that force us to see each other in new ways. Politics is not easy, for it involves not only promoting ideals but understanding the flaws in oneself that might contribute to the construction of public spheres that render individuals superfluous. There is no easy answer to this dilemma, but only the necessity of recognizing our role in constructing the world that produces such evils. Punishment is only one response to evil – another is to look within ourselves, work towards alternatives and hope that the future will bring forth new beginnings.

Appendix 1

A1.1 Interventions from 1950 to 2005

Number	Start date	End date	Intervenor(s)	Target state	Name	Purpose	Punitive
1	1950	1953	United Nations (US)	Korea		Respond to NK attack	Yes P3
2	1950	1950	France	Côte d'Ivoire		Colonial control	No
3	1952	1956	France	Morocco		Colonial control	No
4	1952	1956	France	Tunisia		Colonial control	No
5	1953	1956	United Kingdom	Kenya		Colonial control	No
6	1953	1959	United Kingdom	Yemen		Border conflict with SA	No
7	1953	1953	Soviet Union	East Germany		Ideology	No
8	1953	1953	United Kingdom	Guyana		Regime change	No
9	1946	1954	France	Vietnam		Colonial/rebellion	No
10	1955	1960	France	Cameroon		Colonial control	No
11	1955	1959	United Kingdom	Cyprus		Enosis movement	No
12	1956	1956	Israel	Egypt		Security	No
13	1956	1956	United Kingdom	Egypt		Empire/economics	No
14	1956	1956	France	Egypt		Empire/economics	No
15	1956	1967	United Nations	Egypt	UNEF I	Ceasefire	No
16	1956	1956	Soviet Union	Hungary		Ideology	No
17	1958	1962	France	Algeria		Colonial control	No
18	1958	1976	United States	Vietnam		Ideology	No
19	1958	1959	France	Congo		Colonial/rebellion	No
20	1958	1958	United States	Lebanon		Civil war	No
21	1947	1962	France	Morocco		Colonial/rebellion	No
22	1959	1962	Belgium	Rwanda/Burundi		Control Hutu attacks on Tutsi	Yes, P2a
23	1959	1960	Belgium	Congo		Protect Europeans in Congo	No
24	1960	1964	United Nations	Congo	ONUC	Halt civil war	No
25	1961	1963	United Kingdom	Brunei		Support Sultan	No
26	1961	1975	Portugal	Angola		Colonial control	No
27	1962	1963	United Kingdom	Guinea		Riots	No
28	1962	1963	United Nations	West New Guinea	UNSF	Decolonization transition	No
29	1962	1967	Egypt	Yemen		Ideology	No
30	1963	1966	Indonesia	Malaysia		Territorial disputes	No
31	1963	1974	Portugal	Guinea-Bissau		Suppress independence	No

continued

A1.1 continued

Number	Start date	End date	Intervenor(s)	Target state	Name	Purpose	Punitive
32	1964	1975	Portugal	Mozambique		Suppress independence	No
33	1964	1964	United States	Panama	Flag Riots	Nationalist dispute	No
34	1964	1964	France	Gabon		Topple a coup	No
35	1965	1965	United States	Dominican Republic		Anti-communism	No
36	1966	1967	France	Djibouti		Protect de Gaulle from riots	No
37	1968	1968	Soviet Union	Czechoslovakia		Protect communist government	No
38	1968	1971	France	Chad		Support Tombolbaye government	No
39	1971	1971	India	E. Pakistan		Punitive/humanitarian	Yes, P3
40	1973	1979	United Nations	Egypt	UNEF II	Ceasefire	No
41	1973	1973	Iraq	Kuwait		Territorial disputes	No
42	1974	1975	Zaire	Angola		US Proxy contra Angola	No
43	1974	1988	South Africa	Namibia		Ideology	No
44	1974		Turkey	Cyprus		Territorial disputes	No
45	1975	1988	Indonesia	East Timor		Territorial disputes	No
46	1975	1988	Cuba (Soviet Union)	Angola		Support communism	No
47	1976	1977	France	Djibouti		Respond to hostage taking	No
48	1976	1978	Syria	Lebanon		Civil War	No
49	1977	1978	Rhodesia	Zambia		War over apartheid	Yes, P3
50	1977	1989	Vietnam	Cambodia		Punitive/humanitarian	No
51	1977	1977	OAU	Zaire		Territorial disputes	No
52	1978	1979	Cuba (Soviet Union)	Somalia	Ogaden War	Territorial disputes	No
53	1978	1978	Israel	Lebanon		Security/capture PLO	Yes, P1
54	1978	1989	Soviet Union	Afghanistan		Civil war/ideology	No
55	1978	1978	France, Belgium	Zaire		Territorial disputes	No
56	1978	1979	Tanzania	Uganda		Security/humanitarian	No
57	1978	1987	Libya	Chad		Civil war/territory	No
58	1978		United Nations	Lebanon	UNFIL	Civil war	No
59	1978	1979	France	Chad		Civil war	No
60	1979	1979	France	Central African Republic		Support coup	No
61	1979	1979	South Africa	Angola		Ideology	No

#			Actor	Location	Mission	Objective	Outcome
62	1982	1982	United Kingdom	Falklands	Malvinas War	Territorial disputes	No
63	1984	1982	United States	Lebanon	Multilateral Force	Civil war	No
64	1984	1982	France	Lebanon	Multilateral Force	Civil war	No
65	1983	1982	Israel	Lebanon		Security/capture PLO	Yes, P1
66	1983	1983	France	Chad		Civil war/Libya involvement	No
67	1983	1983	United States	Grenada		Anti-communism	No
68	1988	1983	India	Maldives		Prevent coup	No
69	1990	1988	United Nations	Namibia	UNTAG	Transition to independence	No
70	1992	1989	United Nations	Central America	ONUCA	Demilitarize/implementation	No
71		1989	Syria	Lebanon		Ideology	No
72	1989	1989	United States	Panama	Operation Just Cause	Capture Noriega	Yes P2a
73	1991	1990	Iraq	Kuwait		Territorial disputes	No
74	1997	1990	ECOWAS	Liberia	ECOMOG	Civil war	No
75	1991	1991	Nigeria	Sierre Leone		Civil war	No
76	2003	1991	United Nations	Iraq	UNIKOM	Monitor ceasefire	No
77	1994	1992	United Nations	Mozambique	UNOMOZ	Assist ceasefire implementation	No
78		1992	Russia	Georgia	JCC	Territory/political control	No
79		1992	Russia	Tajikistan		Territory/political control	No
80		1992	Russia	Moldava		Territory/political control	No
81	1992	1992	United States	Somalia		Humanitarian	Yes P2a
82	1994	1992	United Nations	Somalia	UNSOM	Humanitarian/capture Aideed	Yes P2a
83	1996	1992	United Nations	Cambodia	UNTAC	Ceasefire/elections	No
84	1993	1992	United Nations	Former Yugoslavia	UNPROFOR	Ceasefire, later assist Tribunal	Yes P2b, P3
85	1996	1993	Russia	Abkhazia		Territory/political control	No
86		1993	United Nations	Rwanda	UNAMIR	Ceasefire	No
87	1996	1993	United Nations	Haiti	UNMIH	Implement Governor's Island Accords	No
88		1994	France	Rwanda		Halt civil war/genocide	No
89	1999	1994	United Nations	Macedonia	UNPREDEP	Monitor borders with Yugoslavia	No
90	1997	1995	United Nations	Angola	UNAVEM III	Implement peace accords	No
91	1998	1995	United Nations	Croatia	UNCRO, UNTAES	Ceasefire/Human rights	Yes, P2a,b
92	2002	1995	United Nations	Bosnia/Hercegovina	UNMIBH	Ceasefire/Human rights	Yes P2a,b
93	2004	1996	United Nations/NATO	Bosnia/Hercegovina	SFOR	Ceasefire/Human rights	Yes, P2a,b
94	1999	1997	ECOWAS	Sierre Leone		Civil war	No
95		1997	Italy	Albania		Financial scandal	No
96		1997	United Nations	Angola	MONUA	Consolidate reconciliation	No

continued

A1.1 continued

Number	Start date	End date	Intervenor(s)	Target state	Name	Purpose	Punitive
97	1997	2000	United Nations	Haiti	MIPONUH	Professionalize police force	Yes,P2b
98	1998	2000	United Nations	Central African Republic	MINURCA	Institution building	Yes, P2b
99	1999		NATO, UN	Kosovo	KFOR, UNMIK	Prevent human rights abuses	Yes P3
100	1999	2005	United Nations	Sierre Leone	UNAMSIL	Implement Lomé Accord	No
101	2000		United Kingdom	Sierre Leone	Operation Palliser	Evacuate EU citizens/Support UN	No
102	2000		United Nations	Ethiopia/Eretria	UNMEE	Monitor ceasefire	No
103	2000	2003	United Nations	East Timor	UNTAET	State-building/law and order	Yes, P2b
104	2000		United Nations	Congo	MONUC	Monitor/implement Lukasa Accords	No
105	2001	2004	South Africa/AU	Burundi	SAPSD	Implement Arusha Accords	No
106	2001		United States	Afghanistan		Regime change	Yes, P3
107	2001	2002	United States	Afghanistan		Capture bin Laden	Yes, P1
108	2002		UN/NATO	Afghanistan	ISAF	State-building/law and order	Yes, P2b
109	2002	2005	United Nations	East Timor	UNMISET	State-building/law and order	Yes, P2b
110	2002		France	Côte d'Ivoire	Operation Licorne	Ceasefire	No
111	2003		France	Congo	Operation Artemis	Security/support MONUC	No
112	2003	2004	ECOWAS	Liberia	ECOMIL	Ceasefire	No
113	2003		United Nations	Liberia	UNMIL	Ceasefire/state-building	No
114	2003	2004	ECOWAS	Côte d'Ivoire	ECOMICI	Ceasefire	No
115	2003		United Nations	Côte d'Ivoire	UNOCI	Ceasefire/state-building	No
116	2003		United States	Iraq		Capture Saddam Hussein	Yes P1
117	2003	2004	United States	Iraq		State-building/law and order	Yes, P2b
118	2003		Australia	Solomon Islands	RAMSI	State-building/law and order	Yes P2b
119	2004		EU/UN	Bosnia/Hercegovina	EUFOR	Security, assist ICTFY	Yes P2a
120	2004		United Nations	Haiti	MINUSTAH	Security, policing	No
121	2004		United Nations	Burundi	ONUB	Ceasefire/human rights	No
122	2004		United Nations	Côte d'Ivoire	UNOCI	Ceasefire/state-building	No
123	2005		United Nations	Sudan	UNMIS	Ceasefire/state-building	Yes P2b

Appendix 2

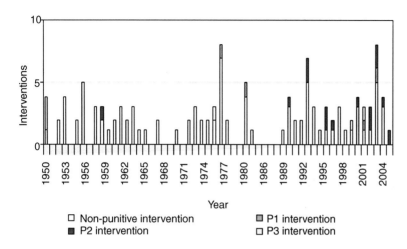

Figure A2.1 Punitive intervention, 1950–2005.

Notes

1 See the introductory essay in Robert Solomon and Mark Murphy, eds, *What is Justice? Classical and Contemporary Readings*, 2nd edn (Oxford: Oxford University Press, 2000): 3–10.
2 Any review of the news suggests this to be the case as well. As I was writing this chapter, then Prime Minister Tony Blair had just proposed a radical rethinking of criminal justice procedures in the United Kingdom, what he wished to see as one of the legacies of his tenure in government. See Patrick Wintourn and Tania Branigan, "Prime Minister Accuses Legal Establishment and Insists on Summary Justice Drive" *The Guardian*, 23 June 2006.
3 Martin Wight, "Why is There No International Theory?" in Herbert Butterfield and Martin Wight, eds, *Diplomatic Investigations* (London: Allen and Unwin, 1966): 17–34. The literature on international political theory is growing rapidly; for a good introduction, see Chris Brown, *Sovereignty, Rights and Justice: International Political Theory Today* (Cambridge: Polity Press, 2002). For a historical context, see Edward Keene, *International Political Thought: A Historical Introduction* (Cambridge: Polity Press, 2005).
4 The "dean" of this field is M. Cherif Bassiouni. See his *Introduction to International Criminal Law* (Ardsley NY: Transaction Publishers, 2003) for a good overview of the legal issues. For a historical treatment, see Gary Bass, *Stay the Hand of Vengeance: The Politics of War Crimes Tribunals* (Princeton: Princeton University Press, 2000). For a very good philosophical treatment of international criminal law, see Larry May, *Crimes against Humanity: a Normative Account* (Cambridge: Cambridge University Press, 2004). For critical analyses of punishment in international criminal law, see Mark Drumbl, *Punishment, Atrocity and International Law* (Cambridge: Cambridge University Press, 2007) and Jan Klabbers, "Just Revenge? The Deterrence Argument in International Criminal Law" *Finnish Yearbook of International Law* 12 (2001): 249–267.
5 There are some attempts to explore punishment more broadly in international relations. For some initial efforts, see Oded Lowenheim, *Predators and Parasites: Persistent Agents of Transnational Harm and Great Power Authority* (Ann Arbour: University of Michigan Press, 2007) and Harry Gould, "State Crime: Conceptual Clarifications" International Studies Association Convention 2007, Chicago.
6 See Anthony F. Lang Jr, Joel H. Rosenthal and Albert C. Pierce, eds, *Ethics and the Future of Conflict: Lessons from the 1990s* (Upper Saddle River, NJ: Prentice Hall, 2004) for a set of essays that emphasizes the transitional nature of this time frame, although in order to make a different point.
7 This section is not a contribution to a disciplinary debate in international

relations; indeed, if it was, I would be examining a much wider array of conceptual positions (constructivism, post-modernism, critical theory, feminism, ad infinitum). Instead, realism and liberalism seem to represent the clearest expressions of a wide array of different understandings of the international.

8 See John Mearsheimer, *The Tragedy of Great Power Politics* (New York: W. W. Norton, 2001).

9 See Robert Keohane, *Power and Governance in a Partially Globalized World* (London: Routledge, 2002).

10 See Mervyn Frost, *Constituting Human Rights: Global Civil Society and the Society of Democratic States* (London: Routledge, 2002).

11 See David Chandler, *From Kosovo to Kabul: Human Rights and International Intervention* (London: Pluto Press, 2002).

12 One exception here is the recent work of Andrew Williams, *Liberalism and War: The Victors and the Vanquished* (Abingdon: Routledge, 2006). Williams explores a range of ways in which liberal states have dealt with victory in war, including punishments as expressed in the reparations debate following the First World War.

13 There is one genre of realist writing that does employ the term punishment, but in a very different way than I employ it here. Strategic theorists, specifically those working on questions of deterrence and coercive diplomacy have argued that certain uses of force are "punitive" in comparison with those that are a form of "denial." The distinction here is between a use of force designed to hurt an opponent's civilians (punishment) and a use of force designed to halt its military (denial). The difference from this use and how I am using it here is that the strategic theorist is interested in a use of force in order to protect one individual agent, while punishment is designed to enforce a set of rules that govern a society as a whole. Deterrence according to the strategist might lead to the enforcement of the rules over the long run, but it is not designed to do that; rather it is only designed to protect the one agent. See Glenn Snyder, *Deterrence and Defence: Toward a Theory of National Security* (Princeton: Princeton University Press, 1961) for a classic statement of this distinction and Robert Pape, *Bombing to Win: Air Power and Coercion in War* (Ithaca: Cornell University Press, 1996) for a use of the term punishment in the context of coercive diplomacy.

14 See Kenneth Waltz, *Theory of International Politics* (New York: McGraw Hill, 1979) for the clearest articulation of this tenet of realist theory.

15 Hans J. Morgenthau, "Views of Nuremberg: Further Analysis of the Trial and its Importance" *America*, 7 December 1946: 266–267.

16 See Benjamin Mollov, *Power and Transcendence: Hans J. Morgenthau and the Jewish Experience* (Lanham: Lexington Books, 2002) for an account of Morgenthau's ethics as resulting from his religious background, which includes this divine command ethic. While Morgenthau's understanding of ethics largely draws on this divine command model, it also includes a more nuanced, Aristotelian inspired dimension; see Anthony F. Lang, Jr, "Morgenthau, Agency and Aristotle" in Michael J. Williams, ed., *Realism Reconsidered: The Legacy of Hans J. Morgenthau in International Relations* (Oxford: Oxford University Press, 2007): 18–41.

17 The one exception to this point is Hans Kelsen, whose work I explore in Chapter 2.

18 For examples from this burgeoning literature, see Chandra Sriram, *Confronting Past Human Rights Violations: Justice vs. Peace in Times of Transition* (London: Frank Cass, 2004); Jon Elster, *Closing the Books: Transitional Justice in Historical Perspective* (Cambridge: Cambridge University Press,

2004); Mohammed Abu-Nimer, ed., *Reconciliation, Justice and Coexistence* (Lanham: Lexington Books, 2001); and M. Cherif Bassiouni, ed., *Post-Conflict Justice* (Ardsley NY: Transnational Publishers, 2002).

19 See David Cortwright, *et al.*, *Sanctions and the Search for Security: Challenges to UN Action* (Boulder CO: Lynne Rienner, 2002) for arguments for smart sanctions.

20 See Mervyn Frost, *Constituting Human Rights: Global Civil Society and the Society of Democratic States* (London: Routledge, 2002) for an analysis of how human rights constitutes the international order. See David P. Forsythe, *Human Rights in International Relations*, 2nd edn (Cambridge: Cambridge University Press, 2006) for how human rights are manifested in particular international practices and institutions.

21 See Anthony F. Lang, Jr, ed., *Just Intervention* (Washington DC: Georgetown University Press, 2003) for some essays on the normative dimensions of intervention.

22 A. John Simmons, "Introduction" in Simmons, ed., *Punishment: A Philosophy and Public Affairs Reader* (Princeton: Princeton University Press, 1993): viii.

23 The literature on punishment is vast. Throughout this book, I will reference texts as they relate to the specific issues I am addressing. Comprehensive edited collections of philosophical arguments about punishment include H. B. Acton, ed., *The Philosophy of Punishment: A Collection of Papers* (London: Macmillan, 1969); Antony Duff, *Punishment* (Brookfield VT: Aldershot Publishers, 1993); and A. John Simmons, ed., *Punishment: A Philosophy and Public Affairs Reader* (Princeton: Princeton University Press, 1995). Single authored philosophical accounts of punishment from which I have benefited include C. L. Ten, *Crime, Guilt and Punishment: A Philosophical Introduction* (Oxford: Clarendon Press, 1987); John Braithwaite and Philip Petit, *Not Just Deserts: A Republican Theory of Criminal Justice* (Oxford: Clarendon Press, 1990) and Matt Matravers, *Justice and Punishment: The Rationale of Coercion* (Oxford: Oxford University Press, 2000). As a historical and social practice, sociologists and historians have also explored punishment in some depth; the most famous such account is Michel Foucault, *Discipline and Punish: The Birth of the Prison*, translated by Alan Sheridan (New York: Pantheon Books, 1977). An excellent introduction to punishment in the domestic legal context of the United Kingdom is Susan Easton and Christine Piper, *Sentencing and Punishment: The Quest for Justice* (Oxford: Oxford University Press, 2005). For two accounts focusing on the United States and punishment, see Thomas L. Dumm, *Democracy and Punishment: Disciplinary Origins of the US* (Madison: University of Wisconsin Press, 1987) and Mark Kann, *Punishment, Prisons and Patriarchy: Liberty and Power in the Early American Republic* (New York: New York University Press, 2005).

24 James Rachels, "Punishment and Desert" in Hugh LaFollette, ed., *Ethics in Practice: An Anthology*, 2nd edn (Oxford: Blackwell Publishers, 2002): 468.

25 Jeffrie Murphy has made this point in various places; see, for example, "Marxism and Retribution" in Simmons, ed., *Punishment: A Philosophy and Public Affairs Reader*: 3–29.

26 See Alan Goldman "The Paradox of Punishment" in Simmons, *Punishment: A Philosophy and Public Affairs Reader*: 30–46 for an attempt to address the problem of excessive punishment.

27 See Simmons, "Introduction" *Punishment: A Philosophy and Public Affairs Reader*: viii.

28 Easton and Piper, *Sentencing and Punishment*: 19.

29 Easton and Piper, *Sentencing and Punishment*: 23–24.
30 Peter Liberman, "An Eye for an Eye: Public Support for War against Evildoers" *International Organization* 60 (Summer 2006): 687–722.
31 See Helena Cobban, "Think Again: International Courts" *Foreign Policy* (March/April 2006): 23–28 for one of the clearest critiques of the international court system, including a critique of punishment.
32 As will be explored in more depth in Chapter 5, the debate over economic sanctions has focused on whether or not sanctions should be punitive or coercive. See David Cortright and George Lopez, with Richard W. Conroy, Jaleh Dashti-Gibson and Julia Wagler, *The Sanctions Decade: Assessing UN Strategies in the 1990s* (Boulder CO: Lynne Rienner Publishers, 2000).
33 Michel Foucault, "History of Systems of Thought" in *Language, Counter-memory and Practice: Selected Essays and Interviews*, translated and edited by Donald Bouchard (Ithaca: Cornell University Press, 1977): 199.
34 Michel Foucault, *Discipline and Punish: The Birth of the Prison*, trans by Alan Sheridan (New York: Vintage Books, 1977).
35 Cesare Beccaria, *On Crimes and Punishments and Other Writings*, Richard Bellemy, ed. (Cambridge: Cambridge University Press, 1995).
36 See Adrian Howe, *Punish and Critique: Toward a Feminist Analysis of Penalty* (New York: Routledge, 1994) for a review of some of these ideas.
37 Foucault, *Discipline and Punish*: 201.
38 "Intellectuals and Power: An Interview with Giles Deluze" in Foucault, *Language, Counter-memory, Practice*: 210.
39 Foucault, of course, follows Nietzsche here, whose ideas would take this work in a completely different direction. Nietzsche's conception of punishment as an instance of power is part of his larger conception of morality and ethics, one that I find interesting but not completely convincing. See Friedrich Nietzsche, *On the Genealogy of Morality*, edited by Keith Ansell-Pearson (Cambridge: Cambridge University Press, 1994).
40 Andrew Hurrell, "Order and Justice in International Relations: What is at Stake?" in Rosemary Foot, John Lewis Gaddis and Andrew Hurrell, eds, *Order and Justice in International Relations* (Oxford: Oxford University Press, 2003): 25. See also Nicholas Rengger's study of order and international relations theory; *International Relations, Political Theory and the Problem of Order: Beyond International Relations Theory?* (London: Routledge, 2000).
41 This distinction between two conceptions of politics comes from Michael Oakeshott; see "Rationalism in Politics" in Michael Oakeshott, *Rationalism in Politics and Other Essays, New and Expanded Edition* (Indianapolis: Liberty Press, 1991): 5–42. For an application of this distinction to international affairs, see Terry Nardin, *Law, Morality and the Relations of States* (Princeton: Princeton University Press, 1983).
42 Hedley Bull, *Justice in International Relations* (Waterloo: University of Waterloo, 1984).
43 Rule following is not as simple a process as this section suggests. For some conceptual issues concerning rules and rule following, see Anthony F. Lang, Jr, Nicholas J. Rengger and William Walker, "The Role(s) of Rules: Some Conceptual Clarifications" *International Relations* 20, 3 (September 2006): 274–294.
44 See Oded Lowenheim, *Predators and Parasites: Persistent Agents of Transnational Harm and Great Power Authority* (Ann Arbour: University of Michigan Press, 2007) for a study of the role that great powers play in enforcing the rules of the international system especially in their punitive treatment of those agents who stand outside the norms of the system, such as pirates or terrorists.

45 Stanley Hoffman, *World Disorders: Troubled Peace in a post-Cold War Era* (Lanham: Rowman and Littlefield, 1998).

46 G. John Ikenberry, *After Victory: Institutions, Strategic Restraint, the Rebuilding of Order after Major Wars* (Princeton: Princeton University Press, 2000).

47 Hans Morgenthau presents the best example of such a theorist; see *Politics Among Nations*, 6th edn (New York: Alfred A. Knopf Publishers, 1986). Nicholas Rengger demonstrates how realists sustain such an order in *International Relations, Political Theory and the Problem of Order*.

48 See, for example, Oliver Richmond, *Making Order, Making Peace* (New York: Palgrave, 2002) and *The Transformation of Peace* (New York: Palgrave, 2005).

49 Robert Keohane, *Power and Governance in a Partially Globalized World* (London: Routledge, 2002): 51–53.

50 See Judith Goldstein, Miles Kahler, Robert Keohane and Anne-Marie Slaughter, eds, "Legalization and World Politics" Special Issue of *International Organization* 54, 3 (2000).

51 See Allan Buchanan and Robert Keohane, "The Preventive Use of Force: A Cosmopolitan Institutional Proposal" *Ethics & International Affairs* 18, 1 (2004): 1–22; Ruth W. Grant and Robert Keohane, "Accountability and Abuses of Power in World Politics" *American Political Science Review* 99, 1 (February 2005): 29–43; Allan Buchanan and Robert Keohane, "The Legitimacy of Global Governance Institutions" *Ethics & International Affairs* 20, 4 (2006): 405–438; and Robert Keohane, "Decisiveness and Accountability as Part of a Principled Response to Nonstate Threats" *Ethics & International Affairs* 20, 2 (2006): 219–224.

52 See, for instance, Robert Keohane, *After Hegemony: Cooperation and Discord in the World Political Economy* (Princeton: Princeton University Press, 1984).

53 Anthony F. Lang, Jr, "Punitive Justifications or Just Punishment? An Ethical Reading of Coercive Diplomacy" *Cambridge Review of International Affairs* 19, 3 (2006): 389–403.

54 Anthony F. Lang, Jr, "Normative Causes and Consequences: Understanding and Evaluating the War with Iraq" in Raymond Hinnebusch and Rick Fawn, eds, *The Iraq War: Causes and Consequences* (Boulder CO: Lynne Rienner Publishers, 2006): 269–282 and "The Violence of Rules: Rethinking the 2003 War against Iraq" *Contemporary Politics* 13, 3 (September, 2007): 257–276. While the war against Iraq can be explained by a wide range of reasons, the point of these two articles is that punishment for violations of norms and rules did play a central role in the decision-making and justification surrounding the war in the US and UK.

55 I use the term criminal here rather than accused because once punishment becomes part of the process, the assumption is that the agent has already been found guilty by some judicial process.

56 John Rawls, *A Theory of Justice* (Cambridge: Belknap Press, 1971).

57 Robert Nozick, *Anarchy, State and Utopia* (Oxford: Blackwell, 1974).

58 Allen Buchanan, *Justice, Legitimacy and Self-Determination: Moral Foundations for International Law* (Oxford: Oxford University Press, 2004) and Simon Caney, *Justice Beyond Borders: A Global Political Theory* (Oxford: Oxford University Press, 2005).

59 It is important to emphasize that harm is inflicted by punishment, but the individual who has committed the violation is the one harmed. So, punishment does not prevent harm in general, but is intended to protect those who obey the rules from being harmed.

60 Gerry Simpson, *Great Powers and Outlaw States: Unequal Sovereigns in the International Legal Order* (Cambridge: Cambridge University Press, 2003). See also Galia Press-Barnathan, "The War against Iraq and International Order: From Bull to Bush" *International Studies Review* 6, 2 (June 2004): 195–212 and Renee de Nevers, "Imposing International Norms: Great Powers and Norm Enforcement" *International Studies Review* 9, 1 (Spring 2007): 53–80.

61 See Robert S. Litwak, *Rogue States and US Foreign Policy: Containment After the Cold War* (Baltimore: Johns Hopkins University Press, 2000), which traces this doctrine back to the first Bush and Clinton administrations.

62 See Toni Erskine, "Assigning Responsibilities to Institutional Moral Agents: The Case of States and Quasi-States" *Ethics & International Affairs* 15, 2 (2001): 67–87 for one account of how certain states should not be labelled as sovereign, yet they are held responsible for specific outcomes in the international system.

63 John Rawls, "Two Concepts of Rules" [1954] in H. B. Acton, ed. *The Philosophy of Punishment: Collected Papers* (London: Macmillan, 1969): 108.

64 See Anthony F. Lang, Jr, "Crime and Punishment: Holding States Accountable" *Ethics & International Affairs* 21, 2 (2007): 389–403.

65 For an intellectual history of constitutionalism, see Charles Howard McIlwain, *Constitutionalism, Ancient and Modern* (Ithaca: Great Seal Books, 1958). For philosophical analyses of constitutionalism, see Larry Alexander, ed., *Constitutionalism: Philosophical Foundations* (Cambridge: Cambridge University Press, 1998).

66 See Jose Alverez, *International Organizations as Law Makers* (Oxford: Oxford University Press, 2005), a text that includes a chapter on constitutional interpretation.

67 Nicholas Onuf, *The Republican Legacy in International Thought* (Cambridge: Cambridge University Press, 1998) and Daniel Deudney, *Bounding Power: Republican Security Theory from the Polis to the Global Village* (Princeton: Princeton University Press, 2006) are two central thinkers on this issue. An older body of literature exploring the idea of internationalism also has relevance here; see Cornelia Navari, *Internationalism and the State in the 20th Century* (New York: Routledge, 2000) and Michelene Ishay, *Internationalism and its Betrayal* (Minneapolis: University of Minnesota Press, 1995).

68 Witnessing the construction of the Iraqi constitutional framework demonstrates the challenges of this task; for an insider's view of this process, see Larry Diamond, *Squandered Victory: The American Occupation and the Bungled Effort to Bring Democracy to Iraq* (New York: Owl Books, 2006).

69 *The International Law Commission's Articles on State Responsibility: Introduction, Text and Commentary*, edited by James Crawford (Cambridge: Cambridge University Press, 2001). For a legal analysis of the ILC's work, see Nina H. B. Jogensen, *The Responsibility of States for International Crimes* (Oxford: Oxford University Press, 2000).

70 See Cian O'Driscoll, "Re-negotiating the Just War: The Invasion of Iraq and Punitive War" *Cambridge Review of International Affairs* 19, 3 (September 2006): 405–420.

71 The concept of "new war" has been popularized by Mary Kaldor in *New and Old Wars* (Cambridge: Polity Press, 1999). Gilbert's book is *New Terror, New War* (Washington DC: Georgetown University Press, 2003).

72 Gilbert, *New Terror, New Wars*: 16–19.

73 He goes on to critique attempts to create justice through international courts as well; see, ibid., pp. 122–126.

74 For a critique of the self-defence claim as a justification for the war with Iraq, see Anthony F. Lang, Jr, "Normative Causes and Consequences: Understanding and Evaluating the War with Iraq" in Raymond Hinnebusch and Rick Fawn, eds, *The Iraq War: Causes and Consequences* (Boulder CO: Lynne Rienner Publishers, 2006): 269–282.

75 For two general introductions to questions of political authority, see Richard Flathman, *The Practice of Political Authority: Authority and the Authoritative* (Chicago: University of Chicago Press, 1980) and Joseph Raz, ed., *Authority* (Oxford: Blackwell, 1990).

76 For a clear and interesting comparison of Hobbes and Locke, although not on the issue of punishment, see Ross Harrison, *Hobbes, Locke and Confusion's Masterpiece: An Examination of Seventeenth-Century Political Philosophy* (Cambridge: Cambridge University Press, 2003). The secondary literature on both these thinkers is voluminous, and I have only drawn on those works that are relevant for my purposes here.

77 See Leo Strauss, *The Political Philosophy of Thomas Hobbes: Its Basis and Genesis*, translated from German by Elsa M. Sinclair (Oxford: Oxford University Press, 1936).

78 Thomas Hobbes, *Leviathan*, introduced by C. B. MacPherson (London: Penguin Books [1651] 1968): chapter 13, p. 183. All page references are to the Penguin edition.

79 Hobbes, *Leviathan*, chapter 14, pp. 190–193.

80 Jean Hampton, *Hobbes and the Social Contract Tradition* (Cambridge: Cambridge University Press, 1986).

81 Hobbes, *Leviathan*, chapter 25, p. 303.

82 The question of obligation in Hobbes work has been the subject of some dispute in twentieth-century studies of Hobbes. See Howard Warrender, *The Political Philosophy of Thomas Hobbes: His Theory of Obligation* (Oxford: Oxford University Press, 1957), who argues that Hobbes' justification for obedience is not based on this fear of harm from each other but upon a divinely grounded natural law. For my purposes in this chapter, the source of that obligation does not matter so much as that obedience to authority is central to Hobbes' whole philosophy.

83 Hobbes, *Leviathan*, Introduction, p. 81.

84 Hobbes, *Leviathan*, chapter 28, p. 353.

85 Hobbes, *Leviathan*, chapter 15, p. 210.

86 Mario A. Cattaneo, "Hobbes' Theory of Punishment" in K. C. Brown, ed., *Hobbes Studies* (Oxford: Basil Blackwell, 1965): 275–298.

87 There is an important puzzle in Hobbes concerning the agreement by those entering the social contract; that no individual would give up his right to defend himself, even if he is being punished for a crime he committed. This dilemma results from Hobbes' focus on the rights of individuals as the foundation for the social contract. I do not explore this issue at all here, but for one treatment of it – which concludes that this dilemma actually undermines Hobbes' overall philosophy – see Thomas S. Schrock, "The Rights to Punish and Resist Punishment in Hobbes' Leviathan" *The Western Political Quarterly* 44, 4 (December 1991): 853–890.

88 Hobbes, *Leviathan*, chapter 28, pp. 356–357.

89 His third law of nature deals with justice, which he defines as the keeping of covenants; Hobbes, *Leviathan*, chapter 15, p. 202. Not only is justice placed after peace, but by defining it as the keeping of covenants, Hobbes does not give it the same importance as peace in his theoretical framework.

90 In his Straussian reading of John Locke, Richard Cox argues that Locke's

premises do not differ that much from Hobbes; see Richard Cox, *Locke on War and Peace* (Oxford: Clarendon Press, 1960).

91 See C. B. Macpherson, "Editor's Introduction" John Locke, *Second Treatise of Government* (Indianapolis: Hackett Publishing Co, 1980 [1690]). For further background on Locke's historical context, see Ian Harris, *The Mind of John Locke: A Study of Political Theory in its Intellectual Setting*, rev. edn (Cambridge: Cambridge University Press, 1994). For an excellent recent biography of Locke, see Roger Woolhouse, *Locke: A Biography* (Cambridge: Cambridge University Press, 2007).

92 Locke, *Second Treatise of Government*, Book VII, sec. 91, pp. 48–49. All page number references are to the Hackett edition.

93 C. B. Macpherson famously argued that the importance of property and bourgeois society more broadly are central to both Hobbes' and Locke's political theories. I find this more plausible in Locke than in Hobbes. See C. B. Macpherson, *The Political Philosophy of Possessive Individualism* (Oxford: Oxford University Press, 1962).

94 Locke, *Second Treatise*, Book I, sec. 3, p. 8.

95 A. John Simmons, "Locke and the Right to Punish" *Philosophy and Public Affairs* 20, 4 (1991): 311–349; for an extension of this argument and other themes in Locke, see A. John Simmons, *The Lockean Theory of Rights* (Princeton: Princeton University Press, 1992).

96 Locke, *Second Treatise*: Book II, sec. 7, pp. 9–10.

97 Simmons, "Locke and the Right to Punish": 316.

98 Locke, *Second Treatise*, Book VII, sec. 88, p. 47.

99 Ibid.

100 Locke, *Second Treatise*, Book II, sec. 9, pp. 10–11.

101 Locke, *Second Treatise*, Book II, sec. 11, p. 11.

102 Locke, *Second Treatise*, Book II, sec. 12, p. 12.

103 Locke, *Second Treatise*, Book II, sec. 13, p. 12.

104 See Hugo Grotius, *The Free Sea*, edited and with an introduction by David Armitage (Indianapolis: Liberty Fund, 2004) for the text, Welwod's critique and Grotius' response.

105 Hugo Grotius, *The Rights of War and Peace*, edited and with an introduction by Richard Tuck (Indianapolis: Liberty Fund, 2005): Book II, chapter 1, sec. I, pp. 393–396. All page references are from the Liberty Fund edition.

106 Terry Nardin "The Moral Basis for Humanitarian Intervention" in Anthony F. Lang, Jr, ed., *Just Intervention* (Washington DC: Georgetown University Press, 2003): 13–14.

107 For an exploration of humanism as it relates to questions of war and peace, see Richard Tuck, *The Rights of War and Peace: Political Thought and International Order from Grotius to Kant* (Oxford: Oxford University Press, 1999).

108 See, for instance, Vitoria's arguments about the foundations of papal authority, which, while supporting, he also carefully circumscribed; "On the Power of the Church" [1532] in Vitoria, *Political Writings*, introduced and edited by Anthony Pagden (Cambridge: Cambridge University Press, 1991): 45–152.

109 Grotius, *De Jure Belli ac Pacis*, Book I, chap I, sec 8, p. 142.

110 See, ibid., the extensive footnote from the French translator of Grotius, Jean Barbeyrac who disputes Grotius' understanding of Aristotle.

111 *De Jure Belli ac Pacis*, Book II, chapter 20, sec. 2, p. 953.

112 Ibid., Book II, chapter 20, sec. 3, p. 955.

113 Ibid., Book II, chapter 20, sec. 38, p. 1018.

114 Ibid., Book II, chapter 20, secs 40–51.

115   Ibid., Book I, chapter 3, p. 250.

116   Although, one could argue that Vitoria precedes Grotius here. My view is that Vitoria is not so much authorizing action in defence of human rights, but seeking to prevent the abuse of rights by those intervening for other reasons. Thanks to Patrick Hayden for pressing me on this point.

117   Ibid., Book II, chapter 20, sec. 43.

118   Hans Kelsen, *General Theory of Law and State* (Cambridge: Harvard University Press, 1946): 19.

119   Kelsen, *General Theory of Law and State*: 106.

120   David Rodin, *War and Self-Defense* (Oxford: Clarendon Press, 2004): 176.

121   Hans Kelsen, *Peace through Law* (Chapel Hill NC: University of North Carolina Press, 1944).

122   See the appendix to *Peace through Law* that lays out a proposed treaty for the creation of a new international institution, the central aspect of which is the judiciary; pp. 127–140.

123   Kenneth Abbott, Robert O. Keohane, Andrew Moravcsik, Anne-Marie Slaughter and Duncan Snidal, "The Concept of Legalization" *International Organization* 54, 3 (2000): 401–419. See also the essays in Part II of Robert Keohane, *Power and Governance in a Partially Globalized World* (London: Routledge, 2002).

124   See John F. Murphy, *The United States and the Rule of Law in International Affairs* (Cambridge: Cambridge University Press, 2004) and Phillippe Sands, *Lawless World: America and the Making and Breaking of Global Rules* (London: Allen Lane, 2005).

125   See Anthony F. Lang, Jr, Nicholas Rengger and William Walker, "The Role(s) of Rules: Some Conceptual Clarifications" *International Relations* 20 (2006): 274–294.

126   See Christopher C. Joyner, ed., *The United Nations and International Law* (Cambridge: Cambridge University Press, 1997).

127   Philip Allot, "Intergovernmental Societies and the Idea of Constitutionalism" in Jean-Marc Coicaud and Veijo Heiskanen, eds, *The Legitimacy of International Organizations* (Tokyo: The United Nations University Press, 2001): 69–103.

128   Jose Alverez, "Constitutional Interpretation in International Organizations" in Coicaud and Heiskanen, eds, *The Legitimacy of International Organizations*: 104–154.

129   Jan Klabbers, "Two Concepts of International Organization" *International Organizations Law Review* 2 (2005): 277–293.

130   Thanks for Torsten Michel for a very rigorous reading of this chapter.

131   Fourth Report of the Prosecutor of the International Criminal Court, Mr Luis Moreno Ocampo, to the UN Security Council Pursuant to UNSCR 1593 (2005), 14 December 2006. Accessed from the ICC website on 16 December 2006; www.icc-cpi.int/library/organs/otp/OTP_ReportUNSC4Darfur_English. pdf: 2.

132   See Fourth Report, pp. 3–4. The section of UNSCR 1591 that details the sanctions system is Operative Paragraph 3. Accessed on 16 December 2006 from the UN Security Council website; daccessdds.un.org/doc/UNDOC/GEN/ N05/287/89/PDF/N0528789.pdf?OpenElement.

133   I have been writing about agency in various contexts for the past few years. As a result, this section is drawn from different published sources: Anthony F. Lang, Jr, *Agency and Ethics: The Politics of Military Intervention* (Albany NY: SUNY Press, 2002), particularly chapter 1; Anthony F. Lang, Jr and John Williams, "Between International Politics and International Ethics" in

Lang and Williams, eds, *Hannah Arendt and International Relations: Reading Across the Lines* (New York: Palgrave, 2005): 221–232; and Anthony F. Lang, Jr, "Morgenthau, Agency and Aristotle" in Michael Williams, ed., *Realism Reconsidered: The Legacy of Hans J. Morgenthau in International Relations* (Oxford: Oxford University Press, 2007): 18–41.

134 Although it is interesting to see how humans often need to explain the results of natural disasters by means of some being's agency. Susan Neiman highlights how the Enlightenment response to the earthquakes in Lisbon in 1755 radically reshaped understandings of evil and agency; Susan Neiman, *Evil in Modern Thought: An Alternative History of Philosophy* (Princeton: Princeton University Press, 2004).

135 Kenneth Waltz, *Theory of International Politics* (Boston: Addison-Wesley, 1979).

136 See Robert Keohane, ed., *Neorealism and its Critics* (New York: Columbia University Press, 1986).

137 Alexander Wendt, "The Agent-Structure Problem in International Relations Theory" *International Organization* 41 (1987): 335–370; see also Alexander Wendt, *Social Theory of International Politics* (Cambridge: Cambridge University Press, 1999): 139–192.

138 Constructivism has become a broad church. While Wendt's work defines one version, other approaches focus on the international law as the primary structure, while others look to moral norms as providing structures. For an early use of the term constructivism, and for one of the best analyses from this legal perspective, see Nicholas Onuf, *World of Our Making: Rules and Rule in Social Theory and International Relations* (Columbia: University of South Carolina Press, 1989).

139 For a recent example of this kind of rigour, see Colin Wight, *Agents, Structures and International Relations: Politics as Ontology* (Cambridge: Cambridge University Press, 2006).

140 One individual who has explored questions of moral agency and responsibility in terms of global politics is Toni Erskine; see Toni Erskine, "Assigning Responsibility to Institutional Agents: The Case of States and Quasi-States" *Ethics & International Affairs* 15 (2001): 67–85 and Toni Erskine, ed., *Can Institutions have Responsibilities? Collective Moral Agency and International Relations* (New York: Palgrave, 2003).

141 Harry Frankfurt, "Freedom of the Will and the Concept of a Person" in John Martin Fischer, ed., *Moral Responsibility* (Ithaca: Cornell University Press, 1986): 65–80, originally published in *Journal of Philosophy* 68 (January 1971): 5–20.

142 Charles Taylor, "What is Human Agency?" in Taylor, *Philosophical Papers Volume I: Human Agency and Language* (Cambridge: Cambridge University Press, 1985): 15–44, originally published in T. Mischel, ed., *The Self* (Oxford: Blackwell Publishers, 1977): 103–135.

143 Peter Strawson, "Freedom and Resentment" in John Martin Fischer and Mark Ravizza, eds, *Perspectives on Moral Responsibility* (Ithaca: Cornell University Press, 1993): 45–66, originally from *Proceedings of the British Academy* 48 (1962): 1–25. Strawson's argument is not without some controversy among philosophers; see the essays following Strawson's in the Fischer and Ravizza book.

144 Strawson, p. 48.

145 Alasdair MacIntyre, "Social Structures and their Threats to Moral Agency" *Philosophy* 74 (1999): 311–329. I am indebted to Amanda Beattie for bringing this article to my attention.

162   *Notes*

146 Hannah Arendt, *The Human Condition* (Chicago: University of Chicago Press, 1958).
147 Arendt, *The Human Condition*: 41.
148 Arendt, *The Human Condition*: 176.
149 Arendt, *The Human Condition*: 182.
150 Hannah Arendt, *Eichmann in Jerusalem: A Report on the Banality of Evil*, revised and enlarged edition (New York: Penguin Books, 1964).
151 See Hannah Arendt, *Responsibility and Judgment*, introduced and edited by Jerome Kohn (New York: Schocken Books, 2003), particularly the essays "Personal Responsibility Under Dictatorship" (17–48) and "Collective Responsibility" (147–158).
152 For a different critique of international punitive institutions modelled on the domestic legal ideal, see Mark A. Drumbl, *Atrocity, Punishment and International Law* (Cambridge: Cambridge University Press, 2007). I return to Drumbl's critical analysis in Chapter 7, one I find quite important and insightful.
153 Letter 43, Hannah Arendt to Karl Jaspers, 17 August 1946 in *Hannah Arendt Karl Jaspers Correspondence, 1926–1969*, edited by Lotte Kohler and Hans Sauer (New York: Harcourt, Brace, Jovanovich, 1985): 54.
154 Arendt, "Collective Responsibility": 149.
155 I am less interested in tracing the origins of Arendt's ideas about political responsibility in this book, although their trajectory is quite interesting. It would appear that some of her ideas on this topic arose from her engagement with the work of Karl Jaspers, particularly her response to his book, *The Question of German Guilt* [*Die Schuldfrage*], trans by E. B. Ashton, introduced by Joseph W. Koterski, S. J., (New York: Fordham University Press, 2000 [1947]). Arendt and Jaspers debated his conception of responsibility briefly in an exchange of letters; see Letters 43, 45 and 50 in *Hannah Arendt Karl Jaspers Correspondence, 1926–1969*: 51–70.
156 Arendt, "Collective Responsibility": 157–158.
157 Arendt, "Personal Responsibility Under Dictatorship": 26.
158 Letter 50, Hannah Arendt to Karl Jaspers, 17 December 1946 in *Hannah Arendt Karl Jaspers Correspondence, 1926–1969*: 69.
159 Lang, "Crime and Punishment: Holding States Accountable."
160 Some of the ideas in this chapter were first developed in my "Punitive Intervention: Enforcing Justice or Creating Conflict?" in Mark Evans, ed., *Just War Theory: A Reappraisal* (Edinburgh: Edinburgh University Press, 2005): 50–70.
161 Anthony F. Lang, Jr, *Agency and Ethics: The Politics of Military Intervention* (Albany: SUNY Press, 2001) and Anthony F. Lang, Jr, ed., *Just Intervention* (Washington DC: Georgetown University Press, 2003).
162 Boutros Boutros-Ghali, *Unvanquished: A U.S.-UN Saga* (New York: Random House, 1999): 98–100.
163 A mission mandate that was reiterated in Security Council Resolution 1706 of 31 August 2006, which increased the size of the force to 17,000 troops from the original 10,000.
164 See www.icc-cpi.int/pressrelease_details&id=107.html.
165 See the website of UNMIS for more information about its various tasks, including special sections devoted to policing and the rule of law; www.unmis.org.
166 See Lang, *Agency and Ethics*: 155–185 for more on this case and the literature surrounding it.
167 See Alex Bellamy, "Responsibility to Protect or Trojan Horse? The Crisis in

Darfur and Humanitarian Intervention after Iraq" *Ethics & International Affairs* 19, 2 (2005): 31–54.

168 See Anthony F. Lang, Jr, "Introduction: Humanitarian Intervention – Definitions and Debates" in Lang, ed., *Just Intervention* (Washington DC: Georgetown University Press, 2003): 1–10.

169 See R. J. Vincent, *Non-Intervention and International Order* (Princeton: Princeton University Press, 1974).

170 See Nicholas Wheeler, *Saving Strangers* (Oxford: Oxford University Press, 2000) for an account of intervention that demonstrates how various Cold War interventions might be understood as humanitarian by focusing on their consequences rather than the intentions of the interveners.

171 Terry Nardin, "Introduction" in Terry Nardin and Melissa Williams, eds, *Humanitarian Intervention* (New York: New York University Press, 2006): 1.

172 J. L. Holzgrefe, "The Humanitarian Intervention Debate" in J. L. Holzgrefe and Robert O. Keohane, eds, *Humanitarian Intervention: Ethical, Legal, and Political Dilemmas* (Cambridge: Cambridge University Press, 2003): 18.

173 Wheeler, *Saving Strangers*.

174 Nardin, "Introduction" in Nardin and Williams, eds, *Humanitarian Intervention*: 20–21.

175 Joseph Boyle, "Traditional Just War Theory and Humanitarian Intervention" and Kok-Chor Tan, "The Duty to Protect" in Nardin and Williams, *Humanitarian Intervention*: 31–57 and 84–116.

176 C. A. J. Coady, "War for Humanity: A Critique" in Deen Chatterjee and Don E. Scheid, eds, *Ethics and Foreign Intervention* (Cambridge: Cambridge University Press, 2003): 274–295.

177 See Gary Bass, *Stay the Hand of Vengeance: The Politics of War Crimes Tribunals* (Princeton: Princeton University Press, 2000).

178 See Daniel Byman and Mathew Waxman, *The Dynamics of Coercion: American Foreign Policy and the Limits of Military Might* (Cambridge: Cambridge University Press, 2002).

179 Anthony F. Lang, Jr, "Crime and Punishment: Holding States Accountable" *Ethics & International Affairs* 21, 2 (Summer 2007): 239–258.

180 Data come from the following sources: Alex Bellamy and Paul Williams, "Who's Keeping the Peace? Regionalization and Contemporary Peace Operations" *International Security* 29, 4 (2005): 157–195; Anthony Clayton, *Frontiersmen: Warfare in Africa since 1950* (London: University College Press, 1999); Herbert K. Tillema, *International Armed Conflict since 1945* (Boulder CO: Westview Press, 1991); Stephen Watts, "Military Interventions and the Construction of Political Order" American Political Science Association Conference, Washington DC, September 2005; and United Nations Department of Peacekeeping website, www.un.org/Depts/dpko/dpko/.

181 Of course, military force has been employed to bring about normative change in the past, although I would argue that there has been a distinct increase in such actions since the end of the Cold War, as the data collected suggest. For a review of past instances of great powers using force to bring about normative change, see Renee de Nevers, "Imposing International Norms: Great Powers and Norm Enforcement" *International Studies Review* 9, 1 (Spring 2007): 53–80.

182 Kurt Mills, *Human Rights in the Emerging Global Order: A New Sovereignty* (New York: Palgrave, 1998): 165.

183 Mervyn Frost, *Constituting Human Rights: Global Civil Society and the Society of Democratic States* (London: Routledge, 2002).

184 Neither of these authors argues that punishment is central to protecting human rights; rather, they suggest that human rights are central to the

international normative order more generally. The evidence I have collected point towards an increase in the use of punitive uses of force in response to violations of human rights.

185 International Commission on Intervention and State Sovereignty, *The Responsibility to Protect* (Ottawa: International Development Research Centre, 2001): 14.
186 Ibid., 66.
187 Scott Carlson, *Legal and Judicial Rule of Law Work in Multi-Dimensional Peacekeeping Operations: Lessons Learned* (New York: UN Department of Peacekeeping, 2006).
188 See, for instance, *Access to Justice*, United Nations Development Programme (UNDP) Practice Note, 9/3/2004, obtained from www.undp.org/governance/docs/Justice_PN_En.pdf, and Report of the Secretary General, "Uniting our Strengths: Enhancing United Nations Support for the Rule of Law" A61/636-S/2006/980 14 December 2006, obtained from daccessdds.un.org/doc/UNDOC/GEN/N06/661/01/PDF/N0666101.pdf?OpenElement.
189 David Chandler, *From Kosovo to Kabul: Human Rights and International Intervention* (London: Pluto Press, 2002): 51.
190 Peter Liberman, "Punitiveness and US Elite Support for the 1991 Persian Gulf War" *Journal of Conflict Resolution* 51, 1 (January 2007): 1–29 and "An Eye for an Eye: Public Support for War against Evildoers" *International Organization* 60 (Summer 2006): 687–722.
191 For the classic account of how a hegemon creates institutions that outlive its particular role in shaping them, see Robert O. Koehane, *After Hegemony: Cooperation and Discord in the World Political Economy* (Princeton: Princeton University Press, 1984).
192 It is important to emphasize that harm is inflicted by punishment, but the individual who has committed the violation is the one harmed. So, punishment does not prevent harm in general, but is intended to protect those who obey the rules from being harmed.
193 Human Rights Watch, "Somalia Faces the Future: Human Rights in a Fragmented Society," 1995. Downloaded from www.hrw.org/reports/1995/Somalia, 8 November 2004.
194 See R. J. Vincent, *Non-intervention and International Order* (Princeton: Princeton University Press, 1974).
195 Or, of course, when acting in self-defence, which is analogous to domestic society as well.
196 See Simon Chesterman, *Just War or Just Peace? Humanitarian Intervention and International Law* (Oxford: Oxford University Press, 2001).
197 See Fernando R. Teson, "The Liberal Case for Humanitarian Intervention," 93–129 and Alan Buchanan, "Reforming the International Law of Humanitarian Intervention" in J. L. Holzgrefe and Robert O. Keohane, eds, *Humanitarian Intervention: Ethical, Legal, and Political Dilemmas* (Cambridge: Cambridge University Press, 2003): 130–174.
198 See Michael Byers and Simon Chesterman, "Changing the Rules about Rules? Unilateral Intervention and the Future of International Law" in Holzegrefe and Keohane, *Humanitarian Intervention*: 177–203.
199 International Commission on Intervention and State Sovereignty, *The Responsibility to Protect* (Ottawa: International Development Research Centre, 2001).
200 See Adam Roberts, "The United Nations and Humanitarian Intervention" in Jennifer M. Welsh, ed., *Humanitarian Intervention and International Relations* (Oxford: Oxford University Press, 2004): 71–97.

201 Robert Keohane, "Political Authority after Intervention: Gradations of Sovereignty" and Michael Ignatieff, "State Failure and Nation-Building" in Holzgrefe and Keohane, eds, *Humanitarian Intervention*: 275–298 and 299–321.

202 Scott Carlson, *Legal and Judicial Rule of Law Work in Multi-Dimensional Peacekeeping Operations: Lessons-Learned Study* (New York: United Nations Peacekeeping Office, March 2006).

203 See *Agency and Ethics*, chapter 1.

204 Robert Jackson, *Quasi-states: Sovereignty, International Relations and the Third World* (Cambridge: Cambridge University Press, 1990).

205 I argue in *Agency and Ethics* that even international organizations construct their agency through interventions, using the example of the United Nations' role in the intervention in Somalia. Rather than simply mirroring what the member states wanted, there were clearly moments in the Somali intervention that the UN bureaucracy, led by Secretary General Boutros Boutros-Ghali, promoted a particular UN view; see *Agency and Ethics*: 178–181.

206 Adam March, "Uganda's Civil War and the Politics of ICC Intervention" *Ethics & International Affairs* 21, 2 (Summer 2007): 179–198.

207 One form of sanctions I do not explore in this chapter are those that arise from disputes in international trade negotiations. These sanctions have recently taken on a more punitive character with the role of arbitral panels authorizing retaliatory sanctions in the context of the World Trade Organization. These sanctions provide some interesting evidence of a system of punishments issued by agents and authorized by an overarching quasi-judicial authority – exactly the type of punitive measure I have been promoting in this book. I chose not to explore them, however, because the cases in this book all revolve around questions of security and violence. The WTO structure provides one possible framework for considering how such sanctions might operate in the contexts I explore here, although the goods being distributed are obviously different.

208 Thucydides, *History of the Peloponnesian War*, translated by Rex Warner (New York: Penguin Classics, 1972): Book IV, 303–310.

209 David Baldwin, *Economic Statecraft* (Princeton: Princeton University Press, 1986).

210 For a sample of this literature, see Gary Clyde Hufbauer, Jeffrey Schott and Kimberley Ann Elliott, *Economic Sanctions Reconsidered: History and Current Policy* (Washington DC: Institute for International Economics, 1986); Lisa Martin, *Coercive Cooperation: Explaining Multilateral Economic Sanctions* (Princeton: Princeton University Press, 1992); Daniel Drezner, *The Sanctions Paradox: Economic Statecraft and International Relations* (Cambridge: Cambridge University Press, 1999); Hossein G. Askari, John Forrer, Hildy Teegen and Jiawen Yang, *Case Studies of U. S. Economic Sanctions: The Chinese, Cuban and Iranian Experience* (Westport: Praeger Publishers, 2003); and Ka Zeng, *Trade Threats, Trade Wars: Bargaining, Retaliation and American Coercive Diplomacy* (Ann Arbour: University of Michigan Press, 2004).

211 David Cortright and George Lopez, "Economic Sanctions in Contemporary Global Relations" in David Cortright and George Lopez, eds, *Economic Sanctions: Panacea or Peacebuilding in a Post-Cold War Era* (Boulder CO: Westview, 1995): 3–16. The Institute for International Economics study (cited first in footnote 3) is the basis for the 30 per cent figure (actually 34 per cent according to their calculations). Robert Pape argued in an influential article in *International Security* that even drawing on the data in HSE, the success rate of economic sanctions is even lower, perhaps 10 per cent; Robert

Pape "Why Economic Sanctions Do Not Work" *International Security* 22, 2 (Fall 1997): 90–136.

212   Hufbauer, Schott and Elliott, *Economic Sanctions Reconsidered*: 2.
213   Meghan L. O'Sullivan, *Shrewd Sanctions: Statecraft and State Sponsors of Terrorism* (Washington DC: Brookings Institute Press, 2003): 12.
214   Drezner, *The Sanctions Paradox*: 2.
215   The Royal Institute of International Affairs, Information Department, *Sanctions: The Character of International Sanctions and their Application* (London: The Royal Institute of International Affairs, September 1935): 5.
216   Ibid., 6.
217   Margaret Doxey, *Economic Sanctions and International Enforcement*, 2nd edn (Houndsmill, Basingstoke, Hampshire: Palgrave Macmillan, 1980): 9. Interestingly, in a previous article, Doxey was more critical of international organizations' abilities to impose sanctions because of their lack of legitimacy. Margaret Doxey, "International Sanctions: A Framework for Analysis with Special Reference to the UN and South Africa" *International Organization* 26, 3 (Summer 1972): 527–550.
218   James C. Ngobi, "The United Nations Experience with Sanctions" in David Cortright and George Lopez, eds, *Economic Sanctions: Panacea or Peace-building in a Post-Cold War Era* ((Boulder CO: Westview, 1995): 20.
219   They have made this argument throughout their publications; see, for instance, Cortright and Lopez, *The Sanctions Decade*: 223.
220   Kim Richard Nossal, "International Sanctions as International Punishment" *International Organization* 43, 2 (Spring 1989): 301–322.
221   Nossal, "International Sanctions as International Punishment": 315.
222   Nossal, "International Sanctions as International Punishment": 313.
223   This response to Nossal raises larger questions about the foundation of moral norms. This is not the place to address those questions, although considerations of the source of ethics that justify punishment could certainly play a role in considering the questions of this book. My response is more pragmatic than theoretical – i.e. there exists a set of norms with concrete manifestation in international law that can create international order.
224   For brief, factual summaries of these sanctions episodes, see Hafbauer, Schott and Elliott, *Economic Sanctions Reconsidered: History and Current Policy*: 236–239 (Iran), 275–279 (Egypt) and 315–323 (Cuba).
225   Idealism and utopianism as descriptions of the League can be found in E. H. Carr, *The Twenty Years Crisis, 1919–1939*, introduced by Michael Cox (New York: Palgrave, 2001 [1981]). For a contextual account of realist critiques of this period and later idealisms, see Michael J. Smith, *Realist Thought from Weber to Kissinger* (Baton Rogue LA: Louisiana State University Press, 1986). For accounts of internationalism, see Michelene Ishay, *Internationalism and Its Betrayal* (Minneapolis: University of Minnesota Press, 1995); Carsten Holbrand, *Internationalism and Nationalism in European Political Thought* (New York: Palgrave, 2003); and Cornelia Navari, *Internationalism and the State in the 20th Century* (London: Routledge, 2000).
226   Alfred Zimmern, *The League of Nations and the Rule of Law, 1918–1935* (London: Macmillan, 1936). For a perceptive analysis of Zimmern and his colleague Gilbert Murray, see Jeanne Morefield, *Covenants without Swords: Idealist Liberalism and the Spirit of Empire* (Princeton: Princeton University Press, 2005).
227   George W. Baer, *The Coming of the Italian-Ethiopian War* (Cambridge MA: Harvard University Press, 1967): 1–24.

228 G. M. Gathorne-Hardy, "Italy and Abyssinia" in Ludwig Schaefer, ed., *The Ethiopian Crisis: Touchstone of Appeasement?* (Boston: D. C. Heath, 1961): 7.

229 Ludwig Schaefer, "Introduction" in Schaefer, ed., *The Ethiopian Crisis*: vii–viii.

230 Geatano Salvemini, "Prelude to World War II" in Schaefer, *The Ethiopian Crisis*: 42.

231 Baer, *The Coming of the Italian-Ethiopian War*: 101.

232 Baer, *The Coming of the Italian-Ethiopian War*: 122.

233 The Peace Ballot was a referendum organized by supporters of the League of Nations in Great Britain in 1935. It demonstrated overwhelming support for the League and peaceful settlement of disputes, including a question that demonstrated stronger support for economic sanctions than for military intervention to enforce international legal norms. See Martin Ceadel, "The First British Referendum: The Peace Ballot, 1934–1935" *The English Historical Review* 95, 377 (October 1980): 810–839.

234 F. S. Northedge, *The League of Nations: Its Life and Times, 1920–1946* (Leicester: Leicester University Press, 1986): 221–254.

235 Inis Claude, Jr, *Swords into Plowshares: The Problems and Progress of International Organization* (New York: Random House, 1959): 80–83.

236 This distinction between the League and the United Nations on the question of enforcement is drawn from F. H. Hinsley, *Power and the Pursuit of Peace: Theory and Practice in the History of Relations between States* (Cambridge: Cambridge University Press, 1963): 336–340.

237 For an accessible history of Rhodesia, see Martin Meredith, *The Past is Another Country: Rhodesia, 1890–1979* (London: Andre Deutsch, 1979).

238 For the relevant sections of the 1923 constitution, see Elaine Windrich, ed., *The Rhodesian Problem: A Documentary Record, 1923–1973* (London: Routledge, 1975): 12–14.

239 Robert C. Good, *UDI: The International Politics of the Rhodesian Rebellion* (London: Faber and Faber, 1973): 77.

240 "Britain and the United Nations: A Demand for Results" *The Round Table* 56, 222 (March 1966): 132–141.

241 "Black Rhodesia's Sense of Betrayal" *The Round Table* 56, 224 (October 1966): 348–353, at 348.

242 Good, *UDI*: 140.

243 For a discussion of views about Rhodesian sanctions within the Conservative Party, see Mark Stuart, "A Party in Three Pieces: The Conservative Split over Rhodesian Oil Sanctions, 1965" *Contemporary British History* 16, 1 (Spring 2002): 51–88.

244 For a good overview of the debate leading up to Resolution 232, see Good, *UDI*: 203–231.

245 Good, *UDI*: 207.

246 T. R. C. Curtin, "Rhodesian Economic Development under Sanctions and the Long Haul" *Africa Affairs* 67, 267 (April 1968): 100–110. See also Johan Galtung, "On the Effects of International Economic Sanctions, with Examples from the Case of Rhodesia" *World Politics* 19, 3 (April 1967): 378–416 for a critical take on sanctions more broadly, but which draws on the Rhodesian case.

247 Margaret Doxey, "International Sanctions: A Framework for Analysis with Special Reference to the UN and Southern Africa" *International Organization* 26, 3 (Summer 1972): 527–550.

248 The intervention originally was presented by Iraq as a response by it to a

request from the Free Kuwaiti Government for aid in a revolution. Soon thereafter, however, Iraq changed its argument to a claim that it simply had annexed Kuwait, a territory to which it had certain historic claims.

249 UN Document S/PV2943 reprinted in Elihu Lauterpacht, ed., *The Kuwait Crisis: Volume I, Basic Documents* (Cambridge: Grotius Publications: 1991): 137.

250 David Campbell, *Politics without Principle: Sovereignty, Ethics, and Narratives of the Gulf War* (Boulder CO: Lynne Reinner Publishers, 1993): 40.

251 Reprinted in Lauterpacht, ed., *The Kuwait Crisis: Volume I, Basic Documents*: 97.

252 Reprinted in *The United Nations and the Iraq-Kuwait Conflict, 1990–1996*, introduction by Boutros Boutros-Ghali (New York: Department of Public Information, United Nations, 1996).

253 UN Document S/22339, reprinted in *The United Nations and Iraq*: 258–259.

254 See Ian Johnstone, *Aftermath of the Gulf War: An Assessment of UN Action* (Boulder Co: Lynne Rienner Publications, 1994): 16.

255 UN Doc. S/22661, reproduced in John Norton Moore, *Crisis in the Gulf: Enforcing the Rule of Law* (New York: Oceana Publications, 1992): 549–551; see also Johnstone, *Aftermath of the Gulf War*: 17.

256 Moore, *Crisis in the Gulf*: 543.

257 UN Doc. S22885, reprinted in Moore, *Crisis in the Gulf*: 553–563.

258 Moore, *Crisis in the Gulf*: 560.

259 See David Cortright and George Lopez, *Sanctions and the Search for Security: Challenges to UN Action* (Boulder CO: Lynne Rienner, 2002): 21–46 for an overview of the efforts to make sanctions less harmful to the civilian population.

260 See, for a brief sample, Albert C. Pierce, "Just War Principles and Economic Statecraft" *Ethics & International Affairs* 10 (1996); Joy Gordon, "Chokehold on the World" *The Nation* (1 January 2001): 27–32; and Geoff Simons, *The Scourging of Iraq: Sanctions, Law and Natural Justice*, 2nd edn (Basingstoke: Macmillan, 1998).

261 For instance, one could explore the different norms in terms of which sanctions were imposed. Tim Niblock, in his study of the sanctions regimes imposed in the Middle East more broadly, highlights the fact that, while sanctions under the Clinton Administration were supposedly about removing a corrupt regime from power, the initial resolution that emphasized Iraq violations of human rights (UN SC Res 688) was kept separate from any enforcement mechanisms; see Tim Niblock, *"Pariah States" and Sanctions in the Middle East* (Boulder CO: Lynne Rienner, 2001): 104–107. This suggests that, like the Rhodesian case, the norms that sanctions were designed to enforce, may not have been entirely clear.

262 kroc.nd.edu/research/econsanc.shtml.

263 www.watsoninstitute.org/tfs/targetedfinsan.cfm.

264 See David Cortright and George Lopez, *Sanctions and the Search for Security*: 34–36.

265 See www.smartsanctions.se for more information on some of these initiatives.

266 Although, for a compelling argument that sanctions might have worked in Iraq, see David Cortright and George Lopez, "Containing Iraq: Sanctions Worked" *Foreign Affairs* (July/August 2004): 90–103.

267 For a list of targeted sanctions imposed by the United Nations, see the Watson Institute Targeted Sanctions Toolkit website, www.watsoninstitute. org/tfs/CD/.

268 See S/2000/1254 Report of the Security Council Committee Established

pursuant to Resolution 1267 on 29 December 2000. All reports and documents obtained from the Committee website, www.un.org/sc/committees/1267.

269 S/2002/101 Report of the Security Council Committee established pursuant to Resolution 1267 on 5 February 2002, paragraph 11.

270 This information comes from the Committee's website, accessed on 15 September 2007.

271 There is another important committee in the UN devoted to terrorism issues, the Counter-Terrorism Committee. This committee was created by UN Security Council Resolution 1368 and is devoted mainly to ensuring general compliance with that resolution and other counter-terrorism procedures in the UN. It does not have a sanctions list, nor does it seek to enforce sanctions. For distinctions between the 1267 Committee and the Counter-terrorism Committee, see UN Security Council Press Release 7827, issued on 28 July 2003 available on the 1267 website.

272 Fact Sheet on Listing, located on 1267 Committee website.

273 Larissa van den Nerik and Nico Schrijver, "Human Rights Concerns in Current Targeted Sanctions Regimes from the Perspective of International and European Law" in *Strengthening Targeted Sanctions through Fair and Clear Procedures*, Report of the Watson Institute for International Studies, March 2006: 13.

274 Ban Ki-Moon, Keynote Address at Enhancing the Implementation of United Nations Security Council Resolutions: A Symposium, New York City, 30 April 2007. Accessed at www.smartsanctions.se/literature/ban_kee_moon_070718%20Final%20symposium%20report.pdf.

275 Iain Cameron, "UN Targeted Sanctions, Legal Safeguards and the European Convention on Human Rights" *Nordic Journal of International Law* 72 (2003): 159–214, at 171.

276 See Cameron, "UN Targeted Sanctions, Legal Safeguards and the European Convention on Human Rights"; Goran Lysen, "Targeted UN Sanctions: Application of Legal Sources and Procedural Matters" *Nordic Journal of International Law* 72 (2003): 291–304; and Nicholas Lavranos, "UN Sanctions and Judicial Review" *Nordic Journal of International Law* 76 (2007): 1–17.

277 Watson Institute for International Studies, *Strengthening Targeted Sanctions through Fair and Clear Procedures*: 43–49.

278 Bardo Fassbender, "Targeted Sanctions and Due Process" Study commissioned by the United Nations Office of Legal Affairs, 20 March 2006; accessed at www.un.org/law/counsel/Fassbender_study.pdf.

279 www.whitehouse.gov/news/releases/2001/09/20010924-4.html.

280 S/AC.37/2003/(1455)/19 Report of the United Kingdom pursuant to paragraphs 6 and 12 of Resolution 1455 (2003); paragraph 8.

281 S/AC.37/2004(1455)/1 Note Verbale dated 5 January 2004 from the Permanent Mission of Egypt to the United Nations addressed to the Chairman of the Committee, Paragraph 2.I.

282 I prefer counter-terrorism policy to war on terror, since labelling it a war makes certain assumption about what constitutes the practice. War is part of counter-terrorism, but it does not encapsulate the entire process.

283 For debates on the definition of terrorism, see Alex P. Schmid and Albert J. Johgman, with the assistance of Michael Stohl, *Political Terrorism: A New Guide to Actors, Authors, Concepts, Data Bases, Theories and Literature* (New Brunswick NJ: Transaction Publishers, 2005).

284 For an understanding of counter-terrorism as a distinct policy, I have drawn

upon the following sources: Paul Wilkinson, *Terrorism and Democracy: The Liberal State Response* (London: Frank Cass, 2001); Graeme C. S. Steven and Rhohan Guarantna, *Counterterrorism: A Resource Handbook* (Santa Barbara: ABC CLIO, 2004); and Boaz Ganor, *The Counterterrorism Puzzle: A Guide for Decision Makers* (New Brunswick: Transaction Publishers, 2005).

285 This distinction is found throughout the literature on terrorism and counter-terrorism. For one critical discussion, see Ken Booth and Tim Dunne, "Worlds in Collision" in Booth and Dunne, eds, *Worlds in Collision: Terror and the Future of Global Order* (Houndsmill: Palgrave Macmillan, 2002): 1–26.

286 Ganor, *The Counterterrorism Puzzle*: 222.

287 See, for instance, the debate between Kenneth Roth, head of Human Rights Watch and Ruth Wedgwood, a conservative international lawyer in the pages of *Foreign Affairs*: Kenneth Roth, "The Law of War in the War on Terror" *Foreign Affairs* (January/February 2004) and Ruth Wedgwood/Kenneth Roth "Response: Combatants or Criminals?" *Foreign Affairs* (May/June 2004) reprinted in James F. Hodge, Jr and Gideon Rose, eds, *Understanding the War on Terrorism* (New York: Council on Foreign Relations, 2005): 302–317.

288 Carl von Clausewitz, *On War*, edited and translated by Michael Howard and Peter Paret (Princeton: Princeton University Press, 1976).

289 Carl Schmitt, *On the Concept of the Political*, translated by George Schwab (Chicago: University of Chicago Press, 1996).

290 George W. Bush, Address to a Joint Session of Congress and the American People, 20 September 2001. www.whitehouse.gov/news/releases/2001/09/20010920–8.html, accessed on 26 October 2007.

291 Richard J. Erickson, *Legitimate Use of Force Against State Sponsored International Terrorism* (Honolulu: University Press of the Pacific,1989): 63.

292 For a fuller development of the role of punishment in the just war tradition, see my "Punishment and Peace: Critical Reflections on Countering Terrorism, *Millennium*," 36,3 (2008).

293 For one, see John F. Murphy, *Punishing International Terrorists: The Legal Framework for Policy Initiatives* (Lanham MD: Rowman and Littlefield, 1985).

294 Steven and Gunaratna, *Counterterrorism*: 101.

295 For a wide ranging selection of essays on the international legal dimensions of counter-terrorism, see Andrea Bianchi, ed., *Enforcing International Law Norms Against Terrorism* (Oxford: Hart Publishing, 2004).

296 Wilkinson, *Terrorism and Democracy*: 94.

297 Ibid., 104.

298 Ibid., 97.

299 Murphy, *Punishing International Terrorists*.

300 Madeline Morris, "Arresting Terrorism: Criminal Jurisdiction and International Relations" in Bianchi, ed., *Enforcing International Law Norms against Terrorism*: 63–82, at 64.

301 See Georges Abi-Saab, "The Proper Role of International Law in Combating Terrorism" in Bianchi, ed., *Enforcing International Law Norms against Terrorism*: xiii–xxiii.

302 Robert Pape, *Dying to Win: The Strategic Logic of Suicide Terrorism* (New York: Random House, 2005).

303 Clive Walker, *Blackstone's Guide to Anti-Terrorist Legislation* (Oxford: Oxford University Press, 2002): 170.

304 See John Horgan, *The Psychology of Terrorism* (London: Routledge, 2005): 140–157; see also Max Taylor and John Horgan, "A Conceptual Framework for Addressing Psychological Process in the Development of the Terrorist" *Terrorism and Political Violence* 18, 4 (2006): 585–601.

305 Bruno S. Fey, *Dealing with Terrorism: Stick or Carrot* (Cheltenham: Edward Elgar, 2004).

306 Ganor, *The Counterterrorism Puzzle*: 203–206.

307 For a review of the Reagan administration's terrorism policies, see David C. Wills, *The First War on Terror: Counter-Terrorism Policy during the Reagan Administration* (Lanham MD: Rowman and Littlefield, 2003).

308 Paul Pillar, *Terrorism and US Foreign Policy* (Washington DC: Brookings Institute, 2003): 80.

309 See "Counterterrorism Before 9/11" 9/11 Commission Staff Statement No. 8, reprinted in Hodge and Rose, *Understanding the War on Terrorism*: 166–181, at 166.

310 "Counterterrorism Before 9/11": 169.

311 Richard Clarke, *Against All Enemies: Inside America's War on Terror* (New York: Simon and Schuster, 2004).

312 Bob Woodward, *Bush at War* (New York: Pocket Books, 2003).

313 This chapter will not address the 2003 Iraq war as part of the "war on terrorism." The war against Iraq raises other important questions about punishment, for it was partly framed as a response to the Iraqi regime's failure to conform to the provisions of the ceasefire resolutions of the 1991 Iraq War, particularly those relating to weapons of mass destruction. Almost no one today accepts that the war was really a central element of the counter-terrorism campaign. For some thoughts on how the Iraq war relates to questions of punishment and rules, however, see my "Normative Causes and Consequences: Understanding and Evaluating the War with Iraq" in Raymond Hinnebusch and Rick Fawn, eds, *The Iraq War: Causes and Consequences* (Boulder CO: Lynne Rienner Publishers, 2006): 269–282.

314 For one early analysis that presents important questions about how the responsibility of al-Qaeda for the attacks was determined, see Steve Smith in Ken Booth and Steve Smith, eds, *Worlds in Collision: Terror and the Future of Global Order* (Houndsmill: Palgrave Macmillan, 2002).

315 For an early, positive summary of the war effort, see Michael E. O'Hanlon, "A Flawed Masterpiece" *Foreign Affairs* May/June 2002, reprinted in Hodge and Rose, *Understanding the War on Terror*: 190–200.

316 Anthony F. Lang, Jr "Punitive Justifications or Just Punishment? An Ethical Reading of Coercive Diplomacy" *Cambridge Review of International Affairs* 19, 3 (2006): 389–403.

317 Barry Buzan, "Who May we Bomb" in Booth and Dunne, eds, *Worlds in Collision*: 85–94.

318 "What We're Fighting For: A Letter from America" reprinted on www.americanvalues.org/html/wwff.html.

319 From *Questions on the Heptatuech*, Book VI, chapter 10, reprinted in Gregory Reichberg, Henrik Syse and Endre Begby, eds, *The Ethics of War: Classic and Contemporary Readings* (Malden MA: Blackwell Publishing, 2006): 82.

320 See Jean Bethke Elshtain, *Just War Against Terror: The Burden of American Power in a Violent World* (New York: Basic Books, 2004) and "Terrorism" in Charles Reed and David Ryall, eds, *The Price of Peace: Just War in the 21st Century* (Cambridge: Cambridge University Press, 2007): 118–135.

321 For details, of the attack, see Walter Pincus, "U. S. Strike Kills Six in Al

Qaeda" *The Washington Post*, 5 November 2002, available at www.washingtonpost.com.

322 "U. S. Kills al-Qaeda Suspects in Yemen" *USA Today*, 5 November 2002, available at www.usatoday.com.

323 For a useful debate about the ethics of targeted killings, see Steven David and Yael Stein, "Debate: Israel's Policy of Targeted Killing" *Ethics & International Affairs* 17, 1 (Spring 2003).

324 Nyier Abdou, "Death by Predator" *Al-Ahram Weekly*, 14–20 November 2002, obtained from weekly.ahram.org.eg/2002/612/re5.htm.

325 Ibid.

326 For one such demand about following the rules, see Philippe Sands, *Lawless World: America and the Making and Breaking of Global Rules* (London: Allen Lane, 2005).

327 Brief history from the US Navy's website devoted to Guantanamo Bay: www.cnic.navy.mil/Guantanamo/AboutGTMO/gtmohistgeneral/gtmohistgeneral.

328 Kathleen T. Rhem, "Government Attorney: Detainees Don't Deserve POW Privileges" 4 March 2005 accessed at www.defenselink.mil/news/newsartlce.aspx?id=31274.

329 Gerry J. Gilmore, "Detention Puts Terrorists out of Action, DoD Official Says" 10 January 2006 accessed at www.defenselink.mil/news/newsarticle.aspx?id=14649.

330 For the text of the law, Public Law 109–366, see www.loc.gov/rr/frd/Military_Law/pdf/PL-109-366.pdf. For commentary, see "Contemporary Practice of the United States Relating to International Law" *American Journal of International Law* 101, 1 (January 2007): 185–195.

331 John Langbein, "The Legal History of Torture" in Sanford Levinson, ed., *Torture: A Collection* (Oxford: Oxford University Press, 2004): 93–105, at 95.

332 Jill Harries, "Contexualizing Torture: Rules and Conventions in the Roman Digest" in Amanda Beattie and Anthony F. Lang, Jr, eds., *War, Torture and Terrorism: Rethinking the Rules of International Security* (Routledge, 2008).

333 Mark Osiel, "The Mental State of Torturers: Argentine's Dirty War" in Levinson, *Torture: A Collection*: 129–143.

334 Sanford Levinson, "Contemplating Torture: An Introduction" in Levinson, ed. *Torture: A Collection* (Oxford: Oxford University Press, 2004): 24.

335 Memorandum for Alberto R. Gonzales, Counsel to the President, Re Standards for Conduct for Interrogation Under 18 U. S. C. Sections 2340–2340A, reprinted in Karen Greenberg, ed., *The Torture Papers* (Cambridge: Cambridge University Press, 2004): 172–217.

336 Memorandum, p. 172.

337 Scott Shane, David Johnston and James Risen, "Secret U. S. Endorsement of Sever Interrogations" *The New York Times*, 4 October 2007, accessed on the same day at www.nytimes.com.

338 Ibid.

339 John T. Parry, "Escalation and Necessity: Defining Torture at Home and Abroad" in Levinson, ed., *Torture: A Collection*: 145–164, at 152–153.

340 Morris, "Arresting Terrorism": 71–72.

341 Samuel Huntington, *The Clash of Civilizations and the Remaking of World Order* (London: Touchstone Books, 1997).

342 While they are often conflated, I would argue that rules and norms should be kept separate conceptually. A norm is a shared social expectation about the world, while a rule is an action-guiding directive concerning how one ought

to behave. Importantly, we are not punished for violating norms but we can be punished for violating a rule.

343 Anthony F. Lang, Jr, Nicholas Rengger and William Walker "The Role(s) of Rules: Some Conceptual Clarifications" *International Relations* 20 (2006): 274–294.

344 Anthony F. Lang, Jr, "The Violence of Rules: Rethinking the 2003 War against Iraq" *Contemporary Politics* 13,3 (September 2007): 257–276

345 See my chapter, "Governance and Political Action: Hannah Arendt on Global Political Protest" in Anthony F. Lang, Jr and John Williams, eds, *Hannah Arendt and International Relations: Reading Across the Lines* (New York: Palgrave, 2005): 179–198.

346 I am indebted to Sean Molloy for this phrase and forcing me to consider this point more carefully.

347 See Richard E. Flathman, *The Practice of Political Authority: Authority and the Authoritative* (Chicago: University of Chicago Press, 1980): 90–108.

348 Anthony F. Lang, Jr, "Crime and Punishment: Holding States Accountable" *Ethics & International Affairs* 21, 2 (2007): 239–257.

349 For one example that relates directly to one of the cases explored here, see Andrew Neal, "Foucault in Guantanamo: Towards an Archaeology of the Exception" ms. University of Edinburgh 2007.

350 Michel Foucault, *Discipline and Punish*.

351 Gary Bass, *Stay the Hand of Vengeance: The Politics of War Crimes Tribunals* (Princeton: Princeton University Press, 2000).

352 Steven C. Roach, *Politicizing the International Criminal Court: The Convergence of Politics, Ethics, and Law* (Lanham MD: Rowman and Littlefield, 2006).

353 Gerry Simpson, *Law, War and Crime: War Crimes Trials and the Reinvention of International Law* (Cambridge: Polity Press, 2007).

354 Mark Drumbl, *Atrocity, Punishment and International Law* (Cambridge: Cambridge University Press, 2007): 61.

355 Ibid., 121.

356 Portions of this section draw from my article, "Crime and Punishment: Holding States Accountable" *Ethics & International Affairs* 21, 2 (2007): 239–257.

357 There is, of course, a wide range of other judicial institutions at regional levels, such as the European Court of Human Rights. Such institutions could well complement the system I am proposing here, but I want to construct a specifically global one. As a result, I will focus on these three institutions.

358 See the website of the ICJ where its basic structure is described in more depth; www.icj-cij.org/icjwww/icjhome.htm.

359 There is a debate about whether the Court simply makes declaratory judgements or actually imposes sanctions. Some believe the Court is moving closer to imposing sanctions; see Malcolm Shaw, "The International Court, Responsibility and Remedies" in Malgosia Fitzmaurice and Dan Sarooshi, eds, *Issues of State Responsibility before International Judicial Institutions* (Oxford: Hart Publishing, 2004): 19–34.

360 David Malone has recently argued that the Security Council shifted from a politico-military role to a legal-regulative role, particularly in its decisions concerning Iraq during the 1990s, which resulted in the creation of a wide range of bodies that were designed to regulate Iraqi behaviour; David M. Malone, *The International Struggle over Iraq: Politics in the UN Security Council, 1980–2005* (Oxford: Oxford University Press, 2006).

361 For an insightful discussion of constitutional legitimacy, see Ian Clark, *Legitimacy in International Society* (Oxford: Oxford University Press, 2005).

362 See William Schabas, *An Introduction to the International Criminal Court*

(Cambridge: Cambridge University Press, 2003) and the ICC website at www.icc-cpi.int/about/ataglance/establishment.html.

363 These include, but are not limited to, the Universal Declaration of Human Rights, the International Covenant on Economic, Social and Cultural Rights and the International Covenant on Civil and Political Rights.

364 See, for one critique of the judiciary in the context of constitutionalism, Richard Bellamy, *Political Constitutionalism: A Republican Defence of the Constitutionality of Democracy* (Cambridge: Cambridge University Press, 2007).

365 See Patrick Hayden, "Superfluous Humanity: An Arendtian Perspective on the Political Evil of Global Poverty," *Millennium*, 35, 2 (2007): 279–300 and Patrick Hayden, *Political Evil in a Global Age: An Arendtian Perspective* (London: Routledge, 2008).

366 Hayden, "Superfluous Humanity": 5.

367 For one of the best analyses of forgiveness, see Peter Digeser, *Political Forgiveness* (Ithaca: Cornell University Press, 2001).

368 The following draws upon my chapter, "Evil, Agency and Punishment" in Renee Jeffery, ed., *Confronting Evil in International Relations: Ethical Responses to Problems of Moral Agency* (New York: Palgrave Macmillan, 2008).

369 William Connolly, *Identity/Difference: Democratic Negotiations of Political Paradox* (Ithaca: Cornell University Press, 1991): 96.

370 Connolly does not borrow uncritically from Nietzsche, however; see *Identity/Difference*, 184–197.

371 Arendt, *The Human Condition*: 238–242.

Bibliography

Chapters 1–3 Works on punishment and international political theory

Abu-Nimer, Mohammed, ed., *Reconciliation, Justice and Coexistence* (Lanham MD: Lexington Books, 2001)

Acton, H. B., ed., *The Philosophy of Punishment: A Collection of Papers* (London: Macmillan, 1969)

Alexander, Larry, ed., *Constitutionalism: Philosophical Foundations* (Cambridge: Cambridge University Press, 1998)

Alverez, Jose, *International Organizations as Law Makers* (Oxford: Oxford University Press, 2005)

Arendt, Hannah, *The Human Condition* (Chicago: University of Chicago Press, 1958)

Arendt, Hannah, *Eichmann in Jerusalem: A Report on the Banality of Evil, Revised and Enlarged Edition* (New York: Penguin Books, 1964)

Arendt, Hannah, *Responsibility and Judgment*, introduced and edited by Jerome Kohn (New York: Schocken Books, 2003)

Bass, Gary, *Stay the Hand of Vengeance: The Politics of War Crimes Tribunals* (Princeton: Princeton University Press, 2000)

Bassiouni, M. Cherif, ed., *Post-Conflict Justice* (Ardsley NY: Transnational Publishers, 2002)

Beccaria, Cesare, *On Crimes and Punishments and Other Writings*, Richard Bellemy, ed. (Cambridge: Cambridge University Press, 1995)

Braithwaite, John and Philip Petit, *Not Just Deserts: A Republican Theory of Criminal Justice* (Oxford: Clarendon Press, 1990)

Brown, Chris, *Sovereignty, Rights and Justice: International Political Theory Today* (Cambridge: Polity Press, 2002)

Buchanan, Allen, *Justice, Legitimacy and Self-Determination: Moral Foundations for International Law* (Oxford: Oxford University Press, 2004)

Buchanan, Allen and Robert Keohane, "The Preventive Use of Force: A Cosmopolitan Institutional Proposal" *Ethics & International Affairs* 18, 1 (2004): 1–22

Buchanan, Allen and Robert Keohane, "The Legitimacy of Global Governance Institutions" *Ethics & International Affairs* 20, 4 (2006): 405–438

Bull, Hedley, *Justice in International Relations* (Waterloo: University of Waterloo, 1984)

Caney, Simon, *Justice Beyond Borders: A Global Political Theory* (Oxford: Oxford University Press, 2005)

Carr, E. H., *The Twenty Years Crisis, 1919–1939*, edited with an introduction by Michael Cox (New York: Palgrave, [1981] 2001)

Cattaneo, Mario A., "Hobbes' Theory of Punishment" in K. C. Brown, ed., *Hobbes Studies* (Oxford: Basil Blackwell, 1965): 275–298

Clark, Ian, *Legitimacy in International Society* (Oxford: Oxford University Press, 2005)

Claude, Inis Jr, *Swords into Plowshares: The Problems and Progress of International Organization* (New York: Random House, 1959)

Coicaud, Jean-Marc and Veijo Heiskanen, eds, *The Legitimacy of International Organizations* (Tokyo: The United Nations University Press, 2001)

Connolly, William, *Identity/Difference: Democratic Negotiations of Political Paradox* (Ithaca: Cornell University Press, 1991)

Cox, Richard, *Locke on War and Peace* (Oxford: Clarendon Press, 1960)

Crawford, James, ed., *The International Law Commission's Articles on State Responsibility: Introduction, Text and Commentary* (Cambridge: Cambridge University Press, 2001)

Deudney, Daniel, *Bounding Power: Republican Security Theory from the Polis to the Global Village* (Princeton: Princeton University Press, 2006)

Duff, Antony, ed., *Punishment* (Brookfield VT: Aldershot Publishers, 1993)

Dumm, Thomas L., *Democracy and Punishment: Disciplinary Origins of the US* (Madison: University of Wisconsin Press, 1987)

Easton, Susan and Chistine Piper, *Sentencing and Punishment: The Quest for Justice* (Oxford: Oxford University Press, 2005)

Elster, Jon, *Closing the Books: Transitional Justice in Historical Perspective* (Cambridge: Cambridge University Press, 2004)

Erskine, Toni, "Assigning Responsibilities to Institutional Moral Agents: The Case of States and Quasi-States" *Ethics & International Affairs* 15, 2 (2001): 67–87

Erskine, Toni, ed., *Can Institutions have Responsibilities? Collective Moral Agency and International Relations* (New York: Palgrave, 2003)

Fitzmaurice, Malgosia and Dan Sarooshi, eds, *Issues of State Responsibility before International Judicial Institutions* (Oxford: Hart Publishing, 2004)

Foot, Rosemary, John Lewis Gaddis and Andrew Hurrell, eds, *Order and Justice in International Relations* (Oxford: Oxford University Press, 2003)

Forsythe, David P., *Human Rights in International Relations*, 2nd edn (Cambridge: Cambridge University Press, 2006)

Foucault, Michel, *Discipline and Punish: The Birth of the Prison*, translated by Alan Sheridan (New York: Pantheon Books, 1977)

Frankfurt, Harry, "Freedom of the Will and the Concept of a Person" in John Martin Fischer, ed., *Moral Responsibility* (Ithaca: Cornell University Press, 1986): 65–80, originally printed in *Journal of Philosophy* 68 (January 1971): 5–20

Frost, Mervyn, *Constituting Human Rights: Global Civil Society and the Society of Democratic States* (London: Routledge, 2002)

Goldstein, Judith, Miles Kahler, Robert Keohane and Anne-Marie Slaughter, eds, "Legalization and World Politics" Special Issue of *International Organization* 54, 3 (2000)

Gould, Harry, "State Crime: Conceptual Clarifications" International Studies Association Convention 2007, Chicago

Grant, Ruth W. and Robert Keohane, "Accountability and Abuses of Power in World Politics" *American Political Science Review* 99, 1 (February 2005): 29–43

Grotius, Hugo, *The Free Sea*, edited and with an introduction by David Armitage (Indianapolis: Liberty Fund, [1605] 2004)

Grotius, Hugo, *The Rights of War and Peace*, edited and with an introduction by Richard Tuck (Indianapolis: Liberty Fund, [1625] 2005)

Hampton, Jean, *Hobbes and the Social Contract Tradition* (Cambridge: Cambridge University Press, 1986)

Harris, Ian, *The Mind of John Locke: A Study of Political Theory in its Intellectual Setting*, Rev. edn (Cambridge: Cambridge University Press, 1994)

Harrison, Ross, *Hobbes, Locke and Confusion's Masterpiece: An Examination of Seventeenth-Century Political Philosophy* (Cambridge: Cambridge University Press, 2003)

Hayden, Patrick, "Superfluous Humanity: An Arendtian Perspective on the Political Evil of Global Poverty" *Millennium*, 35, 2 (2007): 279–300

Hayden, Patrick, *Political Evil in a Global Age: An Arendtian Perspective* (London: Routledge, 2008)

Hinsley, F. H., *Power and the Pursuit of Peace: Theory and Practice in the History of Relations between States* (Cambridge: Cambridge University Press, 1963)

Hobbes, Thomas, *Leviathan*, introduced by C. B. Macpherson (London: Penguin Books [1651] 1968)

Hoffman, Stanley, *World Disorders: Troubled Peace in a post-Cold War Era* (Lanham MD: Rowman and Littlefield, 1998)

Howe, Adrian, *Punish and Critique: Toward a Feminist Analysis of Penalty* (New York: Routledge, 1994)

Ikenberry, John, *After Victory: Institutions, Strategic Restraint, the Rebuilding of Order after Major Wars* (Princeton: Princeton University Press, 2000)

Ishay, Michelene, *Internationalism and its Betrayal* (Minneapolis: University of Minnesota Press, 1995)

Jaspers, Karl, *The Question of German Guilt* [*Die Schuldfrage*], trans by E. B. Ashton, introduced by Joseph W. Koterski, S. J. (New York: Fordham University Press, [1947] 2000)

Jogensen, Nina H. B., *The Responsibility of States for International Crimes* (Oxford: Oxford University Press, 2000)

Joyner, Christopher C. ed., *The United Nations and International Law* (Cambridge: Cambridge University Press, 1997)

Kann, Mark, *Punishment, Prisons and Patriarchy: Liberty and Power in the Early American Republic* (New York: New York University Press, 2005)

Keene, Edward, *International Political Thought: A Historical Introduction* (Cambridge: Polity Press, 2005)

Kelsen, Hans, *Peace through Law* (Chapel Hill NC: University of North Carolina Press, 1944)

Kelsen, Hans, *General Theory of Law and State* (Cambridge: Harvard University Press, 1946)

Keohane, Robert, *After Hegemony: Cooperation and Discord in the World Political Economy* (Princeton: Princeton University Press, 1984)

Keohane, Robert, *Power and Governance in a Partially Globalized World* (London: Routledge, 2002)

Keohane, Robert, "Decisiveness and Accountability as Part of a Principled Response to Nonstate Threats" *Ethics & International Affairs* 20, 2 (2006): 219–224

Klabbers, Jan, "Two Concepts of International Organization" *International Organizations Law Review* 2 (2005): 277–293

Lang Jr, Anthony F., Joel H. Rosenthal and Albert C. Pierce, eds, *Ethics and the Future of Conflict: Lessons from the 1990s* (Upper Saddle River, NJ: Prentice Hall, 2004)

Lang, Jr, Anthony F., "Normative Causes and Consequences: Understanding and Evaluating the War with Iraq" in Raymond Hinnebusch and Rick Fawn, eds, *The Iraq War: Causes and Consequences* (Boulder CO: Lynne Rienner Publishers, 2006): 269–282

Lang, Jr, Anthony F., "Punitive Justifications or Just Punishment? An Ethical Reading of Coercive Diplomacy" *Cambridge Review of International Affairs* 19, 3 (2006): 389–403

Lang, Jr, Anthony F., "Crime and Punishment: Holding States Accountable" *Ethics & International Affairs* 21, 2 (Summer 2007): 239–259

Lang, Jr, Anthony F., "Morgenthau, Agency and Aristotle" in Michael J. Williams, ed., *Realism Reconsidered: The Legacy of Hans J. Morgenthau in International Relations* (Oxford: Oxford University Press, 2007): 18–41.

Lang, Jr, Anthony F., "The Violence of Rules: Rethinking the 2003 War against Iraq" *Contemporary Politics* 13, 3 (September 2007): 257–276.

Lang, Jr, Anthony F. and John Williams, eds, *Hannah Arendt and International Relations: Reading Across the Lines* (New York: Palgrave, 2005)

Lang, Jr, Anthony F., Nicholas J. Rengger and William Walker, "The Role(s) of Rules: Some Conceptual Clarifications" *International Relations* 20, 3 (September 2006): 274–294

Liberman, Peter, "An Eye for an Eye: Public Support for War against Evildoers" *International Organization* 60 (Summer 2006): 687–722

Liberman, Peter, "Punitiveness and US Elite Support for the 1991 Persian Gulf War" *Journal of Conflict Resolution* 51, 1 (January 2007): 1–29

Locke, John, *Second Treatise of Government*, edited and introduced by C. B. Macpherson (Indianapolis: Hackett Publishing Co, [1690] 1980)

Lowenheim, Oded, *Predators and Parasites: Persistent Agents of Transnational Harm and Great Power Authority* (Ann Arbour: University of Michigan Press, 2007)

McIlwain, Charles Howard, *Constitutionalism, Ancient and Modern* (Ithaca: Great Seal Books, 1958)

MacIntyre, Alasdair, "Social Structures and their Threats to Moral Agency" *Philosophy* 74 (1999): 311–329

Macpherson, C. B., *The Political Philosophy of Possessive Individualism* (Oxford: Oxford University Press, 1962)

Malone, David M., *The International Struggle over Iraq: Politics in the UN Security Council, 1980–2005* (Oxford: Oxford University Press, 2006)

Matravers, Matt, *Justice and Punishment: The Rationale of Coercion* (Oxford: Oxford University Press, 2000)

Mearsheimer, John, *The Tragedy of Great Power Politics* (New York: W. W. Norton, 2001)

Mills, Kurt, *Human Rights in the Emerging Global Order: A New Sovereignty* (New York: Palgrave, 1998)

Mollov, Benjamin, *Power and Transcendence: Hans J. Morgenthau and the Jewish Experience* (Lanham MD: Lexington Books, 2002)

Morefield, Jeanne, *Covenants without Swords: Idealist Liberalism and the Spirit of Empire* (Princeton: Princeton University Press, 2005)

Morgenthau, Hans J., "Views of Nuremberg: Further Analysis of the Trial and its Importance" *America*, 7 December 1946: 266–267

Morgenthau, Hans J. and Kenneth Thompson, *Politics Among Nations*, 6th edn (New York: Alfred A. Knopf Publishers, 1986)

Murphy, John F., *The United States and the Rule of Law in International Affairs* (Cambridge: Cambridge University Press, 2004)

Navari, Cornelia, *Internationalism and the State in the 20th Century* (New York: Routledge, 2000)

Neiman, Susan, *Evil in Modern Thought: An Alternative History of Philosophy* (Princeton: Princeton University Press, 2004)

Nevers, Renee de, "Imposing International Norms: Great Powers and Norm Enforcement" *International Studies Review* 9, 1 (Spring 2007): 53–80

Northedge, F. S., *The League of Nations: Its Life and Times, 1920–1946* (Leicester: Leicester University Press, 1986)

Nozick, Robert, *Anarchy, State and Utopia* (Oxford: Blackwell, 1974)

O'Driscoll, Cian, "Re-negotiating the Just War: The Invasion of Iraq and Punitive War" *Cambridge Review of International Affairs* 19, 3 (September 2006): 405–420

Onuf, Nicholas, *World of Our Making: Rules and Rule in Social Theory and International Relations* (Columbia: University of South Carolina Press, 1989)

Onuf, Nicholas, *The Republican Legacy in International Thought* (Cambridge: Cambridge University Press, 1998)

Pape, Robert, *Bombing to Win: Air Power and Coercion in War* (Ithaca: Cornell University Press, 1996)

Press-Barnathan, Galia, "The War against Iraq and International Order: From Bull to Bush" *International Studies Review* 6, 2 (June 2004): 195–212

Rawls, John, "Two Concepts of Rules" [1954] in H. B. Acton, ed., *The Philosophy of Punishment: Collected Papers* (London: Macmillan, 1969)

Rawls, John, *A Theory of Justice* (Cambridge: Belknap Press, 1971)

Rengger, Nicholas, *International Relations, Political Theory and the Problem of Order: Beyond International Relations Theory?* (London: Routledge, 2000)

Richmond, Oliver, *Making Order, Making Peace* (New York: Palgrave, 2002)

Richmond, Oliver, *The Transformation of Peace* (New York: Palgrave, 2005)

Rodin, David, *War and Self-Defense* (Oxford: Clarendon Press, 2004)

Sands, Phillippe, *Lawless World: America and the Making and Breaking of Global Rules* (London: Allen Lane, 2005)

Schrock, Thomas S., "The Rights to Punish and Resist Punishment in Hobbes' Leviathan" *The Western Political Quarterly* 44, 4 (December 1991): 853–890

Simmons, A. John, "Locke and the Right to Punish" *Philosophy and Public Affairs* 20, 4 (1991): 311–349

Simmons, A. John, *The Lockean Theory of Rights* (Princeton: Princeton University Press, 1992)

Simmons, A. John, ed., *Punishment: A Philosophy and Public Affairs Reader* (Princeton: Princeton University Press, 1993)

Simpson, Gerry, *Great Powers and Outlaw States: Unequal Sovereigns in the International Legal Order* (Cambridge: Cambridge University Press, 2003)

Snyder, Glenn, *Deterrence and Defence: Toward a Theory of National Security* (Princeton: Princeton University Press, 1961)

Solomon, Robert and Mark Murphy, eds, *What is Justice? Classical and Contemporary Readings*, 2nd edn (Oxford: Oxford University Press, 2000)

Sriram, Chandra, *Confronting Past Human Rights Violations: Justice vs. Peace in Times of Transition* (London: Frank Cass, 2004)

Strauss, Leo, *The Political Philosophy of Thomas Hobbes: Its Basis and Genesis*, translated from German by Elsa M. Sinclair (Oxford: Oxford University Press, 1936)

Strawson, Peter, "Freedom and Resentment" in John Martin Fischer and Mark Ravizza, eds, *Perspectives on Moral Responsibility* (Ithaca: Cornell University Press, 1993): 45–66 [originally from *Proceedings of the British Academy* 48 (1962): 1–25]

Taylor, Charles, "What is Human Agency?" in Taylor, *Philosophical Papers Volume I: Human Agency and Language* (Cambridge: Cambridge University Press, 1985): 15–44, originally published in T. Mischel, ed., *The Self* (Oxford: Blackwell Publishers, 1977): 103–135

Ten, C. L., *Crime, Guilt and Punishment: A Philosophical Introduction* (Oxford: Clarendon Press, 1987)

Tuck, Richard, *The Rights of War and Peace: Political Thought and International Order from Grotius to Kant* (Oxford University Press, 1999)

Vitoria, Francesco de, *Political Writings*, introduced and edited by Anthony Pagden (Cambridge: Cambridge University Press, 1991)

Waltz, Kenneth, *Theory of International Politics* (New York: McGraw Hill, 1979)

Warrender, Howard, *The Political Philosophy of Thomas Hobbes: His Theory of Obligation* (Oxford: Oxford University Press, 1957)

Wight, Colin, *Agents, Structures and International Relations: Politics as Ontology* (Cambridge: Cambridge University Press, 2006)

Wight, Martin, "Why is There No International Theory?" Herbert Butterfield and Martin Wight, eds, *Diplomatic Investigations* (London: Allen and Unwin, 1966)

Woolhouse, Roger, *Locke: A Biography* (Cambridge: Cambridge University Press, 2007)

Zimmern, Alfred, *The League of Nations and the Rule of Law, 1918–1935* (London: Macmillan, 1936)

Chapter 4 Works on intervention

Bellamy, Alex, "Responsibility to Protect or Trojan Horse? The Crisis in Darfur and Humanitarian Intervention after Iraq" *Ethics & International Affairs* 19, 2 (2005): 31–54

Bellamy, Alex and Paul Williams, "Who's Keeping the Peace? Regionalization and Contemporary Peace Operations" *International Security* 29, 4 (2005): 157–195

Boutros-Ghali, Boutros, *Unvanquished: A U.S.-UN Saga* (New York: Random House, 1999)

Byman, Daniel and Mathew Waxman, *The Dynamics of Coercion: American Foreign Policy and the Limits of Military Might* (Cambridge: Cambridge University Press, 2002)

Carlson, Scott, *Legal and Judicial Rule of Law Work in Multi-Dimensional Peace-keeping Operations: Lessons Learned* (New York: UN Department of Peacekeeping, 2006)

Chandler, David, *From Kosovo to Kabul: Human Rights and International Intervention* (London: Pluto Press, 2002)

Chatterjee, Deen and Don E. Scheid, eds, *Ethics and Foreign Intervention* (Cambridge: Cambridge University Press, 2003)

Chesterman, Simon, *Just War or Just Peace? Humanitarian Intervention and International Law* (Oxford: Oxford University Press, 2001)

Clayton, Anthony, *Frontiersmen: Warfare in Africa since 1950* (London: University College Press, 1999)

Holzgrefe J. L. and Robert O. Keohane, eds, *Humanitarian Intervention: Ethical, Legal, and Political Dilemmas* (Cambridge: Cambridge University Press, 2003)

International Commission on Intervention and State Sovereignty, *The Responsibility to Protect* (Ottawa: International Development Research Centre, 2001)

Jackson, Robert, *Quasi-states: Sovereignty, International Relations and the Third World* (Cambridge: Cambridge University Press, 1990)

Lang, Jr, Anthony F., *Agency and Ethics: The Politics of Military Intervention* (Albany NY: SUNY Press, 2002)

Lang, Jr, Anthony F., ed., *Just Intervention* (Washington DC: Georgetown University Press, 2003)

Lang, Jr, Anthony F., "Punitive Intervention: Enforcing Justice or Creating Conflict?" in Mark Evans, ed., *Just War Theory: A Reappraisal* (Edinburgh: Edinburgh University Press, 2005): 50–70

Nardin, Terry and Melissa Williams, eds, *Humanitarian Intervention* (New York: New York University Press, 2006)

Tillema, Herbert K., *International Armed Conflict since 1945* (Boulder CO: Westview Press, 1991)

Vincent, R. J., *Non-Intervention and International Order* (Princeton: Princeton University Press, 1974)

Watts, Stephen, "Military Interventions and the Construction of Political Order" American Political Science Association Conference, Washington DC, September 2005

Welsh, Jennifer, ed., *Humanitarian Intervention and International Relations* (Oxford: Oxford University Press, 2004)

Chapter 5 Works on sanctions

Askari, Hossein G., John Forrer, Hildy Teegen and Jiawen Yang, *Case Studies of U. S. Economic Sanctions: The Chinese, Cuban and Iranian Experience* (Westport: Praeger Publishers, 2003)

Baer, George W., *The Coming of the Italian-Ethiopian War* (Cambridge MA: Harvard University Press, 1967)

Baldwin, David, *Economic Statecraft* (Princeton: Princeton University Press, 1986)

Cameron, Iain, "UN Targeted Sanctions, Legal Safeguards and the European Convention on Human Rights" *Nordic Journal of International Law* 72 (2003): 159–214

Campbell, David, *Politics without Principle: Sovereignty, Ethics, and Narratives of the Gulf War* (Boulder CO: Lynne Reinner Publishers, 1993)

Cortright, David and George Lopez, eds, *Economic Sanctions: Panacea or Peacebuilding in a Post-Cold War Era* (Boulder CO: Westview, 1995)

Cortright, David and George Lopez, with Richard W. Conroy, Jaleh Dashti-Gibson and Julia Wagler, *The Sanctions Decade: Assessing UN Strategies in the 1990s* (Boulder CO: Lynne Rienner Publishers, 2000)

Cortwright, David, *et al.*, *Sanctions and the Search for Security: Challenges to UN Action* (Boulder CO: Lynne Rienner, 2002)

Cortright, David and George Lopez, "Containing Iraq: Sanctions Worked" *Foreign Affairs* (July/August 2004): 90–103

Doxey, Margaret, "International Sanctions: A Framework for Analysis with Special Reference to the UN and South Africa" *International Organization* 26, 3 (Summer 1972): 527–550

Doxey, Margaret, *Economic Sanctions and International Enforcement*, 2nd edn (Houndsmill, Basingstoke, Hampshire: Palgrave Macmillan, 1980)

Drezner Daniel, *The Sanctions Paradox: Economic Statecraft and International Relations* (Cambridge: Cambridge University Press, 1999)

Fassbender, Bardo, "Targeted Sanctions and Due Process" Study commissioned by the United Nations Office of Legal Affairs, 20 March 2006

Galtung, Johan, "On the Effects of International Economic Sanctions, with Examples from the Case of Rhodesia" *World Politics* 19, 3 (April 1967): 378–416

Good, Robert C., *UDI: The International Politics of the Rhodesian Rebellion* (London: Faber and Faber, 1973)

Gordon, Joy, "Chokehold on the World" *The Nation* (January 1, 2001): 27–32

Hufbauer, Gary Clyde, Jeffrey Schott and Kimberley Ann Elliott, *Economic Sanctions Reconsidered: History and Current Policy* (Washington DC: Institute for International Economics, 1986)

Johnstone, Ian, *Aftermath of the Gulf War: An Assessment of UN Action* (Boulder CO: Lynne Rienner Publications, 1994)

Lauterpacht, Elihu, ed., *The Kuwait Crisis: Volume I, Basic Documents* (Cambridge: Grotius Publications: 1991)

Lavranos, Nicholas, "UN Sanctions and Judicial Review" *Nordic Journal of International Law* 76 (2007): 1–17

Lysen, Goran, "Targeted UN Sanctions: Application of Legal Sources and Procedural Matters" *Nordic Journal of International Law* 72 (2003): 291–304

Martin, Lisa, *Coercive Cooperation: Explaining Multilateral Economic Sanctions* (Princeton: Princeton University Press, 1992)

Meredith, Martin, *The Past is Another Country: Rhodesia, 1890–1979* (London: Andre Deutsch, 1979)

Niblock, Tim, *"Pariah States" and Sanctions in the Middle East* (Boulder CO: Lynne Rienner, 2001)

Nossal, Kim Richard, "International Sanctions as International Punishment" *International Organization* 43, 2 (Spring 1989): 301–322

O'Sullivan, Meghan L., *Shrewd Sanctions: Statecraft and State Sponsors of Terrorism* (Washington DC: Brookings Institute Press, 2003)

Pape, Robert, "Why Economic Sanctions Do Not Work" *International Security* 22, 2 (Fall 1997): 90–136

Pierce, Albert C., "Just War Principles and Economic Statecraft" *Ethics & International Affairs* 10 (1996)

The Royal Institute of International Affairs, Information Department, *Sanctions: The Character of International Sanctions and their Application* (London: The Royal Institute of International Affairs, September 1935)

Schaefer, Ludwig, ed., *The Ethiopian Crisis: Touchstone of Appeasement?* (Boston: D. C. Heath, 1961)

Simons, Geoff, *The Scourging of Iraq: Sanctions, Law and Natural Justice*, 2nd edn (Basingstoke: Macmillan, 1998)

Watson Institute for International Studies, *Strengthening Targeted Sanctions through Fair and Clear Procedures*, Report of the Watson Institute for International Studies, March 2006

Windrich, Elaine, ed., *The Rhodesian Problem: A Documentary Record, 1923–1973* (London: Routledge, 1975)

Zengl, Ka, *Trade Threats, Trade Wars: Bargaining, Retaliation and American Coercive Diplomacy* (Ann Arbour: University of Michigan Press, 2004)

Chapter 6 Works on counter-terrorism policy

Bianchi, Andrea, ed., *Enforcing International Law Norms Against Terrorism* (Oxford: Hart Publishing, 2004)

Booth, Ken and Timothy Dunne, eds, *Worlds in Collision: Terror and the Future of Global Order* (Houndsmill: Palgrave Macmillan, 2002)

Clarke, Richard, *Against All Enemies: Inside America's War on Terror* (New York: Simon and Schuster, 2004)

David, Steven and Yael Stein, "Debate: Israel's Policy of Targeted Killing" *Ethics & International Affairs* 17, 1 (Spring 2003)

Elshtain, Jean Bethke, *Just War Against Terror: The Burden of American Power in a Violent World* (New York: Basic Books, 2004)

Erickson, Richard J., *Legitimate Use of Force Against State Sponsored International Terrorism* (Honolulu: University Press of the Pacific, 1989)

Fey, Bruno, *Dealing with Terrorism: Stick or Carrot* (Cheltenham: Edward Elgar, 2004)

Ganor, Boaz, *The Counterterrorism Puzzle: A Guide for Decision Makers* (New Brunswick: Transaction Publishers, 2005)

Gilbert, Paul, *New Terror, New War* (Washington DC: Georgetown University Press, 2003)

Greenberg, Karen, ed., *The Torture Papers* (Cambridge: Cambridge University Press, 2004)

Hodge, James F. Jr and Gideon Rose, eds, *Understanding the War on Terrorism* (New York: Council on Foreign Relations, 2005)

Horgan, John, *The Psychology of Terrorism* (London: Routledge, 2005)

Levinson, Sanford, ed., *Torture: A Collection* (Oxford: Oxford University Press, 2004)

Murphy, John F., *Punishing International Terrorists: The Legal Framework for Policy Initiatives* (Lanham MD: Rowman and Littlefield, 1985)

Pape, Robert, *Dying to Win: The Strategic Logic of Suicide Terrorism* (New York: Random House, 2005)

Pillar, Paul, *Terrorism and US Foreign Policy* (Washington DC: Brookings Institute, 2003)

Schmid, Alex P. and Albert J. Johgman, with the assistance of Michael Stohl, *Political Terrorism: A New Guide to Actors, Authors, Concepts, Data Bases, Theories and Literature* (New Brunswick NJ: Transaction Publishers, 2005)

Steven, Graeme C. S. and Rhohan Guarantna, *Counterterrorism: A Resource Handbook* (Santa Barbara: ABC CLIO, 2004)

Taylor, Max and John Horgan, "A Conceptual Framework for Addressing Psychological Process in the Development of the Terrorist" *Terrorism and Political Violence* 18, 4 (2006): 585–601

Walker, Clive, *Blackstone's Guide to Anti-Terrorist Legislation* (Oxford: Oxford University Press, 2002)

Wilkinson, Paul, *Terrorism and Democracy: The Liberal State Response* (London: Frank Cass, 2001)

Wills, David C., *The First War on Terror: Counter-Terrorism Policy during the Reagan Administration* (Lanham MD: Rowman and Littlefield, 2003)

Chapter 7 Works on international criminal justice

Bassiouni, M. Cherif, *Introduction to International Criminal Law* (Ardsley NY: Transaction Publishers, 2003)

Bellamy, Richard, *Political Constitutionalism: A Republican Defence of the Constitutionality of Democracy* (Cambridge: Cambridge University Press, 2007)

Cobban, Helena, "Think Again: International Courts" *Foreign Policy* (March/April 2006): 23–28

Drumbl, Mark, *Atrocity, Punishment and International Law* (Cambridge: Cambridge University Press, 2007)

Fitzmaurice, Malgosia and Dan Sarooshi, eds, *Issues of State Responsibility before International Judicial Institutions* (Oxford: Hart Publishing, 2004)

Klabbers, Jan, "Just Revenge? The Deterrence Argument in International Criminal Law" *Finnish Yearbook of International Law* 12 (2001): 249–267

May, Larry, *Crimes against Humanity: a Normative Account* (Cambridge: Cambridge University Press, 2004)

Schabas, William, *An Introduction to the International Criminal Court* (Cambridge: Cambridge University Press, 2003)

Simpson, Gerry, *Law, War and Crime: War Crimes Trials and the Reinvention of International Law* (Cambridge: Polity Press, 2007)

Index

References to notes are prefixed by *n*.

Lightning Source UK Ltd.
Milton Keynes UK
UKOW04f1805140314

228124UK00003B/8/P

9 780415 570312